M000223866

A Black Man's Existence
as a White Jew

ALSO BY ERIC B. WILLIS

The WILLIS Handbook:
An Intersection of Genealogy, Memoirs and
History of a Black American Family – 1835-2003

A Black Man's Existence as a White Jew

ERIC B. WILLIS

PANOPLY HOUSE OF PUBLISHING
MICHIGAN

Copyright © 2023 by Eric B. Willis

All rights reserved. No part of this publication
may be reproduced, in any form or by any means,
including electronic reproduction or reproduction
via the internet, except by permission of the
author.

First Edition, 2023

Published by
Panoply House of Publishing, LLC
P.O. Box 8105
Bloomfield Hills, Michigan 48302-8105
www.panoplyhouseofpublishing.com

Printed in the United States of America
10 9 8 7 6 5 4 3 2 1

Book Design: Eric B. Willis

Library of Congress Control Number:
2020912775

ISBN: 978-0-9895466-0-7 (hardcover)

To God,

Who has blessed me with the ability to overcome obstacles and for opening his doors of wisdom, knowledge, and understanding throughout this wonderful journey and the ones to come in Jesus Christ's name.

To my family,

Past, present, and future—
for their prayers, kindness, generosity, and love.

To my youngest brother Brian Willis,

In loving memory—who is celebrating with our Lord, the angels, and our ancestors.

We wear the mask that grins and lies,
It hides our cheeks and shades our eyes,—
This debt we pay to human guile;
With torn and bleeding hearts we smile,
And mouth with myriad subtleties.

Why should the world be over-wise,
In counting all our tears and sighs?
Nay, let them only see us, while
We wear the mask.

We smile, but, O great Christ, our cries
To thee from tortured souls arise.
We sing, but oh the clay is vile
Beneath our feet, and long the mile;
But let the world dream otherwise,
We wear the mask!

–Paul Lawrence Dunbar

CONTENTS

Introduction   1

Chapter 1:   A Carousel of Yesterday's Detroit   3
             Jazz Greats

        Mrs. Naima Shamborguer   7
        Mrs. Alma Smith   8
        Mr. Charles Boles   9
        Mr. John Duke   26
        Mrs. Jo Thompson   27
        Mr. Kenneth Cox, II   28

Chapter 2:   The Milieu   31

        Verne Merze Tate   31
        The Great Depression and the Black Population   33
        Detroit, Michigan, Around the Time of Carl's Birth   36
        in 1926

Chapter 3:   Dorothy Steger: Like Mother, Like Son—   65
             Musically Speaking

        The Detroit Conservatory of Music   65
        A Woman of Substance and Song   69
        The Bertha Hansbury School of Music   69
        Second Baptist Church (Detroit, Michigan)   74
        The Brewster Homes   79

Chapter 4:   The Conversion   101

        Judaism: A Culture, Religion, Nationality, and More   104

        Harvey Leach   132

Jimmy Hoffa   135

Chapter 5: "Guess Who's Coming to Dinner?"   141

The Other Black American Jewish Entertainer—   147
Sammy Davis, Jr.

Chapter 6: Racial Passing: The Dark Secret in   187
Whiteface

"The Doll Tests"   198
The Last Letter Sent   210

Chapter 7: A Tribute and Historical Collage Through   245
Newspaper Advertisements and Articles

Appendices   261

Endnotes   267

Bibliography   281

Acknowledgments   283

Index   285

INTRODUCTION

"Expect the unexpected." In 2014, this quote was periodically spoken to me by my father about God's blessings. However, my expectation of what I would uncover about one of my cousins within my maternal lineage was well within the realm of the unexpected and over time, it would become a recurring theme.

My journey began around 1997 with my genealogical quest for knowledge—to find out about my mother Brenda (Steger) Willis' lineage and my desire to know more about my great-grandfather Leroy Steger, Sr. After conducting multiple family oral interviews and poring through various records, I discovered that Leroy was born on December 7, 1894, in Maysville, Alabama—about 11 miles east of the Huntsville city precinct, the result of a union between Sarah Steger, a dark-skinned black woman, and William Steger, a Caucasian man of German descent.[1]

It is not known how Sarah and William crossed paths in the hot southern town of the Jim Crow South where illegalized slavery against its black population continued to "rule the roost." Was my 2nd great-grandmother a part of a forbidden secret relationship or was she raped as a part of paramour rights?

Paramour rights was an unwritten law and a widespread practice during the Reconstruction and Jim Crow eras, allowing white men to have sexual relationships with Negro women by force or coercion—regardless of age or marital status. "Those relations, while certainly never mentioned in polite company, had tacitly become so normalized as to be nearly invisible. The proliferation of mixed-race children in the South was the result of such encounters, but like so many ugly realities born of slavery, it was simply too fraught, too painful, or too uncomfortable to acknowledge. And needless to say, the men involved had no interest in publicity."[2]

If the answer to the question is known, it hasn't been spoken about in family history lore. Nevertheless, Sarah, about age 18, continued to live with her family which included her mother Nicey and stepfather Nicholas Bohanon, her siblings, and her interracial newborn son.[3]

While researching through records, I was able to locate a white man named William David Steger in a 1900 Madison County (Huntsville Precinct), Alabama census record. Born in Virginia, he lived with his wife Margaret and their four children—Jesse, Shelby B., Ella J., and Birdie Pauline. William worked as a house carpenter.[4] During the same time on a Huntsville farm in a rented house, Leroy—around age seven—lived with his mother, his grandparents, and several aunts and uncles.[5] Could this William be my 2nd great-grandfather? For me to attempt to solve this mystery, I knew I would have to delve deeper into Sarah and Leroy's past or discover a living descendant of William David Steger with knowledge of their family's ancestral past.

At first, I decided to set my sights and focus on Great-Grandfather Leroy Steger, Sr. What was his childhood like? What were his experiences growing up in a racist society as a mixed-race, teenaged boy? What was the personality of his mother? Did Leroy ever see or meet his father? Was he aware of the origin of his parent's relationship? These questions and more began to spin around in my mind like the colorful horses on a merry-go-round. However, after some preliminary research, I was met with what seemed to be an impossible dilemma to overcome. At age 48, Leroy died of pneumonia on November 3, 1942, in Detroit, Michigan, and the few older living relatives of mine were limited in their knowledge of him.[6] Also, the whereabouts of family papers documenting his early life seemed to be non-existent or were not disclosed. And to my knowledge, there is only one known black-and-white photographic image of Leroy—sitting on a brick stair wall in front of a house, dressed in a nice suit, shoes, and hat, with a cigarette barely hanging from the side of his mouth.[7]

After rethinking my strategy, I decided to search for the whereabouts of an older 4th cousin whose identity was made known to me during previous oral interviews and ongoing record researches. His name is Carl Steger. If Carl were still alive, perhaps he could provide me with the answers I sought about my great-grandfather.

CHAPTER 1

A Carousel of Yesterday's Jazz Greats

"There is not any present moment that is unconnected with some future one. The life of every man is a continuous chain of incidents, each link of which hangs upon the former."

—Hugh Blair

Is he alive or dead? The year was 2003 as I pondered this question, wearing my interwoven genealogist, private eye, and investigative journalist hat. I began searching for my cousin Carl Steger whose engagement with our Detroit Steger family, I eventually found out, was non-existent for over fifty years. The feeling of jubilation would probably overcome me if I were to discover that he was still among the living, being in his latter senior years. I envisioned an initial meeting taking place at his home, consisting of an introductory firm handshake, perhaps followed by a hug, and elaborate dialog filled with a treasure trove of untold knowledge about my great-grandfather Leroy Steger, Sr., his immediate and extended family members, and our Steger ancestors.

It was eight days before Thanksgiving Day and during a cool autumn genealogical hunting expedition at Detroit's main public library on Woodward Avenue when I met a local Detroit black historian named Dr. Jiam Desjardins. He appeared to be in his '70s, sharply dressed in a wool trench coat, fedora-styled hat, black velvet suit jacket, and a bow tie. He reminded me of when I watched television or viewed photographic images of a certain nostalgic era gone by, when it was the norm for most rural and city folk—outside of going to church—to adorn themselves in their Sunday best while taking a trip downtown, visiting a movie house, the library, or the like. This was Dr. Desjardins' standard attire during the several times I saw him there, occasionally and slowly swaying back and forth with his head down, engaging himself in his research project—most likely involving the history of Detroit's east side black business and entertainment districts between the 1920s and 1950s—Paradise Valley. I know this because he once showed me several binders full of pages with his wonderful drawings and photographs of the night clubs, theaters, and the famous people who performed or visited those places that lined Hastings Street in the "Valley." I was amazed with what he had accomplished with his research. On a whim, I asked Dr. Desjardins if he knew a man named Carl Steger. To my pleasant surprise, he did. "I met Carl in the late '40s—early '50s. He was a pianist. He used to play at private clubs such as the Fox and Hounds and the Book Cadillac. They were white clubs. He played popular music at the supper clubs."[1]

Over a year later, on March 30, 2005, I sent the following message to Lars Bjorn and Jim Gallert, two local jazz historians and educators who co-authored the book *Before Motown: A History of Jazz in Detroit, 1920 to 1960*, which currently occupies a valuable space on my personal library shelf.

Date: Wed, 30 Mar 2005 13:39:42 -0800 (PST)
From: Eric Willis
To: Lars Bjorn, Jim Gallert
Subject: Inquiry Pertaining to your Extensive Before Motown Research

Hello Mr. Bjorn and Mr. Gallert,

I am a genealogist. I have researched my African American ancestors in Detroit back to 1919. Several years ago, during my research, I discovered that a distant cousin of mine was a musician in Detroit. His name was Carl Gordon Steger. After a conversation with a noted historian of Detroit black musicians named Dr. Desjardin (whom I met at the Detroit Public Library's Burton Historical Collection), he informed me that he met Carl during the late 1940s or early 1950s. He also told me that he was a pianist in Detroit. He said Carl used to play popular music at private supper clubs such as the "Fox and Hounds" and the "Book Cadillac" which were "white clubs." He also said that he may have "passed for white" because of being allowed to play at those clubs and that he was very fair-skinned. Carl's mother, Dorothy Steger, who was deceased during that time, was also known in Detroit during the 1930s and 1940s for her musical accomplishments and contributions as an operatic choral director, music teacher and singer.

I am continuing to research Carl Steger's life including his musical career. Therefore, I would like to know if you or Mr. Gallert have come across any information pertaining to Carl Steger during your extensive historical research into Detroit's black musicians?

P.S. I truly appreciate the valuable information that's contained within your book *Before Motown*. I also enjoyed the informative session that was broadcasted on the television as well.

Thank you very much for your review and for any assistance that you could provide.
Eric Willis

Afterward, the following responses were received from the authors.[2]

Date: Wed, 30 Mar 2005 23:12:42 -0500
From: Lars Bjorn
To: Eric Willis
Subject: RE: Inquiry Pertaining to your Extensive Before Motown Research

Mr. Willis,

I have checked my files and have nothing on Carl Steger. If he played the Book Cadillac (hotel) he might have been advertised in the *Detroit Free Press* or the *Detroit News*. I would check the Musicians Union (Detroit Federation of Musicians, Local 5 of the Am Fed of Musicians) to find out if and when he was a member. They also might know of any jobs he had.
I will let you know if I find anything.
Lars

Date: Sat, 2 Apr 2005 18:46:41 EST
From: Jim Gallert
To: Eric Willis
Subject: Your Inquiry

Dear Eric,

Sorry, haven't heard of the gentlemen. Lars had the right idea, ask the union— Naima Shamborguer is a fine vocalist and a nice person. She will probably be able to check for you. Please tell her I said 'hello.'

Another avenue you may want to explore is musicians. Pianist Charles Boles was around Detroit at that time, and he may recall your cousin. His number is   . Please tell him I gave you his number— he's a good friend and shouldn't mind your call.

Jim Gallert

Mrs. Naima Shamborguer

On April 5, 2005, as suggested by Lars Bjorn, I called the Detroit Federation of Musicians union and spoke with Naima Shamborguer.

"I'm a genealogist and I'm trying to locate my cousins Dorothy Steger and her son Carl Steger. She was a noted chorus leader, singer, and voice teacher in Detroit between the '30s and '40s. Her son Carl was a pianist. I would like to know if they were members of the musicians union?"

She responded, "I will try to locate Dorothy and Carl in the database."

"Naima Shamborguer is a fine vocalist and a nice person," said Jim Gallert about the Detroit native from a family of professional musicians.[3] She "developed her highly artistic and fine, polished vocal abilities as a youth. Naima sang at church and in concerts performing classical and jazz music" and later jazz standards, Latin jazz, and bebop. "A 'Motown' treasure, Naima has performed nationwide with the finest jazz masters known throughout the world including Larry Willis (no relation), Geri Allen, Freddie Hubbard, Kenny Burrell, James Carter, Steve Turre, Rodney Whitaker, Wendell Harrison, Donald Walden, Dwight Adams, Marion Hayden, and Marcus Belgrave."[4]

On the following day, April 6th, Ms. Shamborguer called and provided me with the next genealogical puzzle pieces of information in my quest. "I could not locate Dorothy Steger but do have a card for Carl Steger. He played the piano, drums, clarinet, and vocal. He joined on November 14, 1945. Carl played at Jakks Restaurant [and Lounge] in Oak Park, Michigan, in 1980. He played at the Red Cedars five nights a week (dated: June 16, 1983). His first wife was named Florence ("Fern") June Steger and his second wife was named Carol Ann Steger. His beneficiary card listed his mother as Dorothy Steger and her address as 438 Hague Avenue."

Afterward, I asked Ms. Shamborguer if I may have a copy of the information. She responded, "I cannot make a copy of his information because he may still be alive."

"Does he have an address listed," I inquired. She provided me with his most current home address.

I asked, "Do you know of anyone who may have known Carl?"

"Alma Smith may have known Carl," she replied. "I'll give you her telephone number and let her know I gave it to you."

During the 1944 fall season, Carl's parents purchased a Detroit west side home on **438 Hague Avenue**.[5] Several years later after their deaths, Carl inherited the two-story dwelling. The house (above) was vacant in April 2001 (l) and remodeled and occupied several years later in 2003 (r). From the author's photograph collection.

Mrs. Alma Smith

Mary (Alma) Foster Smith, born on May 15, 1922 in Montgomery, Alabama, was raised as a child along with nine other siblings in the North End community of Detroit, Michigan.

Influenced by her mother who played the piano as a child, Smith began to play the piano as a youth. As a Cass Technical High School music major, she performed after school as a pianist for the King's Aces—a big band composed of teenagers which included the noted Milt Jackson, Willie Anderson, and Lucky Thompson.

Between the 1940s and several years into the millennium, Smith traveled and performed with The Counts and Countess, recorded several albums and "soundies" (short films), and played with other well-known performers including the tenor saxophone player Eddie "Lockjaw" Davis and singer Lou Rawls. She performed at various jazz and lounge clubs in Cleveland and Detroit and mentored numerous young musicians as a jazz music teacher within the Detroit Public School system. She also played the vibraphone and the Hammond organ. Smith was awarded the Legends of Jazz International Award (1995) and the SEMJA Award (2006).[6] "Wonderful woman, wonderful woman. My dear friend," as another noted jazz pianist Charles Boles recalled. "She had quite an interesting career."[7]

I called Ms. Smith, introduced myself, and asked her about Carl. She said, "I somewhat knew Carl because we worked at the same club on different nights. The club was on 8 Mile and Greenfield roads in the northwest area of Detroit. I don't remember the name, but I will look through some clippings and get back with you." I asked her if she knew of anyone else who may have known Carl. She said, "Jo Thompson or Thomas may have known Carl. She was a pianist and singer in Detroit. She played at the Piano Bar. Her son writes for the *Michigan Chronicle*" (a black-owned newspaper since 1936).[8]

On April 7th, I called Ms. Shamborguer at the Detroit Federation of Musicians union and asked her about Jo Thompson, and I requested her telephone number. She said, "I cannot recall her maiden name. You may want to contact Jim Gallert." Afterward, I called Mr. Gallert, who informed me that Thompson's maiden name was Dunmoore.

Mr. Charles Boles

That same day, I conducted a telephone interview (which was followed, years later, with a face-to-face interview) with Detroit jazz legend and pianist extraordinaire Charles Boles and his wife in their spacious and cozy apartment on Detroit's east side.

Author: Hello Mr. Boles. I'm researching my family history and I would like to know if you knew a man named Carl Steger. He is my cousin. I was provided with your telephone number by Jim Gallert. He said you may be able to provide me with some assistance.

CB: I knew Carl very well. He played at a club called Club 49. It was on Jefferson. It was quite a nice club.

Author: What was Carl's complexion?

CB: Carl was very light-skinned.

Author: How did you and Carl meet?

CB: I was introduced to him by John Duke. He was a trumpet player. He became quite big—another one of those people who played for stars. You don't make money—you make some money, but you don't make the kind of money that the star makes. You can make a livin'—a good livin'. But John Duke, I think he was the one who carried me over to Carl Steger's house. I remember going to his house on Hague [Avenue].

> *"Well, if I depended only on jazz,*
> *I wouldn't make a living."*

Seem like I did remember him having some emotional problems and heard that he had tried to commit suicide several times. That I didn't know for sure. You know musicians do that all the time. We just had another musician commit suicide earlier this year. When I said I knew Carl, I knew him very well as a musician. But he and I didn't hang out—we didn't hang in the same circles. I went to his house and I remember talkin' to him about music and that he could play more commercial and play classical. Because he played quite well—classical piano.

Author: Oh. Okay. And that probably stemmed from—

CB: It probably is a part of his entertaining.

Author: Yes. But his mother was also a classical pianist. She sang opera—

CB: Carl played good classical piano with a tinge of jazz in there. He seemed like he either left jazz altogether or he was a crossover—from jazz to classical. The reason why I say that is because he—one of the statements he made to me was 'Well, if I depended only on jazz, I wouldn't make a living.' And he played in a lot of clubs and mostly what we would call today, and in that day too, 'white clubs.' The clubs he played in were mostly frequented by white folk. He played at an 8 Mile and Greenfield club, but I can't recall its name.

I have a 2002 [Detroit Federation of Musicians] union book. Let me see if Carl's name is listed in it [Pause]. No. It's not in there.

Author: I'm going to show you some more pictures [of Carl].

CB: See now, he was even younger than this when I seen him. He didn't look nothin' like this. He was a real young-looking . . . . The club I'm taking about was across the street. It was called Club 49. That building is still there, I thought, but the club is gone.

"The more things change,
the more they stay the same."

Author: Were black artists known to have performed there?

CB: Yeah. It's one thing about black musicians—if you had a way about you, you can make a livin'. And I played in a lot of clubs and I ain't seen two blacks in there the whole time I played there. So, I play in clubs two and three and four and five years and you don't hardly see no blacks in there, you know. I remember playing in one club out in— it was called the Indianwood Golf Club. I was there like six years. One of the few blacks I ever seen in there was Huel Perkins [a noted local Detroit television newscaster].

Author: Oh really?

CB: But I think he had just come to town in that day and was just getting hired at channel two. But he's one of the few blacks that I ever saw. There was a lot of white people that came in there like Wayne Fontes [a former NFL Detroit Lions head football coach] and people like that. Ray Lane [a former local radio and television sportscaster] was doing the Tiger games and he was also on hockey—people like the ABC Warehouse man that owned the ABC Warehouse. The one thing I remember about him most is that he carried a gun back here [pointing to the small of his back near his waist]. He always carried a gun back there. He always took his coat off. I guess he was lettin' everybody know he wasn't going for no crap or something. I don't know what that was about. But you know a lot of musicians in that day played in clubs that would be called "white clubs." And these musicians—a lot of times they played classical or they were crossover.

Author: Did they have to enter in through the back [door]?

CB: Not necessarily! Not necessarily! I don't remember that. I never entered into the back in any club. I'm trying to think—if I ever—No! And I've been playing around in so-called white and black clubs since the late '40s.

Author: Now would you say that that was more conducive with performing up north? If you were to perform down south maybe that—

CB: Well, down south was a whole different— I didn't get down south to play until I got with B. B King. I went down south in the '30s with my parents and in '36, I was four years old. Went down there again in '39 and then I went down there again in 1945. And I remember getting off the sidewalk and lettin' white people by—going to the theater in '45 in Atlanta and going up the back way and sittin' in the balcony. I remember those times. And I remember getting on buses and streetcars and sitting in the back. I remember that very, very well. I remember the white and black faucets. In '36 and in '39, I went to a place called Savannah, Georgia. In '45, I went to Atlanta. But it was still very, very racist there. And in some parts of the South, it's still racist today even. You got to be very, very careful—very diplomatic and keep your mouth shut. 'The more things change, the more they stay the same.' Ain't nothin' changed. It's just the surface.

Author: As evidenced by a lot of the incidences going on across the country.

"...if he weren't there."

CB: Right! Right! So yeah, I don't ever remember entering into a back. The only incident I ever remember—I do remember this. Back, oh, I would say it might have been in the '50s or maybe '60s—probably in the '50s, I was playing in a club. I think the street was called Clifford. It's downtown now. It's still there [the building]. I know the club's long gone. But I remember the owner's name was Mr. Stoller. And I remember playing in there, and I would go and get a drink, and I go in the kitchen.

And I just happen to be in the kitchen one time when he had this older black woman go into the basement to get some ice. And I looked at this lady comin' up those steps bleeding and it just hurt my heart. But the thing that occurred that pissed me off was he said, 'Charlie,' the owner standing there in the kitchen, 'help Mamie with the ice.' Now, ordinarily I would have helped her with the ice if he weren't there. But because he was there, I said, 'You didn't hire me to do that, you hired me to be the piano player.' But I would have jumped—I would have fell over three chairs to help that woman with that ice if he weren't there. But because he said what he said, I said, 'I'm not gonna do it.' I said, 'you didn't hire me to do that, you hired me to play the piano and that's what I'll do.' I wouldn't help her, and it hurt me to my heart not to have helped her. Because my heart went out to her to see an older—at that time she might have been, and I might have been maybe late '20s or earlier. She might have been sixty something doing that kind of work, working in the kitchen, havin' to hustle ice out of the basement in a big heavy a** tub or some damn thing. And she was not a young person and it just hurt me to my heart. But I wouldn't do it.

You know incidents like that—you know, um . . . but I never had any. I never ran. I've had people you know insult me. I remember one incident though, years ago. I was playing at the same place called—not that place but another place up in—it was called Bellaire, Michigan. [You] probably never even heard of it. I think the population is maybe 800 or 1000 now. In the '60s, I was playing there. And Bill Milliken, who became the governor of the state, he came up there with Sonny Eliot [a noted Detroit television news weatherman] and a football player. I think his name was Vince Banonis or something like that. I can't remember his name right now.

"He doesn't have to like me—he doesn't have to like my music, but he should be a little more respectful."

So, during the time we were in intermission, I went over and got me a drink. This guy kept saying things like you know ah, 'Can you play the Chattanooga Shoeshine Boy?' or 'Can you play I'm Alabamy Bound?' But it wasn't the asking, but the tune. You see he was making [a] reference to the fact that I was black, and he was being demeaning. So, I didn't say anything to him. But I went to Bill Milliken who was the lieutenant governor and I said to him, 'Bill—ah, you might very well want to run for governor one day.' I said, 'You would hate to have me go to the *Chronicle* [*Michigan Chronicle*] and document this situation that's occurring now with this friend of yours that's in your party.' But I said, 'I wouldn't have a problem doin' it.' I said, 'You should speak to him and tell him to be a little more respectful. He doesn't have to like me. He doesn't have to like my music, but he should be a little more respectful.' And Bill Milliken went and done it. I didn't vote for him because of that. I voted for him because I always thought he was a Democrat dressed as a Republican or somethin' because he was a Republican. But he really—I think he really was democratic in his ways and in his thoughts. Just like you know Snyder [Michigan governor, 2008-2016] is a Republican from day one. You don't have to think—guess about it. But I think Bill Milliken was Democrat—in his heart. He's a good guy. And ah, he went to the guy and told him. And the guy apologized and he never said another word to me. He kind of sheepishly offered to buy me a drink which I wouldn't accept and I just sort of slunk away from them.

*"You find somebody else to sit in that red—
that room back there."*

It's a funny thing. I do remember one other club where I played. It's funny because it's an all-black area today. Show you how things change. [I] played in a club—it was out on Chicago Boulevard years ago. It was around Chicago and Meyers. You know it's all-black now. The first night I went there to play, the guy says um—when I first got there, he took me—and there was a little room— had a red curtain in front of the door. And it was just a room with a light, a table with a red tablecloth on it, and he had a deck of cards there. And he said, 'Now Charlie, when you go in intermission—it's not me now,' and he went right into this spiel, 'I want you to sit back here. I don't want you intermingling with the customers.' So, you know I said, 'Really?' So, I did it, you know, the first two sets, but the third set, being the kind of gregarious person I am, I just ignored his a** and I went out there and talked to the people anyway.

So, at the end of the night I told the guy—I said, 'You know what? I'm really broke,' and I said, 'I don't have a way to get home. I don't usually draw money for tonight, but I need to draw that money down.' So, he paid me. So, I told him, 'Jim, thank you very much,' and I said, 'I'll never be back again.' I said, 'Thanks for the job, but I won't be back again. You find somebody else to sit in that red—that room back there.'

Author: What was the name of that club?

CB: I don't know, but the club is still there. It's called The Black—the name has probably changed a million times since then, but it was on Chicago and Meyers and I think it was called The Black Dimers. I ain't gonna get it right, but the club—I don't know what it was called then. But I remember playing in that club and I remember him doing that.

Author: You had mentioned Carl playing at Club 49. Did you perform there?

CB: No.

Author: What was Club 49 like?

CB: It was a mostly white club. It was like this area mostly. In the '60s—it was in the '60s. This area was mostly white. This building was probably all white. Well, not all white. I shouldn't say that because the judge that just died—Judge Walker or Walfer, the basketball player that just died—they all lived here in the '60s.

      You know, I remember years ago I was playing at this same club, Indianwood Golf Club. And on a Saturday night going to that job, Minister Farrakhan would come on the radio with his usual anti-white speech. And now, I am not racist at all, but I know the score. And I always tell my kids all the time, 'Know who the enemy is and act accordingly.' But I would listen to Minister Farrakhan and by the time I got to the gig, I be so mad, and somebody say, 'Hi Charley,' and I go [mimicking sounds of anger]. And so, you know what I said, 'I can't listen to this guy and drive out there. Because if I do that, I'm just going to be—' And people just be speaking, you know.

Every white person ain't always thinkin' 'kill the nigger' when they say hello. Although we know they don't really give a s***. But the bottom line is they ain't saying kill the nigger because you're there for a reason—to entertain the white folk. But I entertain them and get some money, and I did very well entertaining them. So, I don't back down and all that. And Carl did very well. He did very well. Of course, he would do better as a white pianist because let me tell you one thing—white pianists, they get more money than a black pianist ever thought they wanted to get.

Author: Yeah. I can imagine.

CB: And the money just changes.

I had people throw quarters at me, man. [*Pause*] Yeah, and make all kind of remarks. But you know that's one of the things you have to go through in playing in a white— because most of the clubs I played in were white when I was in Detroit playing. I played for gangsters. Now those people treated me better than some of those other normal white people. I played for the Giacalones and people like that. Them people treated me fine. I had no trouble out of them, man. If you play for the ordinary white man, he's gonna treat you like—he's gotta talk down to you and try to treat you like—

Mrs
Boles: They look down on black women too.

Author: My father was born in '42 and he remember Aretha
         Franklin because she grew up in the North End [Detroit
         community] too, several blocks away. And he remembers
         seeing her father [Pastor C.L. Franklin].

CB: He was quite a guy. You know I played with her in '64.

Author: Oh. Okay.

CB: And I remember him leaving his radio broadcast at 11:00
         and coming to the 20 Grand [Detroit's most popular
         night club during the 1950s and '60s] to see his
         daughter. He would bring half his church members down
         there and get the table across the front of the 20 Grand—
         a table of twenty, twenty-five people. He'd have them all
         in there, probably 25, coming to see Aretha. She was a
         beautiful young person in those days. No problem. I
         loved her.

"It would make your money go up
to play classical music."

Author: So, you said Carl would mix classical with jazz when he
         performed?

CB: Well, you know what? I just remembered him being
         more classical than jazz. He did play some jazz, but he
         was more classical. It appeared to me because I
         remember him playing something like the "Warsaw
         Contralto." But you know that ain't no joke piece now. I
         don't know if you're familiar with it.

Author: No. I'm not.

CB: Paderewski's [Ignacy Jan] "Warsaw Contralto"—not an easy piece to play—can't even think of how it goes, can't even hum it now. But I remember him playing something like the "Warsaw Contralto" which is a Polish—you know Warsaw. So, I remember him. He was a classical pianist man. So that's how that conversation came about, about me saying to him, 'But jazz . . . ,' and he said, 'Well, I never really—I'm not making any money playing jazz so that's what I want.' But I think he was more classically orientated anyway.

Author: Oh. Okay.

CB: I believe that in my heart.

Author: So, he probably played more—

CB: But I'm pretty sure he could play some jazz. You know if you could play popular music of the day—they used to call it back in the day 'something from the Top 40,' and mix it in with some classical music, it made your money go up even all the more. Because white people wanted to hear classical music even though they may not have— You know like I used to play the first four bars and they hear that, and they start talkin'. And then you get through playing it and they go 'Yeah!' [followed by sounds of clapping]. You done played four measures of the damn song. But it would make your money go up to play classical music.

Jazz music is like classical music. It's an acquired taste. When you cut the radio on and if you're lookin' for jazz, you better be prepared to sit there awhile unless you know the dials or the numbers of where to find jazz because maybe two stations out of a hundred will have jazz on it. The rest of them is gonna have either some country or western or they're gonna have some pop music on the different—them people rapping and disrespecting the black race, talking about black women—treating them like they ain't nothin'. So, it's the same thing with classical music. If you were lookin' for classical music you better be prepared to sit there all day dialing across the dial. I know of maybe one or two stations that play classical music in the daytime. The rest of them you got that rap and all that other crap.

I know there's room for everybody, but it's what they say it is. It's just like . . . you take rap. In order for rap to save their lives and to become international, they had to accept somebody like an Eminem [a noted white rap artist]. And until they accept him in—see what white people do is they'll take it, they'll crush your music if you don't let them in and let them have a half-washed somebody doing a—bumbling through your music and making them seem like they're the greatest star that's come along in a hundred years. They will take and squash it. They'll mash it down like an ant.

Mrs.
Boles: You're thinking about Nina Simone, who was a great, great artist?

CB: Have you seen her special?

Author: No, I haven't.

CB: Are you familiar with her?

Author: Oh yes. I'm familiar with her.

CB: You definitely got to get it—Nina Simone documentary.

Mrs.

Boles: What they did to her was she made this song "Mississippi GD" and they used that to bring her down. Because she was wandering the streets in some foreign country down there [inaudible]. She came back finally. But when she came, she was never in her [right] mind again. But she was so hurt. It was a horrible thing for them to do. But they were looking for an opportunity because she made that song "Mississippi GD."

CB: Well, once again it's really what they say it is.

Author: Yeah. Like the Hollywood industry and all that—

CB: Well, you know you think about the '30s, man. You think about [Bill] "Bojangles" Robinson. If you weren't a "Bojangles" Robinson, who's probably one of the greatest tap dancers who ever lived, and you put a little white girl there with some curls on, suddenly she's bigger than—a bigger and better dancer than "Bojangles" because she's a little white girl.

Author: Right.

CB: And "Bojangles" was probably one of the greatest tap dancers that ever lived.

Author: Right.

CB: But with Shirley Temple there, the only way he's gone get in the movies he's gotta be subservient to her.

Author: Um-hmm. Just like Hattie McDaniels—the different roles—

CB: Well, I love Hattie McDaniels because she said, 'I rather be a movie actress playing a maid rather than being a maid.'

Author: Right, in the natural.

CB: I love her. You know because everybody was talking about her. What the hell is that? She got an Academy Award for that.

Author: Right. Exactly.

CB: And then people started talking about—putting her down and she said, 'Well. I'm a movie actress.' And she took the roles that she had that was gone give her—the same thing here today. None of the roles have changed! Nothing has changed—then it was 50 or 60 years ago. It's just a little more subtle, [today].

Author: Exactly.

CB: But it's the same BS and it ain't gonna change.

Author: And I know the white movie power establishment—they still, for the most part, don't allow blacks as a whole to play certain roles and—

CB: Or they'll pick one guy and they'll let him play, like a Denzel Washington. They'll give him more of a free reign.

Author: Or Morgan Freeman.

CB: But the rest of them—stay in line.

Author: Right.

CB: And you gotta make a typical kinda stereotype movie.[9]

Charles Boles, a black-American "Detroit-born jazz pianist, raised in the city's Black Bottom district, has been playing for nearly as long as he can remember—encouraged at an early age by his adoptive mother's cousin, the legendary jazz stride pianist, organist, string bassist, singer, composer, band leader and comedic entertainer Thomas Wright "Fats" Waller.[10] During the ensuing years, Boles has racked up an impressive résumé that includes stints recording and touring with artists such as B.B. King, Aretha Franklin, Marvin Gaye, Etta James, Moms Mabley, Dinah Washington, and many others." He's been a fixture around Detroit from Hastings Street to his latest regular gig every Tuesday night at the Dirty Dog Jazz Cafe in Grosse Pointe, Michigan. An album of his own has eluded Boles until 2015's release of "Blue Continuum," produced when he was 81-years-old.[11] For his contributions to jazz in Detroit, Boles was awarded the Ron Brooks Award by the Southeastern Michigan Jazz Association.[12]

On September 29, 2015, the author visited with the 82-year-old legendary jazz pianist **Charles Boles** at the Dirty Dog Jazz Cafe in Grosse Pointe Farms, Michigan. From the author's photograph collection.

Mr. John Duke

John Duke, born as John Samuel, was a "big trumpet player" and later "a bass player" who "played for the stars," as referenced by Mr. Charles Boles in my interview with the legendary jazz pianist.

> "It seems like the guy that introduced me to him [Carl] was John Duke who was originally a trumpet player that had a face paralysis. I'm trying to think of that disease he had. It's a disease that goes away automatically because my wife even had it. He ended up suing the Army because of the fact that he said it messed up his career as a trumpeter. But he ended up being a bass player and did very, very well. And he ended up with people like Count Basie and them. So, he did very well for himself as a musician. You know he ended up playing the bass. He couldn't play the trumpet no more because his embouchure wouldn't allow [it]. His face was paralyzed on this side. He couldn't bat his eye. It just stayed opened."[13]

Perhaps the disease which Boles was trying to remember is called Bell's palsy.

> "Bell's palsy is a condition in which the muscles on one side of your face become weak or paralyzed. It affects only one side of the face at a time, causing it to droop or become stiff on that side. It's caused by some kind of trauma to the seventh cranial nerve. This is also called the 'facial nerve.' Bell's palsy can happen to anyone. But it seems to occur more often in people who have diabetes or are recovering from viral infections. Most of the time, symptoms are only temporary."[14]

Mrs. Jo Thompson

On April 15, 2005, I called Mrs. Jo Thompson. She said, "Carl played the piano and sang. He was light skinned. He performed at the Scotch 'n Sirloin club on James Cousins at Eight Mile and Greenfield. He married a white girl. She had about six or eight children (when she married him). I don't know if he had any children. He lived on a farm—he lived way out."[15]

Jo (Josephine) Thompson has been a pianist and singer since the 1950s. The Detroit native performed as a cabaret singer in elegant segregated clubs in Miami Beach.

"My favorite club was the Cork Club in Miami. Although I was the first black person to ever perform there (on the trendy 79th Street Causeway of Miami), I was really well-received and the audiences, who were all white due to segregation in the South, were respectful and made me feel like a superstar."

"As an African American female, I, along with other female entertainers such as Lena Horne, had to de-

JO THOMPSON at the piano bar of Jakks Lounge on Greenfield and 10 Mile, isn't just an ordinary entertainer . . . she rolls a fun-filled ball of fast-paced enjoyment that folks are enjoying more and more on Wednesdays through Saturdays.

Jo's versatile ways at the keyboard and vocals range from songs of yesterdays and today with much style and class as she takes command of the microphone to give all-out effort for her appreciative audience who listen intently to her every word and bar . . . This comes from a true professionalism within that has built up throughout the years . . . Jo far from looks it, but she goes back to the days of the Clover Bar and Town Pump of early 50's and Alamo, Baker's, etc. . . . Her outstanding repertoire is filled with every type song imaginable . . . from blues to ballad to upbeat . . . On the romantic ballads, she sings with closed eyes as lovers listen to her every phrase.

It can be said that Jo Thompson shows no partiality when it comes to song writers . . . Her huge storage of songs runs the gamut of almost every known lyric great . . . and she intermingles an individual style with takeoffs on Ivy Anderson, Lena Horne, Carol Channing, etc. . . . even Louie Armstrong.

The action pace at Jakks is continued as Jo takes very few breaks . . . keeping it going withoug stopping while answering requests galore from low down blues to you-name-it tempos.

Jo gets better as the evening passes . . . playing with much feeling that oozes from within her to a lot of happy guys 'n gals who have been fans of hers before . . . and those who revel in their new entertainment "find."

Jo Thompson reviewed in the May 14, 1976 ed. of *The Detroit Jewish News*[16]

fine class and sophistication. We tried to dispel and disprove ugly stereotypes that labeled Black Americans."[17]

Thompson performed "from blues to ballads, old and new love songs, and interesting ditties only Jo Thompson knows" across the United States, including New York's Carnegie Hall and in various European cities. She also performed with the J.C. Heard Orchestra and worked with many great musical talents, including Lena Horne, Bobby Short, and Lionel Hampton.[18]

Like a railroad caboose connected to the rear of a steam-engine locomotive, I concluded my conversation with Mrs. Thompson with the question I'd posed during my previous interviews with the other noted musicians: "Do you know of anyone who may have known Carl?" She responded, "You may want to call Kenn Cox."[19]

Mr. Kenneth Cox, II

On October 19, 2005, I called Mr. Kenneth "Kenn" Cox and asked him if he knew Carl Steger. "I knew Carl Steger, but not that well. I heard him perform a couple of times."[20]

Kenneth Louis Cox, II was a pianist, a composer, and an historian in Detroit. He performed at Detroit clubs such as the West End Hotel, Del Ray, The Minor Key, and the Paradise Theater. He also played the bass, bassoon, and trumpet.

Cox, a Detroit native and Cass Technical High School alumni, studied at the Detroit Conservatory of Music and the Detroit Institute of Musical Arts.

"Through the years, Cox played with trombonist George Bohanon's quintet and guitarist Wes Montgomery. He was a regular at Detroit's legendary jazz-spot Baker's Keyboard

[Lounge]. His albums, 'Introducing Kenny Cox and the Contemporary Jazz Quintet' and 'Multidirection,' were reissued on the Blue Note label" in 1968 and 1969.[21]

CHAPTER 2

The Milieu

"Carl had a deformity in both index fingers.
He was born with no muscles in his fingers."
—Kimberly Steger-Sherrill[1]

On July 21, 1921, Carl's parents Gordon William Steger and Dorothy Ann Williams were married in Battle Creek, Michigan, which was also the town where his maternal grandparents Robert and Elizabeth Williams lived.[2]

Battle Creek, also known as "Cereal City" for W. K. Kellogg's invention of corn flakes, had a station on the Underground Railroad during the antebellum era that was used by escaped slaves in their quest for freedom. After her escape from slavery, Isabella Baumfree, who later became known as the renowned Sojourner Truth—the charismatic preacher, Underground Railroad agent, abolitionist, and lecturer of women's rights—made the city her home in 1866 after living in the nearby settlement of Harmonia.[3]

The Steger's marriage ceremony was officiated by Minister V. M. Meeds. Gordon's uncle George R. Bohanon and Dorothy's friend and former Battle Creek Central High School alumna Merze Tate were present as witnesses. Afterward, the newlyweds moved to Detroit, Michigan.[4]

Vernie Merze Tate

Vernie Merze Tate, born on February 6, 1905, in the village of Blanchard in Rolland Township, Michigan, overcame obstacles to have a distinguished academic career as a professor, scholar, author, and an authority on United States diplomacy.

As a descendant of early black settlers of farmers and lumbermen in the nearby Mecosta County town around the 1860s, Tate completed her educational studies through the tenth grade in the one-room Blanchard High School on her parents' farm and finished her remaining two years at Battle Creek (Central) High School about 135 miles away to the south.[5]

In 1927, Tate became the first black woman to earn a Distinguished Alumni Award and a Bachelor of Arts degree in education at Western Michigan Teacher's College (now Western Michigan University {WMU}). In 1930, she graduated from the University of Columbia with a Master of Arts degree. In 1935, she became the first black American to earn a Bachelor of Literature degree at England's Oxford University. She worked as a professor at Barber-Scotia College and Bennett College. In 1941, she received a Ph.D from Radcliffe College (currently Harvard University) in government and international relations, the first black female to do so. She became an associate professor of political science and Dean of Women at Morgan State College. A year later, she "became professor of history at Harvard University where she and Dr. Caroline Ware were the first women faculty members in the Department of History."[6]

Dr. Tate's other accomplishments included speaking five languages, a world traveler (twice), a Fulbright lecturer in India, an international relations advisor to General Dwight Eisenhower, a Howard University College history professor (1942-1977), an international reporter for Baltimore's Afro-American newspaper, and a United States State Department researcher, photographer and filmmaker.[7]

Dr. Tate never married or had any children before her death at age 91 in 1996, but her legacy continues to live on. In 1990, she was inducted into the Michigan Women's Hall of Fame. During the same year, she created the Merze Tate Student Education Endowment Fund at WMU with a $1 million donation. She also provided monetary gifts and personal documents to other colleges including Radcliffe College which assisted her with her education. In 2016, the Helen Dwight Reid Award was renamed the Merze Tate Award and "is awarded annually for the best dissertation successfully defended during the previous two years in the field of international relations, law, and politics." Furthermore, the Merze Tate Explorers were created "to inspire girls to travel the world and make strides in areas they otherwise could never imagine."[8]

On May 26, 1922, the Steger family had their first child in Detroit, a daughter who was also named Dorothy. However, tradegy occurred when the infant died 14 days after her birth due to melena neonatorum. The medical ailment consists of "the passage of dark tarry stools by a newborn" which is usually caused by "the alteration of blood pigment associated with hemorrhage."[9]

Around 1924, Carl's father Gordon, a World War I Army veteran, "owned a dry cleaner" [business] [but] lost everything during the depression."[10]

The Great Depression and the Black Population

The United States suffered its worst economic catastrophe on October 29, 1929, when the country's stock market crashed in its Wall Street financial district. The depression, which also eventually expanded worldwide, was considered to have lasted for about a decade. As a result, millions of Americans became unemployed due to monumental reductions or total losses of industrial and farming production which led to vast business closures, including banks and farms, and greatly reduced workforces. Massive poverty and low wages quickly followed.

By most accounts, the nation's disaster was caused by the tremendous and unequal distribution of wealth a decade earlier within the so-called "new era of abundance and prosperity" as the stock market and urban land increased in record values.

A record of Return of Marriages in the county of Calhoun, Michigan includes the July 21, 1921, marriage of Gordon Steger and Dorothy Williams – No. 485.
Public Domain.

However, those "working in agriculture, shipbuilding, coal mining, and the textile and shoe industries" did not enjoy such riches.[11]

Many blacks, both in the South and the North, were already experiencing "The Great Depression" during the mid-1920s when the early evidence of a recession began to appear. Thousands of blacks became unemployed; they were thought of as "casualties of a technological age in which several million people were expected to be unemployed." By 1927 in Detroit, 14,454 blacks were employed compared to 20,404 during the previous year.[12]

Within a few years, as the depression took hold of all sectors of society, black suffrage was even greater than the depressed and improvised state of the white population.

"In the cities they lost their jobs rapidly, while in rural areas they were driven to starvation wages. Added to the denial of freedom and democracy was the specter of starvation. Even in starvation there was discrimination, for in few places was relief administered on a nonracial basis. Some religious and charitable organizations, in the North as well as the South, excluded blacks from the soup kitchens they operated to relieve the suffering. In many of the communities in which relief work was offered, blacks were discriminated against, while some early programs of public assistance showed as much as a $6 differential in the monthly aid given to white and black families. This discrimination was final proof for blacks that democracy had escaped."[13]

Gordon also worked as a porter for over 27 years at several noted Detroit hotels, including the Frontenac. Dorothy worked as a schoolteacher.[14]

With several aliases throughout his life, Carl Gordon Herbert Steger, who was also known as "Gordon Carl Steger," "Gordon W. Steger," and "Gordon Herbert Steger," was born on January 1, 1926, to Gordon and

Dorothy in Detroit.[15] According to oral family history, he was born with a "deformity in his index fingers" and "no muscles in his fingers."[16]

The Steger family lived in their bungalow-styled home on 6712 Scotten Avenue near Tireman Street on the west side of the city. This was the family's residence for almost ten years. According to the historian Thomas J. Sugrue:

> Although the majority of Detroit's black population was confined to a section in the Lower East Side between the 1920s through the 1940s, "pockets of several hundred to several thousand blacks lay scattered throughout the city; on Grand River and Tireman on Detroit's West Side, on the northern boundary of heavily Polish Hamtramck, and in the Eight Mile-Wyoming area in northwest Detroit."[17]

Detroit, Michigan Around the Time of Carl's Birth in 1926

- In 1914, the owner of Highland Park, Michigan's Ford Motor Company, Henry Ford offered employees a high wage of $5 a day, and the mass production of the inexpensive Model T automobile helped to revolutionize labor relations, transportation, and the American industry.[18] Although Ford is often credited with his methods of mass production, it is his friend George Washington Carver—a black American agricultural scientist and inventor of hundreds of plant-based products using peanuts, sweet potatoes and soybeans—who gave him the idea that altered his assembly method of producing one complete car at a time. After the inception of mass production, cars were being produced from the assembly line at a rate of one every forty seconds. Mass production all over the world also became known as "The Plant." [19] Hugh labor demands were filled by European immigrants, blacks from the South, and other ethnic groups. By the mid-1920s, Ford's competitors, General Motors and

Chrysler, began to outsell Ford due to their offering of credit payment plans, plus an emphasis on upscale quality and variety.[20]

- Between 1910 and 1920, "Detroit's population more than doubled, growing from 465,766 people in 1910 to 993,678 people by 1920." Blacks migrating from the South, seeking to leave behind the oppression of Jim Crow and work within the expanding automobile industry, contributed to the city's growth as their population grew from just over 5,741 in 1910 to 40,838 in 1920.[21]

- By 1920 and due to discriminatory housing practices, the black community could live in a few small segregated older neighborhoods, which eventually became overcrowded.[22] "Blacks who attempted to cross the city's invisible racial boundaries regularly faced violence. The result was the creation of two separate cities, one black and one white."[23]

One designated area on the lower east side, the Black Bottom neighborhood, consisted of sixty-square-blocks and was bounded by Gratiot Avenue, Brush Street, Vernor Highway, and the Grand Trunk Railroad tracks. Paradise Valley, located north of Black Bottom on Hastings Street, was the area's commercial and entertainment district. Blacks owned around 350 businesses in these communities including a movie theater, pawn shop, co-op grocery, and a bank. "The community included 17 physicians, 22 lawyers, 22 barbershops, 13 dentists, 12 cartage agencies, 11 tailors, 10 restaurants, 10 real estate dealers, 8 grocers, 6 drugstores, 5 undertakers, 4 employment offices, a few service stations and a candy maker."[24]

- "For years, several thousand Negroes had been living in a small triangle of streets wedged between two of the near west side's largest thoroughfares, West Grand Boulevard and Tireman

Avenue. Compared to Black Bottom, the west side enclave was prosperous and stable, and whites who surrounded it had never seen it as threatening. Though the neighborhood's borders were clear enough, they had also been somewhat porous." "But in the summer of 1925, the whites who encircled the enclave suddenly became passionately and violently committed to preventing Negroes from crossing the color line."[25]

On the evening of September 9, 1925, an angry white mob of several hundred people tried to force the black physician Dr. Ossian Sweet and his family from a bungalow-styled house, a few miles east of Black Bottom, which they had purchased in an all-white Detroit neighborhood on the corner at 2905 Garland Avenue. After defending themselves with gun shots from the house into the crowd, Dr. Sweet, his wife Gladys, and nine of their friends were charged with murder and eventually acquitted during an illustrious trial in the spring of 1926.[26]

According to the scholar and historian Kevin Boyle:

> The owners who sold the Sweet family their home on August 1st "were more than pleased to find the Sweets. By all appearances, Ed and Marie Smith were a completely conventional white couple, hardly the sort one would expect to shatter the neighborhood's color line. But the Smiths were not exactly what they appeared to be. Mrs. Smith was indeed Caucasian, but her husband was a light-skinned colored man who had spent most of his adult life passing as white. The deception had given him the ability to build a successful business selling real estate in areas no black real estate agent could operate, while his brother, who was just as light-

skinned, had risen to the rank of sergeant in the Detroit Police Department."

Because the Sweets had no other place to live and were subjected to bank discriminatory lending restrictions, the Smiths profited greatly from the sale of the house and "they offered to finance the purchase themselves."[27]

Walter White, an NAACP (National Association for the Advancement of Colored People) investigator, was dispatched to Detroit to investigate the Sweet case by the organization's secretary, James Weldon Johnson. White, a black man, once said, "I am a Negro. My skin is white, my eyes are blue, my hair is blond. The traits of my race are nowhere visible upon me." "White's ability to move freely in a Caucasian world was his, and the NAACP's, greatest asset." Passing as white and sometimes going undercover in roles such as a traveling salesman and a member of a white posse, he was able to investigate and expose violence related to lynch mobs, race riots, and elections across the South.

The work was also perilous. "There's a damn yellow nigger down here passing for white and the boys are going to get him," a train conductor once told an escaping White in 1919 while he was on an undercover assignment in Helena, Arkansas. White, with a voice of innocence, asked, "What will they do with him?" The conductor responded, "When they get through with him, he won't pass for white no more."[28]

HENRY SWEET ACQUITTED IN DETROIT SLAYING CASE

Colored Man Was Accused in Murder of Leon E. Briener During Race Disturbance.

By the Associated Press.

DETROIT, May 14.—Henry Sweet, negro, was acquitted of a charge of murder by a jury here late yesterday in connection with the slaying of Leon E. Briener during a race disturbance here last September. Briener was shot by volleys which police said were fired from the house of Ossian H. Sweet, negro doctor.

The house, which was located in a section occupied exclusively by white persons, had been purchased by the negro doctor. Ossian Sweet, his wife, his brother, Henry, and eight other negroes, and a quantity of arms and ammunition were taken from the house after the shooting. Ossian was tried first, the hearing resulting in a mistrial when the jury disagreed.

Clarence Darrow, Chicago criminal lawyer, acted as chief of defense counsel in both trials, and Arthur Garfield Hays of New York was associated with the defense in the first trial.

Robert M. Toms, prosecuting attorney, announced after Henry Sweet's acquittal that he had not decided whether the other 10 negroes would be brought to trial on the same charges on which Sweet was acquitted.

The Evening Star, May 14, 1926   Washington D.C.

- "American cities didn't simply sparkle in the summer of 1925. They simmered with hatred, deeply divided as always." "Many native-born whites didn't have wealth or power to buffer them from the changes sweeping over the cities" like Henry Ford and his millions. "Many resented the foreigners who intruded on their world. Now the cities were filling with Negroes as well . . . " and "many native-born whites were appalled by the cities' celebrations of immigrant and black cultures."

In the early 1920s, native-born whites braced themselves against the threats the city posed: shopkeepers' associations boycotting against foreign-born competitors, church groups campaigning for the enforcement of prohibition and against lewd entertainment, veterans' organizations attempting to remove public school textbooks that didn't glorify Anglo-Saxon culture with an adamant amount of zeal, foremen and tradesmen meetings to prevent immigrants and Negroes from obtaining better paying factory jobs, and thousands of people joining the KKK (Ku Klux Klan). The new KKK of the North was founded by businessmen and "made sure that all those who threatened the nation—blacks, of course, but also

Catholics, Jews, and the foreign-born—were kept in their place." Expanding beyond the South and into small Midwestern and Western towns and big cities, "the money rolled in, for memberships, robes, rulebooks, and the hatred spewed out from the Klan rallies and marches, protests and political campaigns that spread across urban American." By 1924, thirty-five thousand people had joined the Detroit chapter of the Klan.[29]

- In 1926, Dr. Carter Godwin Woodson, a distinguished black scholar, historian, author, editor, and publisher, proposed and launched the annual observance of "Negro History Week" which became Black History Month in 1976.[30]

- During the 1920s and '30s, the notorious Detroit lower east side organized crime syndicate called the Purple Gang, led most often by the Jewish brothers Ray and Abe Bernstein, controlled "all of Detroit's underworld including the city's gambling, liquor and drug trade."[31]

- By 1930, Detroit had become the fourth largest city in America with a population of 1.6 million including a 9.1% black population increase to 149,119.[32]

On April 19, 1926, a historical perspective about the state of Michigan, the city of Detroit, and its noted black and white leaders was written by one of its Negro citizens, Pastor Robert W. Bagnall, for the now defunct *Messenger* magazine. The article (below and on the following four pages) was reprinted in the August 19, 1939, edition of the *Detroit Tribune*.[33]

PAGE TEN   THE DETROIT TRIBUNE, SATURDAY, AUGUST 19, 1939   2146 St. Antoine Street, Corner Columbia—Clifford 2814

BAGNALL REVIEWS EARLY PROGRESS OF RACE IN MICHIGAN

Editor's Note:—The following article from the pen of the Rev. Father Robert W. Bagnall, a former Detroiter, is reprinted from the Messenger magazine, April 19, 1926. It is pregnant with historical information about Michigan and outstanding leaders, white and colored, who have contributed to the growth and progress of the Wolverine State. Many changes have taken place in Detroit and Michigan since 1926 when Father Bagnall published this splendid article in the Messenger. The magazine itself has ceased to be published. Some of the leaders mentioned still live and are active in the various walks of life among our people, and many new dynamic figures have come upon the scene, including Joe Louis, Willis Ward, Eddie Tolan, Bill Watson, Senator Charles C. Diggs, Louis C. Blount, Fred Allen, Father E. W. Daniel, the Rev G. W. Baber, Snow F. Grigsby and numerous others.

By Robert W. Bagnall

Michigan—"The land of the great waters" as the Chippewas aptly named it, is the 22nd state in size and the 7th in population. It is really two states in one, for the Upper and Lower Peninsulas are so different one from the other that they have little in common.

It is a state whose shores are lapped by all the great inland seas—the uncertain and treacherous Lake Erie; the wide reaches of Lake Michigan; the rolling waters of Superior, and the blue waters of St. Clair and Huron.

In addition that straight known as the Detroit River and many other streams and lakes are found within the 58,000 square miles which comprise her territory. In the north there are many resorts and m e d i c i n a l springs. There you find the famous Macinaw Islands.

Its mean temperature is just over 46 degrees and the summers, which are short, hover around a mean of 68 degrees and the winters around 23 degrees. However, zero is frequent and 15 below is by no means uncommon as the wind races over hundreds of miles of ice hummocks and the frigid waters of the Great Lakes.

The Upper Peninsula is rugged, wild and barren, but rich in mineral deposits. Copper and iron are there in rich quantities as well as deposits of coal and statuary marble. Gold, silver and lead are also found in small quantities. There, yesterday the great lumber industry flourished and the name of Michigan pine became famous. Even yet in some sections of the state the lumber industry is very important, and like Maine, each year sees the forest fires jeopardize millions in property as well as human life.

In some parts of the Upper Peninsula the frontier yet remains, and Indians in considerable numbers earn their l i v i n g as trappers, while others are found in the settlements. Deer, bear, and the wolverine, together with the great timber wolf are by no means scarce. In fact, a few winters ago packs of timber wolves invaded villages and towns in the Upper Peninsula attacking the live stock. It is here that we find the only mountains in the state—the Pocupine which are about 2,000 feet above the sea. Here is the great Sault Ste. Marie Canal which accommodates more tonnage than the Suez, Panama or any other canal in the world.

It is interesting to note that when the writer some years ago had the present Civil Rights Bill introduced in the Michigan Legislature, and organized a lobby for its passage, the principal objection in the Legislature to its passage was offered by members from the Upper Peninsula where there are few Negroes. They objected to the bill because they did not want Indians to eat in the restaurants with them.

It is the Upper Peninsula in which old Father Marquette worked and even today it suggests hardship and heroism. It is the Lower Peninsula however where Cadillac and his soldiers played their part, and it is this section of the state which makes Michigan today famous as the great capitol motordom.

Detroit Tribune, August 19, 1939

Here we find the great agricultural region of the state with its crops of waving corn, wheat, oats, rye, barley, buckwheat and hay; with its potato and sugar beet fields; its beans, peas, and famous celery, and along Lake Michigan, its vineyards and fruit orchards. Quite a number of these farms are owned by colored people,—old residents of the state. It is in this region too that we find stock and dairy farms, and sheep herds.

In the Lower Peninsula we find the principal cities of the state and consequently most of its educational institutions, among which is the famous State University. Here abound foundries, iron and steel mills, grist and salt mills, machine shops, furniture factories; the manufacturing of wagons and farm implements, and a great multitude of automobile factories and plants for automobile accessories.

Grand Rapids suggest the idea of furniture; Battle Creek that of breakfast food and sanatoria; Kalamazoo, succulent celery; Port Huron, steel mills and shipping; Saginaw, salt and lumber; and Jackson ,Lansing, Pontiac, Flint and Detroit, the great automobile industry, for in these places more cars are made than anywhere else in the country.

Detroit is the dynamic city of Michigan and it dominates the whole state. It is a name to conjure with; the largest growing great city in the Union, bursting out of its clothing, with a polygot population of over a million souls. It has been so busy making money that it has never had time to stop to find itself.

Just as Detroit dominates the state, so is it dominated in the mind of the world by the remarkable figure of Henry Ford, whose genius for mass production of a cheap car has enabled him to build up the biggest motor factory in the world, covering miles of ground.

In his Detroit plant are employed around 8,000 Negroes, mostly doing heavy work. A considerable group however do skilled a n d semi-skilled work, and there is a Negro foreman, several Negro clerks, and one Negro, Glenn Cochran, a young graduate of the University of Michigan, who is employed in the experimental department as an electrical engineer. Detroit in 1919 had 2176 manufacturing establishments with about 176,-000 workers. Ford employs, over 50,000 or nearly one third of all the city's factory workers.

Detroit h a s developed other notable figures—the Dodge brothers, the Lelands—father and s o n; Chalmers, Chrysler, Willys, Couzins, Lee, Norval Hawkins, among others.

But Ford's name dominates all others like Pike's Peak the surrounding mountain tops. His personality has caught the imagination of the world as it is a peculiar combination of the naive and sophisticated, the efficient and the erratic.

His stunts have been so extraordinary that t h e y have startled the world, nor were they advertising schemes, but sincere efforts. His peace ship, his notion that every criminal could be reformed merely by giving

him a job, his anti-semitic campaign—all reveal a peculiar type of mind. S. S. Marquis, who for years was head of his social service department, says that he has the most disorganized organized mind in America.

Detroit—the city reminds one of Ford—the man. It has the same disorganized organized characteristic. Skyscrapers and unsanitary hovels that few modern cities would permit, are in stone throw of one another. Reeking alleys with six foot piles of manure can be found in the heart of the city along with dirty, miserably paved streets. On the other hand, not many minutes ride away, one finds wonderfully paved broad streets with beautiful homes and even magnificent show places.

Everywhere there seems to be a struggle between the small town and the great industrial city—a physical body politic in internal dissension. And this too is true of its government which certainly cannot be said to be noteworthy for economy, efficiency or freedom from corruption. When one remembers that Detroit in 1910 had only around 376,-000 people and now numbers over a million you have the explanation for much of this.

Some one has said Detroit is Michigan and Michigan is Detroit. While this is hardly true of the state as a whole, it is true of Negro Michigan. The bulk of the Negro population in Michigan is found in Detroit and in cities near by.

Michigan has always had its Negro contingent and many of them have been noteworthy characters. William Lambert, a successful tailor in the old days together with Charles Webb and E l d e r Munroe conducted there the underground railway on a large scale, safely piloting it is said, thousands of slaves to Canada.

Lambert is reputed to have been the author of the code of the underground railway and he and Munroe were friends and advisors of John Brown. Lambert was the founder of St. Matthews Episcopal Church and Munroe its first minister. It was this church which g a v e Bishop Holly to the ministry and where he was ordained, although he was living in the East when he lead a colony to Hayti.

Dr. Levi Johnson in the early days enjoyed a lucrative practice as a physician among the whites of the city, these forming a majority of his patients. His son, Dr. Albert H. Johnson, yet is called into the families who were served by his father and until recently he and his brother continued the drug store his father founded. William Cole had one of the principal moving and trucking firms for many years in Detroit and for a long while his sons carried on the business. Pelham, a colored man from Virginia, whose sons and daughters are well known, lead the fight which removed the "black laws" from the statute books of Michigan and ended compulsory separate schools and the prohibition of intermarriage. He was the father of Robert Pelham of the Census Bureau in Washington.

Negroes had won s o m e place in the arts and inventions in Detroit at this time. Shoecroft had gained a number of important commissions as a portrait painter, Mollie Lambert had won a local literary reputation, and Elijah McCoy had invented the automobile lubricator from which developed the whole principle of automobile lubrication of moving machinery, and on which the great Michigan Lubrication Works w e r e built up. McCoy of course, got little as the result of his work.

In Detroit at this time there had been a few Negro private secretaries to important officials like Charles Webb, a number of clerks and carriers, a number of teachers in the m i x e d schools, a few clerks in political jobs, a county account, tant, some seven or eight physicians, and a few prominent lawyers like Judge D. Augustus Straker, who was elected a magistrate. Samuel Thompson, Francis Warren, Robert Barnes, Walter Stowers. To these could be added the names of a few younger men, some of whom now have considerable practice. There was very little in the way of Negro business, and most of the 8,000 Negroes, were settled around the Antoine district within walking distance of one another, and were served by four churches, whose ministers worked together in civil matters in perfect accord.

Among the names mentioned above several are worthy of notice. D. Augustus Straker was not only a good lawyer but a man of considerable literary attainment and the author of several volumes of interest. Francis Warren was a most unselfish champion of his peoples' rights, but never received the honors he deserved because himself a mulatto, he chose to take a white woman as a second wife,—a woman who at all times proved an excellent helpmate. Warren—stocky, with a leonine head crowned with a thatch of white hair and big voice, was absolutely fearless and utterly militant, and was always on the battleline when the rights of his race were challenged. He was a single-taxer, a democrat, a radical in many ways, and a generation in advance of the provincial group about him. His death robbed Detroit of one of her most valuable Negro citizens.

Around this time the Rev. Robert L. Bradby began his rise to prominence in Detroit. He is perhaps, today the largest Negro figure in Detroit and a force to be recognized. Bradly is a born leader, an excellent organizer, a good business man, and an unusually able orator who makes full use of his nearly 3,000 devoted parishioners and while keen for an opportunity to make money, he is ever ready to champion a race cause.

W. C. O s b y should be mentioned in this connection—for he, too, did much to help Detroit to give Negroes justice. The Reverend Doctor Gomez, a young West Indian clergyman of the A. M. E. church, should also be mentioned as one of the outstanding leaders in the life of Detroit—a dynamic personality with a very large following. He too, has been interested in most public matters concerning the Negro. When the migration came, Negroes poured forth into Detroit at the rate of 100 a day from all parts of the South. Jobs begged for men. Wages were sky-high. Labor was King. Night and day the factories were kept at full speed. Money was plentiful, and the Negro got his full share. He saved money so that later when unemployment came, it was found that h i s g r o u p was the last to ask for charity. He made good; established bank accounts and bought homes. He broke into semi-skilled and skilled work. The masses of him were followed by doctors, lawyers, business men, and a great company of preachers. Negro Detroit jumped from 8,000 in 1914 to 85,000 in 1926, for Detroit became the mecca of the Negro.

But along with him came the whites from the South until now they say these number between 200,000 and 300,000. A surprising number of these joined the police force and stupid commissioners have permitted many of these to be assigned to Negro districts with resultant had relations between the police and Negroes.

Just this last year police shot nearly seventy Negroes in Detroit, and evidence indicates that most of these shootings were unwarranted. No police officer, however, has been punished as the result of such shootings.

With the coming of great numbers of southern whites and Negroes, with the necessity of whole districts being taken over to house the Negroes, prejudice grew apace. Discriminations became frequent, and the prejudice terminated in the succession of riots to prevent Negroes from occupying homes in districts which previously had none of them, riots which culminated in the now famous affair of Dr. Sweet.

The Sweet case was not an isolated instance. As f a r back as 1919 there had been threats and slight overt acts when colored people moved into so-called white districts. But with the coming of southern whites and the rise of the Ku Klux Klan, these demonstrations against colored people living in white neighborhoods took organized and determined form. A colored blacksmith who fired into a mob who stoned his home, was arrested but released when he agreed to move; a colored woman, the mother of a young baby, was arrested and kept in jail over night when she fired on an attacking mob that stoned her house; and Dr. Bristol, a young Negro, moving with companions into his house on American Avenue, had to open fire before an attacking mob retired.

The most important of the cases prior to that of Dr Sweet's was the case of Dr. A. L. Turner. Dr. Turner was a successful surgeon who was on the staff of Grace Hospital and had been most instrumental in founding the Negro hospital in Detroit. He was a graduate in arts and medicine from the University of Michigan, and had studied elsewhere as well.

His wife and mother-in-law had inherited a considerable fortune from "A. L Loudin of the Jubilee singer fame, and their means and his earnings permitted the Turner family to live in a comfortable manner.

Dr. Turner was regarded as one of the Negro leaders in Detroit in business and in his profession, and had been long known as a public-minded citizen. He bought a home in the district wholly peopled by whites—a community where the Klan was very strong.

A mob of 6,000 gathered in front of his home, and when the police came, they stood idly by as onlookers. The mob stoned the house, breaking windows but the police did nothing.

Within the house were Negro men with an ample supply of ammunition, who wished to fire into the mob when they s t o n e d the house—but this T u r n e r would not permit. Finally Turner opened his front door to let in the police, and these were followed by a group of the mob who destroyed the furniture, tore down hangings ,and threatening Dr. Turner with a gun, compelled him to sign an agreement to sell—the police meanwhile looking on.

The mob then loaded Turner's furniture on a van, the police hurried him to his car which was stoned, and he was moved back to his old house. Dr. Turner's wife refused to sign the agreement to sell, but Turner did not return to the new house, in spite of offers of help from many colored citizens and promises of protection from the police.

The Turner incident encouraged the mob in Detroit to believe that they could easily segregate Negroes by force and intimidation. It aroused much indignation on the part of the colored people who felt that Dr. Turner should have returned and protected his home. These determined not to be intimidated.

Dr. Ossian H. Sweet, a young Negro physician who had studied in America and Europe bought a home in a district largely peopled by artisans and factory people. On his coming to the neighborhood the white people of the community organized the Water Works Association whose raison d' etre was to force the Sweets to move. There the steps to be taken were planned.

On the night the Sweets moved in a demonstration in front of his home was held. On the second night, his home was assaulted with stones and shots were fired from within and without. The inmates of the Sweet home opened fire above the heads of the mob, but one of the mob was killed, and a second wounded. The Sweets and the nine other inmates of the house were arrested and indicted for murder in the first degree. The N. A. A. C. P. employed Clarence Darrow, A. Garfield Hayes, Walter F. Nelson, and three local colored attorneys—Cecil W. Rowlette, Charles Mahoney and Julian Perry, to defend them.

The first trial ended in a hung jury and the second will shortly be held.

Weeks before the Turner and Sweet incident, Detroit papers insisted that Negroes must surrender their rights to live wherever they please and accept segregated districts—ghettoes—or else be held responsible for race riots. The police in all these cases were notoriously lax in protecting the Negro homes, and in some instances aided the mob.

The Sweet trial resulted in many Detroiters gaining a new viewpoint and today many whites of that city acknowledge the rights of any racial group to live wherever it can buy.

In spite of the increased prejudice, Detroit gives promise of being one of the most prosperous cities in the country for the Negro. Its business opportunities are many and are rapidly developing. The city as yet lacks a crystallized Negro leadership, but one will, of a certainty, shortly emerge.

The overflow population of Negro Detroit is rapidly building up other cities in Michigan such as Flint, Saginaw, Alpena, Pontiac, and Jackson.

In these places there are a few outstanding figures like Oscar Baker, prominent lawyer and leading citizen of Bay City, who is highly esteemed by both races. A number of such individuals will steadily increase as the Negro population grows and the smaller cities will play a large part in the future of the Negro in Michigan.

The coming of the large number of migrants not only precipitated many problems but set in array against one another many of the older Negro residents and t h e newcomers. On the other hand, a number of the older residents realize that their strength lay in combining with the newcomers and systematically assisting them to adjust themselves to their new environment. The older residents who remained aloof from the newcomers, regarded them as a menace to their numbers, and found their crudities obnoxious— as was inevitable. The smallness of the numbers of these older citizens caused them to be overwhelmed by the great horde of newcomers, so that their influence lessened until it has now become almost nil in Detroit.

In looking over the names of candidates for the Legislature and t h e common council among the Negroes, it is to be noted that the names of those who lived in Detroit before the migration are conspicuously absent. The great mass of Negro migrants for the first time are beginning to pause to consider their cultural life. Heretofore they have been too busy making money and seeking to adjust themselves to their new world.

They have now in Detroit a well-furnished clubhouse; and a well-organized social life is rapidly crystallizing such established social life as we find in the major cities of the South.

The Negro is destined to play a large part in the life of Michigan. He is yet in a period of storm and stress. Just how big that part shall be, no man can say.

As recalled by Ernest Goodman, a noted Jewish attorney and former Detroit resident who represented the poor and oppressed in legal battles since 1928 (and a founding member of the National Lawyers Guild and cofounder of the first interracial law firm in the United States):

In 1911, "I lived the life of a young Jewish kid growing up in Detroit's ghetto. I went to Hebrew school and to synagogue services regularly. My family kept a kosher home. I had that sort of upbringing.

The Jewish ghetto, before it moved to the west side of Woodward Avenue, consisted of housing which was always infested by cockroaches and bedbugs. Rats were another enemy which you had to be constantly chasing, avoiding, and destroying. These ghetto scenes have always been a sharp part of the recollection of my childhood.

To the south of the Jewish ghetto lived the black community in its own ghetto. As we moved north, the black people would take over the ghetto housing of the Jewish people.

I lived in this way, within a completely Jewish environment. I hardly knew any gentiles. We, like most families, didn't own a car. We traveled primarily by streetcar and lived, when we could, near where we worked and where our synagogue was located. Ours was an insular life for most of my childhood years.

I went through Central High School, and the experiences there were tied into the Jewishness of my life, especially being singled out as Jewish and not being able to participate in the life of the non-Jewish WASP [White Anglo-Saxon Protestant] students who politically ran the school. It resulted, during the last part of my high school life, in a bloody battle that occurred at the school between the WASPs and the roughhouse Jewish guys, out of whom arose the notorious Purple Gang in the late 1920s. We considered them our friends because they protected us. This battle between the WASPs and the Jews helped open my eyes to the racial, religious, and ethnic divisions within our society.

When the depression came and I was faced with it, I began to find out that the work I was doing as a lawyer—all of it—was on behalf of small retail stores that sold furniture and jewelry on credit to working people. Our job was to try to collect these accounts or repossess if they couldn't pay, especially when they were laid off. The black community was particularly victimized by this practice. The more I did that kind of work, the more I felt that it was something I didn't want to spend my life on. I read and studied. I became aware that the Thirteenth, Fourteenth, and Fifteenth Amendments had utterly failed to provide any protection to black people.

I began to understand that people were being destroyed for no reason I could see that was logical or necessary. I then began to understand what I had been doing as an individual, as a lawyer. I had been working on behalf of a system that was destroying the people around me. I began to realize that I was becoming a part of this system. I made the decision I didn't want that. I wanted to fight on behalf of the people who were being opposed and do something to help them. The only thing I began to feel sorry about was that I had wasted all these years when I could have been doing something that was useful and constructive.

For the first time, I met black people. I had never before met black people on a social level. In the organizations I had joined were black people as well as white—also, non-citizens who were living here from different countries, different cultures and with different personalities. I began to find out all the wonderful things I could learn from them. Their ideals were so different, and they helped me to expand my view of life and of the world at the same time.

I'm getting into about 1935, 1936, and 1937. These were great years in the sense that there were tremendous organizing movements all over the city—organizing labor unions, organizing tenants, trying to get food for people in some fashion. All these were political struggles. Of course, most important was the labor union struggle. Detroit was nationally known as an open shop-town with no unions of any consequence. They had been kept out for years. The state law made it very, very difficult for a union to organize. Peaceful picketing was not permitted. Injunctions would be issued, people put in jail for peaceful picketing. There was no way in which working people could peacefully organize a labor union except in the small side businesses. What we now consider a right under the Constitution, necessary to a democratic society, was not possible in cities like Detroit. Other means had to be used. Usually it was by violating the law—going on a picket line, trying to close the plant to force the employer to bargain for a contract so they'd be arrested, put in jail as law breakers.

It was this kind of atmosphere that presented just the kind of opportunity I was looking for. As a lawyer, I could fight effectively within a larger struggle with which I identified myself, on behalf of the oppressed and virtually defenseless, against the clearly etched wealthy and powerful. It was a wonderful opportunity to be of help, instead of using the instrumentalities of law to evict people from houses and to take away their furniture when they failed to make the payments.

When the National Lawyers Guild was formed in 1937, I finally had an opportunity to belonging to a law society which embodied the concepts I held. Through the Guild I became acquainted with lawyers across the country who held social and political views similar to my own. They formed a network of lawyers who were involved in the development of labor law, civil rights and liberties, and other areas of people's struggles. The American Bar Association primarily represented big business and finance. It opposed everything Roosevelt and his New Deal represented and excluded black lawyers.

In those days, the police were solely under the control of the employers of the state. They dominated them top to bottom; in addition, the employers had private detectives and agencies working full-time for them. We called them goons or company goons. As the number of strikes increased, violence increased. Employers used every means at their disposal to preserve Detroit as an open-shop town.

Most of the violence came from the police, and much of it was directed toward black people. They were treated differently than whites in all encounters with the judicial system. I soon observed the treatment by the police of the black community was in complete disregard of their rights. They would arrest a black person, hold him for about as long as they wanted—a week, two weeks, sometimes longer. If a lawyer attempted to get him out because no charges had been brought against him, the police could transfer him from one precinct to another, and the judges would not acknowledge this common practice. Unless you served the subpoena at the precinct where the prisoner actually was at the time, the police would win this merry-go-round game.

White policemen—there were only a few that were black—didn't want to go into the black community to try to solve a crime. They had little communication within the black community. But they wanted to solve crimes in the black community so as it wouldn't look as though they were overlooking criminal conduct. So, they used the easy method—beat out a confession. The crime was solved. That was typical. I don't know how many hundreds or thousands of people were sent to prison for crimes to which they confessed but didn't commit.

We have to eradicate these four hundred years of slavery which makes a distinction between the white and black color, which emphasizes all the other attitudes and makes it something different from and greater than the kind of difficulty that people generally have in relating."[34]

Between 1926 and the mid-1930s, the Steger family lived in this west side Detroit house on **6712 Scotten Avenue**.[35] The house was photographed in April 2002. From the author's photograph collection.

On May 8, 1933, Gordon and Dorothy were divorced in Detroit when Carl was seven years old. Gordon was accused of being "guilty of extreme cruelty."[36] The previous year, Dorothy moved to New York City to study and work within the music industry.[37] Nevertheless, over two years later, on November 26, 1935, the estranged couple celebrated their Thanksgiving holiday with their remarriage at the Hartford Avenue Baptist Church in Detroit. Pastor Charles A. Hill was the clergyman who presided over the ceremony.[38] Between 1937 and 1940, the family lived in Apartment No. 2 of the Lodge Apartments on 4180 Brush Street between Superior Street and Willis Avenue in the city's Black Bottom area.[39]

Although Carl was too young to partake in the musical nightlife where he lived, living in that environment may have broadened his musical taste to include the playing of jazz later in his life. Jazz and blues clubs dotted the main thoroughfare of Hastings Street in Black Bottom's Paradise Valley and nearby streets. The MDL Club, Chocolate Bar/Cotton Club, Ace Bar, Cozy Corner, and the Harlem Cave were grouped near the family's home. Several other clubs existed in the city's other black-designated regions, including the North End and the West Side. During the night, music blared out into the streets from within these establishments and musicians performed outside on sidewalks during the day to lure those passing by within their range.[40]

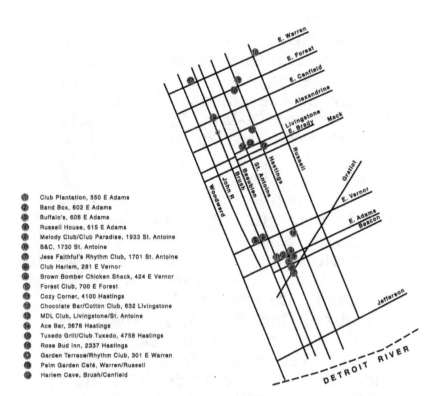

① Club Plantation, 550 E Adams
② Band Box, 602 E Adams
③ Buffalo's, 606 E Adams
④ Russell House, 615 E Adams
⑤ Melody Club/Club Paradise, 1933 St. Antoine
⑥ B&C, 1730 St. Antoine
⑦ Jess Faithful's Rhythm Club, 1701 St. Antoine
⑧ Club Harlem, 281 E Vernor
⑨ Brown Bomber Chicken Shack, 424 E Vernor
⑩ Forest Club, 700 E Forest
⑪ Cozy Corner, 4100 Hastings
⑫ Chocolate Bar/Cotton Club, 632 Livingstone
⑬ MDL Club, Livingstone/St. Antoine
⑭ Ace Bar, 3678 Hastings
⑮ Tuxedo Grill/Club Tuxedo, 4758 Hastings
⑯ Rose Bud Inn, 2337 Hastings
⑰ Garden Terrace/Rhythm Club, 301 E Warren
⑱ Palm Garden Café, Warren/Russell
⑲ Harlem Cave, Brush/Canfield

Detroit's Paradise Valley and Black Bottom area clubs listed on a map during the 1930s. The red dot designates the location of the Lodge Apartments where the Steger family lived between 1937 and 1940. Courtesy of Borkin and Kaplan.

Mrs. Sarah Anna Byrd

Mrs. Sarah Anna Byrd, 80, colored, a resident of Battle Creek for 62 years, died at 11:30 p. m. Friday at the home of her daughter and son-in-law, Mr. and Mrs. Robert Williams, 38 West Rittenhouse avenue. She had been ill for about five years. Born Oct. 8, 1857 in London, Ont., Mrs. Byrd came here in 1875. Besides her daughter, she is survived by one granddaughter, Mrs. Dorothy Steger, Detroit; one grandson, Arley Williams, Detroit; and one great-grandson, Carl Steger, Detroit. Funeral services will be held at 2 p. m. Wednesday from the Mt. Zion A. M. E. church. The Rev. S. S. Harris will be in charge, assisted by the Rev. E. L. Todd, and burial will be in the Reese cemetery.

Carl Steger's maternal great-grandmother **Sarah Anna Byrd's obituary** appeared in the March 13, 1937, edition of the *Battle Creek Enquirer* (Battle Creek, Michigan) newspaper.

"An unusual harmonica solo was given by Master Carl Steger, the son of the hostess who seems to be very talented along musical lines also."

—*Michigan Chronicle*, February 19, 1939

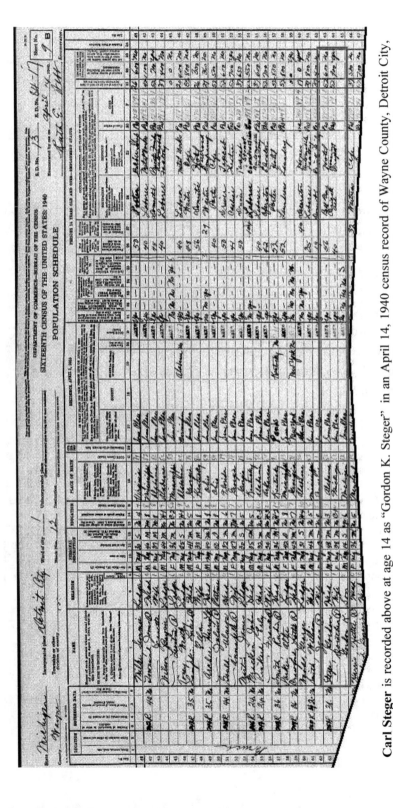

Carl Steger is recorded above at age 14 as "Gordon K. Steger" in an April 14, 1940 census record of Wayne County, Detroit City, Michigan. His parents Gordon and Dorothy, whose name was recorded as "Dorathea," are also listed in the household.[41] Public Domain.

A closer view of the **Gordon Steger household in 1940** with a 14-year-old Carl who was also known as "Gordon K. (or C.) Steger."

Between 1941 and 1944, the Steger family lived in Apartment 204 within the Cevera Apartments at 435 Holbrook Avenue in the city. Carl was a student at Detroit's Northern High School.[42]

According to an oral family history account, Carl "graduated from Wayne State University" after high school.[43]

The **Cevera Apartments** is where the Steger family once lived during the early '40s. These photographs, taken in 1999 of the abandoned apartment building at 435 Holbrook Avenue in Detroit, "was once a luxurious art deco architectural beauty" as shown in detail by the entrance arch. From the author's photograph collection.

During the fall of 1944, the Steger family purchased a house at 438 Hague Avenue in Detroit.[44]

On August 31, 1945, Carl's father Gordon died of a heart attack after a six-month stay at the Fort Custer Veteran Hospital in Battle Creek, Michigan. Four days later, his funeral ceremony was held at the family home. Afterward, he was buried in the Reese Cemetery in Battle Creek.[45]

8. State below the name of each living child of the deceased veteran, including adopted children and stepchildren, under 18 years of age and unmarried, or over 18 years of age and under 21 years of age, unmarried and attending school; or of any age who is insane, idiotic, or otherwise permanently helpless or incapable of self-support by reason of mental or physical defect. (See Instruction No. 4.)

| NAME OF CHILD | DATE OF BIRTH | | | NAME AND ADDRESS OF PERSON HAVING CUSTODY OF EACH CHILD |
	DAY	MONTH	YEAR	
Carl Steger 19 yrs. unmarried, attending school	1	1	1926	Dorothy Steger 438 Hague

9. Which, if any, of the children is (a) a stepchild ___None___; (b) an adopted child ___None___; (c) an illegitimate child ___None___; or (d) a helpless child ___None___. (See Instruction No. 4(b).)

10. If any child was a stepchild, was such child a member of the veteran's household at the time of his death? ___None___

11. (a) What is the amount of the claimant's annual income? ___2.6.00.00.___ (b) From what source is this income derived? ___Dept. Parks and Recreation, Detroit___

(c) Was the claimant exempt from the payment of a Federal income tax during the preceding year? ___No___

12. Is the claimant now holding any office or position, appointive or elective, under the United States Government, or the municipal government of the District of Columbia, or under any corporation, the majority of stock of which is owned by the United States? ___No___ If so, give salary and name of employer ___None___

Carl was referenced above as being in the custody of his mother Dorothy Steger in her application for veteran death benefits after her husband Gordon's death in 1945.[46]

On October 4, 1946, Carl, age twenty, enlisted into the United States Army Air Corps branch as a private and was stationed at Eglin Field, Florida.[47]

During the spring of 1953, Carl married Shirley Marie Lewis.[48] However, their matrimony ended abruptly, and the couple divorced in August.[49] On October 24th, he married his second wife during the year—Florence Onameega Varden—in Bowling Green, Ohio. Florence, a native of Detroit, worked as a typist.[50]

It isn't known if the Florence referenced above is the same one mentioned below, but according to a family member's oral history account, Carl married a woman twice. Florence or "Fern" June Steger "had two children—two or three daughters. I recalled mail coming to the house. The woman can cook." According to another, "She was a good cook. She had a cooking show and a book."[51]

> WEDDINGS It was love at first sight for Carol Jean Lewis,
> N. Y. School of Social Work freshman, and Dr. Thomas
> M. Matthews, whose engagement and late summer wed-
> ding have been announced by her parents, executive sec-
> retary Edward S. Lewis of the New York Urban League,
> and Mrs. Lewis. The prospective bridegroom is chief resi-
> dent in neuro-surgery at the Boston Veterans Admin-
> istration Hospital and a Meharry graduate. They are
> planning a home in Boston and Carol will continue work
> on her master's in social work at Simmons . . . Carl
> Steger, who recently wed the hazel-eyed charmer, Shirley
> Lewis, is the orphaned scion of an old Detroit family . . .
> The Bay State relatives of Dorothy and Ted Yates, around
> Boston, Cambridge, Dorchester, Bedford and Wellesley,
>
> **42**

Carl's marriage to Shirley Lewis was referenced on the Society page
of the May 14, 1953, edition of the black-owned news publication *Jet*
magazine.[52]

Carl's future and second wife Florence Onameega Varner as a
senior in her 1947 Battle Creek Central High School yearbook.[53]

IN THE MATTER OF

_____ and

The undersigned respectfully make application for a Marriage License for said parties, and upon oath states:

That said _____
is ___ years of age, on the ___ day of _____ 19__,
his residence is _____
his place of birth is _____
his occupation is _____
his father's name is _____
his mother's maiden name was _____
that he was _____ previously married _____
and that he has no wife living.
Divorced _____ Date _____ Case No. _____
_____
Minor Children _____

Name of former wife _____

To the Honorable Judge of the Probate Court of said County:
No. _____ MARRIAGE LICENSE APPLICATION

That said _____
is ___ years of age, on the ___ day of _____ 19__, Sandusky County, Ohio
her residence is _____
her place of birth is _____
her occupation is _____
her father's name is _____
her mother's maiden name was _____
that she was _____ previously married _____
and is _____ a widow or divorced woman, her married
name being Mrs. _____
and that she has no husband living.
Divorced _____ Date _____ Case No. _____

Minor Children _____

Name of former husband _____

That neither of said parties is an habitual drunkard, epileptic, imbecile or insane, and is not under the influence of any intoxicating liquor or narcotic drug. Said parties are not nearer of kin than second cousins, and there is no legal impediment to their marriage.
It is expected that _____ is to solemnize the marriage of said parties.

Consent of Father _____
Consent of Mother _____
Sworn to before me and signed in my presence, this ___ day of _____ 19__
_____
Probate Judge.
By _____ Deputy Clerk.

x _____
_____

Consent of Father _____
Consent of Mother _____

ENTRY
Marriage License was this day granted to _____

Probate Court, Sandusky County, Ohio, _____ 19__
_____ and
_____ Probate Judge
By _____ Deputy Clerk.

MARRIAGE CERTIFICATE   No. 21970
I do Hereby Certify, That on the 24 day of October A. D. 1953, I solemnized the Marriage
of Mr. Gordon H. Steger with Miss Onameega Varner
Filed and Recorded October 26, 1953.
Robert J. Gabel, Probate Judge.

The State of Ohio, Sandusky County, ss

_____
Justice of the Peace
Bowling Green, Ohio

The 1953 **Marriage License Application and Certification** for Gordon H.
Steger (alias Carl) and (Florence) Onameega Varner. Note: Carl's first and
former wife Shirley Marie Steger is also listed on the document.[54]

Sometime between 1954 and 1966, Carl and Florence's marriage
ended with a divorce.[55]

Calero, Francisco Hernandez.
  Tu promesa. ©
Calhoun, Gene.
  I want to know.
Calhoun, Henry.
  I want to know.
  My love for you.
  Payday lover.
  Well.
Calkins, Ernest.
  If I had a sweetheart like
    you. ©
Call, Idaho.
  Cryin' my heart out with the
    blues.
Callahan, Joe Walter.
  I have shifted gears. ©
Callaway, Lillie Estella Brough-
    ton.
  Holy Spirit, speak to me. ©
  Teach me Thy way. ©
Callejo, Fernando Ferrer.
  Soñando.
Callejo, Rafael Correa.
  Soñando. ©
Callejo Y Ferrer, Fernando. SEE
  Callejo, Fernando Ferrer.
Callender, George.
  Blow Mr. Norris.
  Blues for J. T.
  Early times.
  Empty ice box blues.
  Lonesome Rebecca.
  Loose pork chops.
  Mississippi blues.
  Way-Out Inn.
Callis, Emma Louise.
  Go on and say it. ©
  (I don't want no) sophisticated
    fellow. ©
  I'm a hillbilly deep down in my
    heart. ©
Calvachio, Alex M.
  On the Mississippi down in
    New Orleans. ©
Calvert, Herbert Stanley.
  My little goats. ©
    __t Rachel.
      __rats. ©

I'm lonely. ©
  That innocent look. ©
Camp, Edith.
  The waits for you. ©
Camp, James Joseph.
  Free me. ©
Camp, John Hall.
  I'll never change. ©
Camp, Michael, pseud. SEE
  Anselmo, Mary Immaculate.
Campbell, A. Spotswood.
  Amaranth. ©
Campbell, Adelaide McBride.
  Fascination. ©
  January. ©
Campbell, Dorothy Lee.
  Too many dreams. ©
Campbell, Ella Patch.
  Aloha. ©
Campbell, Esther W.
  Why do I have to leave you. ©
Campbell, Florence L.
  Let's lend a hand. ©
Campbell, Fred Earnest.
  Blue mountain blues. ©
  Wild fern. ©
Campbell, Gail Anna.
  Deep down heartaches. ©
Campbell, Guy.
  Golden moon.
Campbell, Hannah Barnet.
  Shenandoah Valley.
Campbell, Harold James.
  He is coming for His own. ©
Campbell, Ian.
  Too shy. ©
Campbell, Leola.
  Mistletoe and rice. ©
  That Arizona moon. ©
Campbell, Mark.
  Don't let it end this way. ©
  I whisper to myself. ©
  It's a mistake. ©
Campbell, Medford John.
  Stay out of my dreams. ©
  This chick ain't nobody's
    fool. ©
Campbell, Merle Richmond.
  Anyone but me. ©
  The goodbye waltz. ©
Campbell, Neva Alice.
  March of the little clowns. ©

Candiloro, Angelo.
  It's summer's end, let's not
    pretend.
Candiloro, Charles I.
  It's summer's end, let's not
    pretend. ©
  Stingy miser. ©
Candiloro, Charles Ignatius.
  Lessons in love. ©
Candierr, James Boyd.
  Money spending blues. ©
Candriano, Camillo Ruspoli di.
  Las aguas del mariel.
  Canti della steppa.
  Neva fiorita.
  Santa Maria dei fiori.
Candriano, Margherita di.
  Canti della steppa. ©
  Neva fiorita. ©
Candriano, Margherita Ruspoli di.
  Las aguas del mariel. ©
  Santa Maria dei fiori. ©
Candrix, Pud.
  Tangolita.
Candullo, Joe.
  Ev'ryone knows I love you.
Canfield, Charles Robert.
  Heartaches, rain and tears. ©
Canfield, Jeannie Dexter.
  A voice from the blue. ©
Canham, William A.
  So my love. ©
Canis, David.
  My gal Ruby. ©
  One moment of love. ©
Canisales, Tonie C.
  Darling. ©
Cannan, Gerald F.
  The front porch swing. ©
Cannan, Jean D.
  The front porch swing. ©
Cannavan, Marie Bette.
  Dollar, dollar, you must go. ©
Cannin, Jimmy, pseud. SEE
  Von Heide, James Alan.
Cannon, Charles Floyd.
  A picture of home. ©
  Stolen heart blues. ©
Cannon, Eva Lee. ©
  My Saviour in the garden. ©
Cannon, J. L.
  You're a hit with every
    heart. ©
      __ee Eddie.
        __n around. ©
          __nigan.
            C__

Carbonell, Cecil Eugene.
  Broken-hearted. ©
  The Carolina waltz. ©
  Queen of the Smokies. ©
Carder, Dick.
  I don't care.
Cardinal Music Publications.
  I can't help but dream. ©
  I'll keep on trying. ©
Cardini, George.
  One love alone. ©
  Too many dreams. ©
Cardwell, Alma.
  Waiting for your call. ©
Cardwell, Charlie Haggie.
  My broken heart. ©
Care, Ralph.
  Always love me.
  For your love.
  Go you where you go.
  I'll never make you cry
    again.
  Say what you mean.
  Suddenly my heart remembers.
  Up-side down, down-side up.
Carew, Victor Eugene.
  I should have told you. ©
Carey, Bill.
  Albuquerque.
  Chicago.
  Cleveland.
  Pittsburgh.
  St. Louis, Missouri.
  San Francisco.
  Tulsa.
  Washington.
Carey, Helen Anne.
  Dance adagio, ©
Carey, Jill, pseud. SEE
  Johnsen, Ruthelia.
Carey, Myrna Frank.
  Doin' the drum major strut. ©
Carey, Ruby Evelyn.
  I get a funny feeling. ©
Caribbean Music Co.
  Coldest woman. ©
  I wanna but me mama say
    no. ©
Carideo, Americo Anthony.
  Soft eyes. ©
  When you fall in love. ©
Carl, pseud. SEE
  Steger, Gordon Herbert.
Cari-Hatais, pseud. ___
  Hatzigoga.___
  Tela___

Stancel, Prince.
  Gee, it's rough. ©
Standard Brands, inc.
  Royal puddings. ©
Standley, Johnny Kenneth.
  It's in the book. ©
Standring, John A.
  I'm in love with you. ©
Stanfield, William Carroll.
  Take care, my heart. ©
Stanford, John Rufus.
  Don't hold me close. ©
Stang, Joseph R.
  My confession.
Stanley, Beverly Jean.
  I went sailing. ©
Stanley, Carter.
  Sweetest love.
Stanley, Edward Leroy.
  I don't care what people say. ©
Stanley, Hal, pseud. SEE
  Solomon, Harold.
Stanley, Harold Eugene, Jr.
  I went sailing. ©
Stanley, Huself.
  Juanita. ©
Stanley, Lorna.
  Blushin' skies.
  Skywriting dreams of you.
Stanley, Ralph.
  Sweetest love.
Stanley, Viola.
  I'm going home. ©
Stansbury, David Arthur.
  Take me home. ©
Stansbury, Katherine Louise.
  Take me home. ©
Stanski, Mary Dorothy.
  If it's for the last time. ©
Stanton, Francis Hayward.
  Skeleton in the closet.
Stanton, Frank.
  Half pint boogie.
  Heartbroken.
Stanton, Hellen Elizabeth.
  A special one. ©
Stanton, Jeanne Wynne.
  May I remind you. ©
Stanton, Paul.
  It is more than a wish, it's a
    prayer. ©
  So little time. ©
Star Dust, pseud. SEE
  Barker, Frank Ellsworth.
Star Hit Publications.
  Mama lushun. ©
Star Light, pseud. SEE
  Light, Fannie West.
Star Printing & Pub. Co.
  Rendezvous for love.
    __er, Marvin.
      __ blue.

I'm afraid you've waited too
  long.
Jump, Jack, jump.
  The last song tonight.
  Rosie.
  There's room in my heart.
  Till the cows come home.
  When you make up your mind,
    I'll be around.
Starr, Billy.
  Baby, don't cry.
Starr, Nat.
  Come back, my love. ©
Starr, Norman, pseud. SEE
  Rosenblum, Norman.
Starr, Tony.
  He asked me.
  The rose of roses.
  Somewhere.
Starr Songs Pub. Co.
  Kay's lament. ©
Stasik, Peggy Stark.
  The one that I loved. ©
  So once you said you loved
    me. ©
Stauffer, Mildred Elsie.
  Leave me alone. ©
Staw, Morris.
  Wake up, my darling. ©
Steagerman, LeRoy John.
  My heart sings a hullaby. ©
  Tender lips. ©
Stearn, Jack, pseud. SEE
  Stryker, Fred.
Stearns, Larry.
  On the trail of tomorrow.
  Pussycat shag.
  Sailboat of dreams.
Stebbins, Beth.
  That ain't nice at all. ©
Steele, Charley William.
  A roamin' cowboy. ©
Steele, Elved Milden.
  My special love. ©
Steele, Ethel Irene.
  Million little lovers. ©
Steele, Helen.
  Cu-chi-chi. ©
  Donde. ©
  Don't say adiós. ©
  Tumba, tumba. ©
Steele, Lois.
  Keep your promise, Willie
    Thomas.
Steele, Theodore.
  Dewdrops of love. ©
  I got it, you got it. ©
Steele, Thomas C.
  I've got you on my mind. ©
Stefanski, Daniel.
  One heart in two. ©
Steffman, Mrs. George.
  Be a good neighbor. ©
Steger, Gordon Herbert.
  Janie. ©
  Stei___

Steinhilber, Joyce.
  Our last goodbye. ©
Steinkler, Ruth Lee.
  And you'll be mine again. ©
Steinman, Gertrude S.
  So did you. ©
  When. ©
Steinreich, Al.
  Let's talk it over.
Steinreich, Alexander M.
  Afraid to sleep. ©
  Easy come love, easy go
    love. ©
  How to build a house. ©
  I wanna. ©
  Is there a way. ©
  Let's talk it over. ©
  The loneliest gal in town. ©
  My love from the past. ©
  Not the marrying kind. ©
  Try again. ©
Steibsky, Josef.
  Eisenhower march.
  Everyone loved fairy tales.
  Ike's polka.
  Konvalinka.
  O. K.
  Praha je krasna.
  Večer nad prahou.
Stella, Albert Sidney.
  If I had to do without you. ©
  Remember when we used to
    ride the ferry. ©
Stella, Albert Sidney, Jr.
  Baby's on her way back
    home. ©
Stella, Gaye.
  Believe in me or I'll be
    leaving you.
Stella Music Co., inc.
  Cheesecake. ©
  Connecticut oberek. ©
  Duck huntin'. ©
  Magda za piec. ©
  Marysiu, Marysiu. ©
  Moja dziewczyna. ©
  Oj nasza kasia. ©
  Pansy milody walc. ©
  Polskie wesele. ©
  The thief. ©
  Wesela, wesele. ©
Stella Record Co.
  Lubie sobie spac. ©
  Finochie polka. ©
  Smutno mi. ©
  Sunshine kolomyjka. ©
  The village. ©
Stelker, Russell Carl.
  For you were heaven sent. ©
  Here come the fighting
    Badgers. ©
  Since I met you. ©
Stelton, John Morgan.
  Christmas time. ©
    __ook. ©

I keep her picture hanging
  upside down. ©
Stephens, Charlotte Mae.
  Here is a dream. ©
Stephens, G. S.
  Word of God. ©
Stephens, George C.
  Dream of me, darling. ©
  Si, senorita, si. ©
Stephens, Harry.
  Foot printer's song. ©
  Won't that be the day. ©
Stephens, Leah May Reeves.
  Word of God. ©
Stephens, Sara Belle.
  My lonely heart. ©
Stephenson, Russell.
  I'm quite a guy. ©
Stephenson, William Eaton.
  The barnyard rag. ©
  Give 'em a smile. ©
  Little cowboy from the western
    part of town. ©
  The little Dixie girl. ©
  The shivering snow man. ©
Stepping Tones.
  Collection of Cecchetti
    musical arrangements. ©
Stept, Sam H.
  The Army's always there.
  Danny's hideaway.
  Don't say you love me if you
    don't mean it.
  Hear my plea.
  I feel a polka coming on.
  My guardian angel.
  Sam Stept tune.
  There's a new bird this year in
    last year's nest.
  (You can just feel) Christmas
    in the air.
Stept, Sam Howard.
  Let's start over again.
  Serenade for a tin horn.
  You get me so excited.
Stergin, Lillian Viola.
  This is my diary. ©
Sterling, Bob, pseud. SEE
  Schneider, Sidney.
Sterling, Will, pseud. SEE
  Lingafelt, Wilsie S.
  Lingafelt, Wilsie S., Sr.
Sterling Recording & Music Co.
  Glad rags. ©
  Valeta waltz. ©
  Waltz enchantment. ©
Stern, Henry R.
  Pappy's Snowland. ©
Stern, Jack.
  You can't lose me.
Stern, Melvin.
  The home that y___
Stern, Melvin. R___
  Sterns, M___
Stern, Mil___
  Dou___

According to the 1952 *Catalog of Copyright Entries*, Gordon Herbert Steger used "Carl Steger" as a pseudonym to copyright a song named "Janie." The song's music and lyrics were also written by Steger.[56]

> Steger see also Steiger
> " Albert P (Eliz) musician Det Symphony
>   Orchestra h19320 Derby av
> " Carl G h438 Hague av

As recorded above in a 1957 Detroit City Directory, **Carl G Steger**
lived in his inherited house at **438 Hague Avenue**.[57]

The **Carl Steger Duo**, consisting of Carl (seated) and an unidentified
wood bass player, performed at the Au Sable Lounge, 15123 E. Warren
Avenue in Detroit, Michigan, ca. 1958. Photographer unknown. Courtesy of
Historic Images, Inc.

WOULD YOU BELIEVE? w June Steger, m
Carl Steger. Appl. states prev. reg.
1966, EU942943. NM: additional words
& music. © Carl Steger & June Steger;
25Aug66; EU952748.

A SUMMER SONG; w June Steger, m Carl
Steger. © Carl Steger & June Steger;
27Sep66; EU958911.

Carl wrote the music, June Steger wrote the lyrics, and together they copyrighted several songs as referenced above in a 1966 edition of *Catalog of Copyright Entries*.[58] The song "Would You Believe" was later recorded on side # 2 of his record (below).

Carl Steger, as a jazz and lounge singer, released several records during the '60s including the 45 phonograph disc records (above) through Charade Records, a former Detroit music label and Jewel Records[59] located in Mount Healthy, Ohio.

Carl lived in the North Park Towers in Southfield, Michigan, until 1972.[60]

In May 1973 and while performing at Scotch 'n Sirloin, Carl met Carol Ann Schwikert during her birthday celebration at the restaurant. In June of the following year, they were married at the Oakland County Courthouse in Pontiac, Michigan. Carol, a widow, had six children between the ages of two and twelve. Sometime after the union, Carl adopted her children.[61]

> Piano bar master **Carl Steger** will marry a lady named **Carol** next month and settle into a new home at White Lake with her and her three girls and three boys ages two to 12. Understandably, **Carl** is looking for a piano bar near home . . .

The impending marriage between **Carl Steger** and **Carol**, his third wife to be, was announced in the May 27, 1974, edition of the *Detroit Free Press*.

During the fall of 1984, Carl and his family moved to the southwestern coastal city of Sarasota, Florida. The city is known for its amenities of culture, water, and land activities. It also has a rich black history heritage despite its presence of racism and discrimination that was endured by the early black migrants to the area.[62]

"For over 100 years, African American residents played a major role in the development of Sarasota. Black labor cleared snake-infested land for real estate developers, laid railroad ties, harvested celery, helped plat golf courses and labored in the homes of Sarasota's influential power brokers—cooking, cleaning, ironing and rearing children."[63]

Although Lewis and Irene Colson are mainly regarded as Sarasota's first black settlers in 1884, a community of blacks— "free people of color, formerly enslaved Africans, some of whom were called Black Seminoles and Seminole Indians," were living in the area before their arrival when Florida was a sovereign territory of Spain. In 1885, Lewis Colson, a former slave, assisted Robert E. Paulson with surveying and platting the original town of Sarasota for the Scottish-owned company Florida Mortgage and Investment Company. In 1899, the first black church—Bethlehem Baptist Church—was constructed by blacks and Colson was named its first minister. In 1912, the first black children's school was created in the Knights of Pythias Hall.[64]

During the turn of the 20th century, Overtown became Sarasota's first black and segregated enclave. But in 1914, the Newtown neighborhood, consisting of 240 lots on 40 acres, was established "not to make money but to provide the Negroes with better places in which to live." Schools, churches, and family were the most important institutions for the community. During the 1920s, the city's black population in both neighborhoods grew because of the Florida real estate boom. Black-owned businesses increased during the enforcement of Jim Crow laws. In 1925, Sarasota Grammar School became the first public educational institution built for blacks in the city. As with most blacks during and after slavery in the South, agriculture was a major industry and farming was a main source of work in Sarasota—harvesting citrus crops and celery. The production of turpentine in camps during the early 1900s was another important industry for black workers.[65]

In 1998, Carl released the lounge music compact disc *Sarasota: Carl Steger—Live at Café L'Europe* in the city through his own label, Opy Records. He wrote four of the CD's twenty songs, including a special tribute track for his wife titled "Carol."[66]

CHAPTER 3

Dorothy Steger: Like Mother, Like Son— Musically Speaking

"She had been credited with the development of a city-wide music appreciation program which included thousands of adults and children, both White and Negro, throughout the city."
—*Michigan Chronicle*, December 20, 1947

Dorothy Anna Steger, Carl's mother, was born on February 7, 1902, in Detroit, Michigan, to Negro parents Robert and Anna Williams.[1] Her family lived in a rented house at 268 Randolph Street in Detroit. Robert was a native Kentuckian and worked as a hotel waiter in the city. Anna, born in Canada, was employed as a cook.[2]

In 1910, Dorothy, the oldest of three children, and her family lived in Noblesville, Indiana. Her father Robert worked as a farmer. Sometime between 1910 and 1916, the Williams family moved into a rented house at 38 West Rittenhouse Street in Battle Creek, Michigan —about 121 miles west of Detroit. The children went to school in the area and eventually became students at the Battle Creek Central High School.[3]

At age fourteen, Dorothy began her study of music under a woman named Allen Minor in the city.[4]

In June 1923, Dorothy completed her high school education and graduated from Detroit's Northwestern High School. Afterward, she attended the Detroit Conservatory of Music, majored in voice while studying under Archibald Jackson, and graduated in 1924.[5]

The Detroit Conservatory of Music

In 1874, the Detroit Conservatory of Music was established by J.H. Hahn, one of the foremost musical educators in America.

Steger, Dorothy Williams
Battle Creek High School; Detroit Conservatory of Music.

Dorothy Steger's 1923 Northwestern High School graduation photograph. She was also a member of the Girl's Glee Club. *The NOR'WESTER*, June 1923, Detroit Northwestern High School yearbook, 56. Public Domain.

Steger's photograph appeared in the Detroit Conservatory of Music yearbook. Public Domain. The school as it appeared in 1924 at 5035 Woodward Avenue. Courtesy of the Detroit Public Library, Burton Historical Collection.

DETROIT   CONSERVATORY   OF   MUSIC

1914

LORAINETTA L. HENDERSON (1913)   HENRIETTA BRINDSEN (1913)
MRS. ADELAINDE MAY JUDSON (1913)

1915

HELEN M. HOWARD (1914)   NEVA GRACE KENNEDY (1914)
KATHRYN F. NEWBEGIN (1914)   PEARL T. NEWELL
ELDA M. THOMPSON (1913)

1916

ESTHER A. GARDNER (1915)   MRS. FLORENCE GODDARD (1915
ADELGATHA MORRISON (1915)

1917

MRS. GRACE BUCHANAN (1916)   LOUIS STANLEY HOOPER (1916)
MRS. ETHELYN R. CRANSON (1916)   INA MARIE WESTCOTT (1916)
ZAE ARBUTUS HANNAFORD (1916)   CARRIE F. TRAVERS (1916)

1918

MRS. ALVA HART BOSTICK (1908)   MRS. FRANCIS HALL COMLY (1917)
IRENE M. RENSHLER (1917)

1919

EVA E. CAPLIN   NORMAN O. REAUME
ROBENA COPELAND   WILLIAM GEORGE SCHENK
FLORENCE ELLEN McKENZIE   LENA GERTRUDE SQUIRE
VERA WAGNER   LAUREECE WALFORD

1920

SARAH LEVI (1919)   BERNICE M. MASON (1919)
ELOISE C. HALL (1918)   CLARA B. SIPPEL (1919)
CLARA KRUEGER (1919)   MAYME W. WESTON (1919)
ANGELINE D. WILLIS (1919)

1921

MILDRED CAMPBELL   ROSE RUBENSTEIN
DORA GUTTENTAG   LOIS WHEELOCK
ELIZABETH HOLDEN-HARRISON   HENRIETTA DAVIS

1922

MISS FLORENCE E. CHARLES   MR. ELMER L. MUNDT
MISS IONE L. SHEPARD

1923

MISS ELSIE DOYING, Birmingham   MISS IRENE MESSIER, Royal Oak
MR. MORRIS GRAY FOWLER, Detroit   MISS FLORENCE BESSIE M. ORT, Detroit

1924

MISS MARIE A. BECK, Detroit   MISS ELIZABETH McGHIE, Detroit
MISS LOLA EMMA SZATHMARY, Detroit

Graduates

Class of 1924

MISS ROXIE ANDREWS, Royal Oak   MISS DONNA MAE PIERCE, Allegan
MRS. MARION HOLDER CRAGGS, Detroit   MISS GRACE ELLEN ROSS, Detroit
MISS CLAIRE ELSIE DEISS, Detroit   MRS. PATTY DISMUKE WHEELER, Detroit
MRS. ADA COX LaPOINTE, Ann Arbor   MISS JESSIE B. WOOLFENDEN, Detroit
MISS EVA MARIE CRAGG, Detroit   MISS CLARE C. WISSMUELLER, Mt. Clemens
MISS FLORENCE RUTH KRIEGER,   MISS LOLA EMMA SZATHMARY, Detroit
MISS AUDREY KATHERYN KIRCHNER   MISS ELIZABETH McGHIE, Detroit
MISS RUTH WILHELMINE BAUERLE,   MISS ALINE D. SCHILLER, Detroit
                          Lansing   MISS THELMA ELIZABETH STEALY, Detroit
MISS MARY MAGDELINE KOKOWICZ,   MRS. DOROTHY A. STEGER
                          Detroit   MISS ZELLA E. TOWNE, Detroit
MR. PAUL BUKANTIS, Detroit   MR. JOSEPH HAWTHORNE THOMAS, Detroit
MRS. MARTHA SALO BIRCH, Negaunee   MISS BERNICE E. LAREAU, Detroit
MISS KATHERINE CHIUMINO, Detroit   MISS ALINE D. SCHILLER, Detroit
MISS HELEN ELIZABETH FRIERS,   MISS ELLEN M. MILLSPAUGH, Oxford
                          Port Huron   MISS EMILY BURROWS, Detroit
MRS. BEULAH YOUNG, Detroit   MISS ELIZABETH McGHIE

Detroit Conservatory of Music, Yearbook 1924-1925, Fifty-first Year.
Courtesy of the Detroit Public Library, Burton Historical Collection.

"Following the death of Mr. Hahn, its president, in 1902, Mr. James H. Bell and Francis L. York acquired control of the conservatory, which now ranks with the best in the country."

By 1922, "It is generally conceded that Detroit has greater musical advantages than any other city of its size in the United States and no one has contributed more effectively toward the attainment of this end than has Mr. Bell, secretary, treasurer and manager of the

The former **Detroit Conservatory of Music building** where Dorothy Steger attended as a student. ca. 2018. From the author's photograph collection.

Detroit Conservatory of Music." "Being recognized as one of the foremost institutions of this character in the country" and "since its organization has enjoyed a prosperous and steady growth, twenty-four new studios have been added within the past three years. It has taken over the Detroit College of Music, formally under the direction of Mrs. Louise Unsworth Cragg..." Located at 5035 Woodward Avenue since 1913, the building contained "fifty-five studios, a commodious recital and concert hall, and is situated in the new art and educational center of Detroit, being opposite the new art museum and public library..." "A very complete musical library, both circulating and reference, is at the disposal of the students."

"In 1908, the Detroit Conservatory Orchestra of fifty players was organized for the purpose of giving pupils the necessary practice in ensemble playing and sight reading..." "A choral society is also maintained in connection with the school and among the light operas which they have successfully produced may be mentioned—the Mikado, Pinafore, Patience and the Chimes of Normandy."

"Over twenty-eight hundred students have been enrolled in the various departments of the conservatory, and a staff of eighty of the most competent instructors is maintained. The institution numbers among its graduates and teachers many of the most accomplished musicians in America and wields a power for good in musical matters that can scarcely be overestimated."[6]

A Woman of Substance and Song

In 1926, Dorothy taught students at the Bertha Hansbury School of Music.[7]

The Bertha Hansbury School of Music

During the 1920s, Bertha Hansbury-Phillips and her husband William H. Phillips purchased an 1890's styled-Victorian home on 544 Frederick Street in Detroit. In 1925, the black couple opened the Bertha Hansbury School of Music from their home. Hansbury, a native of the city and pianist, was a graduate (1907) and post-graduate (1908) in the study of pianoforte at the Detroit Conservatory of Music and in Berlin, Germany. The music school "was the first black school in the city of Detroit, and perhaps the country, to bring together a faculty of talented black instructors and students. The instructors of the school were gifted in the arts of pianoforte, voice, instruments, interpretive dancing, English, harmony and history." "Miss Hansbury sacrificed her ambition to become a concert pianist for that of a teacher, so that thousands of young blacks might receive the musical training that they desired but could ill afford."[8]

During the early years of the Great Depression, the school became The Household Art Guild. It was "the first state-licensed employment agency for African Americans in Detroit"—"predating the first widely used government-supported job agency by more than ten years." "Blacks were taught the basic skills of domestic work" and wealthy people in Detroit used the "community assistance headquarters" to acquire the use of their domestic services. Around 1930, the school closed due to the nation's population shift in focus to simply surviving.[9]

Students posed in front of the **Bertha Hansbury School of Music** on 544 Frederick Avenue in Detroit, Michigan. ca. early 1920s. Public Domain.

The former and now vacant school (l) where Dorothy Steger once taught students in 1926 was photographed in November 2017.
From the author's photograph collection.

In 1926, Steger began working as a voice teacher for Detroit's Department of Parks and Recreation.[10] She sang, performed, and orchestrated choirs in public and private events throughout Michigan and cities such as New York and Boston.[11] According to a relative, "I heard that she sung opera."[12]

- On September 27, 1927, Steger participated at the 40th session of the Michigan Annual Conference of A.M.E. Churches by singing as a soloist. The conference opening was held at the St. Stephens African Methodist Episcopal Church in Detroit.[13]

> **Guest of Parents—Mrs.** Gordon Steger and son Gordon Hubert, of Detroit, are the guests of Mrs. Steger's parents, Mr. and Mrs. Robert Williams, 36 West Rittenhouse. Mr. Steger was a week-end visitor. Mrs. Steger will be remembered as Miss Dorothy Williams, former popular soloist of Battle Creek. She sings over the radio in Detroit.

Battle Creek Enquirer, May 29, 1928

- On August 26, 1931, Steger gave a concert Wednesday evening beginning at 8:15 P.M. at the Second Baptist Church at 323 East Michigan Avenue in Battle Creek, Michigan.[14]

Gold Star Mothers Hear Impromptu Recital By Mrs. Dorothy Steger

On Thursday, June 9, at 1 o'clock, the group of forty Gold Star Mothers, enroute to the war cemeteries in France where their sons are buried, as guests of the United States Government, were treated to a short musicale by Mrs. Dorothy Williams Steger, soprano, of Detroit, and Miss Olive Arnold, pianist, of Minneapolis.

It was an impromptu affair, arranged at a few minutes' notice by Mrs. Cecelia Cabaniss Saunders, executive secretary, when she discovered that Mrs. Steger and Miss Arnold were both in the West 137th street branch Y. W. C. A. at that time, and the lobby of the Emma Ransom House was the improvised concert hall.

Mrs. Steger sang "Go down, Moses" and "Nobody knows the trouble I see," Spirituals, and a Gypsy song, and then gave an unusual and enjoyable whistling number. Miss Arnold displayed pianistic ability of a high order, exhibiting unusual technical development and a matured understanding that belied her tender years.

The group of mothers enjoyed the recital and gave every evidence of fullest appreciation.

Mrs. Steiger, who is visiting in New York, is attached to the Department of Recreation, City of Detroit, as a playground leader. She is director of music also for the Lucy Thurman Branch Y. W. C. A., and serves also at the Central branch for white girls. She is a graduate of the Detroit Conservatory, 1924, and has done post graduate work with Thaddeus Wromsker.

When the Detroit Civic Opera Co., Mr. Wromsker, director, gave a performance of the grand opera, "Aida," in April, Mrs. Steger trained and led a group of colored singers who were incorporated in the cast, and which was given a tremendous ovation.

She is in negotiation with one of New York's leading concert bureaus, and there is a possibility that she might become a permanent New Yorker. She is stopping at 300 West 141st street.

Miss Arnold studied with private teachers attached to the McPhail School of Music, and for the past year and a half with teachers in the Conservatory of Music of the University of Minnesota, where she is a sophoomore. While in high school, taking part in the annual statewide music contest, she won second prize the first year, and first prize the second year, after having won first places in both county and district preliminaries. During her freshman year, she was the only member of her class selected to play in the Thursday musicales, presented every week.

Dorothy Steger was referenced in an article in the June 18, 1932 edition of *New York Age*. The weekly was one of the most influential black newspapers since its inception as the *Globe* in 1880, the *Freeman* in 1884, and *New York Age* in 1887.
Courtesy of the Library of Congress. Public Domain.

- In 1933, Steger moved to New York City where she continued to perform and study music and voice. She was employed as a teacher of piano and voice. She also worked for the Heckscher Foundation, whose mission is to "level the playing field for underserved youth, principally in New York" by supporting "innovative, results driven programs and partnerships," and focused giving to education.[15]

On August 7th, she traveled back to Detroit to perform as one of the "star soloists"—contralto and mezzo-soprano—at the 4th annual Negro Music Night on Belle Isle in Detroit. She sang a song called "Swing Along."[16]

On August 19th, she performed as a guest soloist at the noted Second Baptist Church at 441 Monroe Avenue in Detroit.[17]

Second Baptist Church (Detroit, Michigan)

The Second Baptist Church is the oldest black congregation in Michigan. In 1836, it was founded by 13 former slaves after leaving the First Baptist Church (of Detroit) because of its practice of discrimination. According to the church's historical marker:

"From its beginnings, the church has occupied a prominent place in Detroit's black community. In 1839, it established the city's first school for black children, and its first pastor, the Reverend William C. Monroe, was a noted anti-slavery activist. In 1843, he presided over the first State Convention of Colored Citizens, which met at the Second Baptist Church. Delegates demanded the right to vote and an end to slavery. On January 6, 1863, Detroit's blacks celebrated the Emancipation Proclamation here. Located at this site since 1857, the church has expanded its facilities through the years."[18]

The Second Baptist Church also became a northern stop on the Underground Railroad for escaped slaves seeking their freedom just miles from the Canadian border. "Its leaders helped to form the Amherstburg Baptist Association and the Canadian Anti-Slavery Baptist Association, both of which supported abolitionism" and fugitive slaves "spiritually and materially."[19]

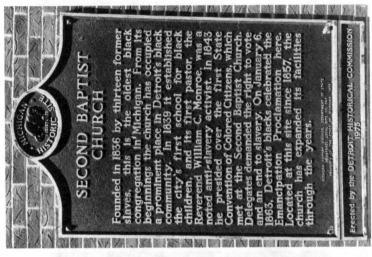

The Second Baptist Church historical marker.

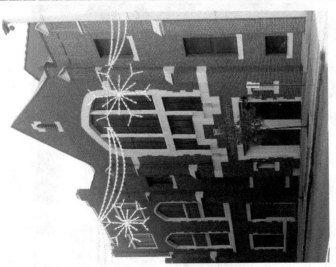

The Second Baptist Church in Detroit is the oldest black congregation in Michigan. ca. 1836. Both photographs are from the author's photograph collection.

The marker above references the Second Baptist Church as an **Underground Railroad Site**. The marker below discloses when the church's **Educational Building** was created in 1968. The photographs are from the author's collection.

- In 1936, Steger was employed at the Utopia Children's House and as a social worker at the Congregational Church in New York. She taught private pupils, did radio work, and "mastered several languages to assist her in her work."

One of the recent visitors in the city is Mrs. Dorothy William Steger, formerly of Detroit, but now of New York City. She is a well-known musician. Mrs. Steger and her son have been visiting her mother in Battle Creek and her husband, Gordon Steger of this city. It will be remembered that while Mrs. Steger was living in ████t, she graduated from the ██ Conservatory as contralto ████ soprano soloist, but her ████ ████ New York has raised her voice to that of a lyric soprano. Mrs. Steger has been employed in New York for the past few years, as teacher of voice and piano and a worker in the Heckscher Foundation. She is now employed at the Utopia Children's House and social worker for the Congregational Church, in New York City, as well as teaching private pupils and doing radio work. She reports she has studied and mastered several languages, to assist her in her work.

Dorothy's many musical accomplishments were listed in the *Detroit Tribune* on January 18, 1936. Her husband Gordon and son Carl were also referenced in the newspaper article. Courtesy of the Library of Congress. Public Domain.

Around the spring, she moved back to Detroit and worked as a teacher of voice, piano, and French at 290 East Hancock Avenue in the city.[20]

On May 17th, she sang in French, English, and Italian for the Clef Club's "Symphonic Hour" concert at the Lucy Thurman Y. W. C. A. (Young Women's Christian Association).[21]

- In 1938, Steger worked as the director of girls and women activities at the Brewster Community Center.[22]

On March 6th, she sang as a contralto in an all-star musicale that was presented by the New Light Baptist Church choir at their house of worship at 6300 20th Street in Detroit.[23]

On May 15th, she sang as the soloist in a Negro version of the Aida at the Second Baptist Church. The musicale was presented by the Detroit Musicians Association.[24]

On June 3rd, she participated in a Department of Parks and Recreation sponsored Musical Elaboretta at the Detroit Institute of Arts on Woodward Avenue. She was the teacher and director of a singing group of approximately forty men and women from the Brewster Center, Birdhurst Center, and Sampson and Washington Schools. She also sang three songs as a part of The Dream Trio group.[25]

West Side Congenial Singers Club

The West Side Congenial Singers club celebrated their first social affair of the year Saturday, Feb. 25 at the home of Mrs. Jacobs, 6505 Whitewood. It was a very enjoyable affair.

Guests present included Mr. and Mrs. Norman McCall, Mr. and Mrs. Garland Bugg, Mr. and Mrs. Osborn Wilson, Mr. and Mrs. Kirk Hunter, Mr. and Mrs. James Burrell, Messrs. George Diles, George Counts, Thaddeus Marinovicn, John Easton, Arthur Glover, J. Dennis, Lawrence Dilworth, Roosevelt Rughess, Alvin Smith, Charles Shorter, E. A. Rose, A. L. Williams, A. H. Smith, Prof. William Hensen, Mrs. Dorothy Steger and son, Carl, also Mesdames C. B. Mitchell, B. Carson, Mary Smith, J. Dennis, R. M. Williams, president; Mildred Halliday, secretary; Miss P. Bethel, Ada Phillips, Kate Elliott, Rose Dilworth, Virginia Dennis, Lillian Jennings, C. Thomas, H. J. Phillips.

On February 25, 1939, Dorothy and Carl performed as members of the West Side Congenial Singers Club. *Detroit Tribune*, March 18, 1939. Public Domain.

• In March 1939, Steger accepted a clerk position at the Brewster Homes (Brewster Housing Project) which were managed by the Department of Parks and Recreation.[26]

The Brewster Homes

"Between 1910 and 1940, Detroit's African American population increased dramatically. Faced with restrictions on where they could live, many African Americans were forced into substandard housing." In 1935, the United States first lady Eleanor Roosevelt traveled to the city to break ground and begin the construction of the Brewster Homes. In 1938, the 701 units in low-rise buildings, bounded by Beaubien, Hastings, Mack, and Wilkins Streets, became the "nation's first federally funded public housing development for African Americans." This and other governmental housing programs throughout the nation were devised under Franklin D. Roosevelt's New Deal initiative after he assumed the role as America's 32nd president in 1933. Attempting to provide relief to the suffering during the Great Depression by stabilizing the economy and providing jobs over the next eight years, the New Deal consisted of a series of experimental projects and programs.[27]

In 1934, the Federal Housing Administration (FHA) was established. However, its policies "furthered the segregation efforts by refusing to insure mortgages in and near African-American" neighborhoods—a policy known as 'redlining.' At the same time, the FHA was subsidizing builders who were mass-producing entire subdivisions for whites—with the requirement that none of the homes be sold to African Americans." In doing so, they were forced to live in urban housing projects. Jewish families were also affected by the government's discriminatory housing practices.[28]

During World War II, the planned construction of a Detroit housing development on the city's northwest side and near a mostly black neighborhood would not be permitted by the FHA. However, a developer proposed to build a six-foot-high cement wall to divide his development from the black neighborhood to make sure no black families could move or walk into the newly constructed white subdivision. Afterward, the construction loans were approved by the FHA and the development was erected.[29]

Black children posing in front of the **Detroit Wall**—erected in 1941 to separate the black and white neighborhoods. The concrete barrier was also known as the "Wailing Wall" and the "Eight Mile Wall." The Detroit Wall as it appeared in the background of the black section (below-left) and from the side of the white subdivision (below-right). ca. August 1941.
The photographs are courtesy of the Library of Congress, Public Domain.

The Detroit Wall in 1951.
The Detroit Jewish News, January 25, 2018.

The Detroit Wall—graffiti covered, six-feet-high, one foot thick, and one-half mile long—still exists today as visual evidence of Detroit's racial segregation. Within the now majority black neighborhood, artists painted murals on the wall's exposed side depicting symbolic scenes of "remembrance and harmony"—from the civil rights movement to unison in housing.[30] The photographs are from the author's collection.

"The Brewster Homes were completed in 1941 with 941 units. Residents were required to be employed and there were limits on what they could earn. Former residents described Brewster as 'a community filled with families that displayed love, respect, and concern for everyone' in a 'beautiful, clean and secure neighborhood.' The original Brewster homes were demolished in 1991 and replaced by 50 townhouses.[31]

Dorothy Steger Wins New Job

Mrs. Dorothy Steger has accepted the position of director of public relations in addition to her choral work at the Brewster Recreation Center, 637 Brewster. In June of this year Mrs. Steger transferred from the Housing Commission to Parks And Recreation to conduct singing classes, throughout the city. This new office comes as a natural consequence of her fine work.

Detroit Tribune,
October 11, 1941

- In 1942, Steger continued to work as a choral specialist for the Department of Parks and Recreation. She taught singing, sight reading, and elements of piano music in various centers throughout the city including the Mount Vernon Recreation Center, the Brewster Center, St. Cyprians Parish House, Duffield Elementary School, and the Metropolitan Baptist Church.[32]

On November 8th, she directed the Recreation Victory Chorus during their annual musical elaboretta presentation at the Brewster Center.[33]

ARTISTS ON SECOND "ALL STAR MUSICALE" FRIDAY, MARCH 13–8:15 P.M.

At St. John's Presbyterian Church, cor. Jos. Campau and Clinton
Auspices of the Church Choir

OSCAR B. PLANTE,
Dramatic Baritone,

Is the son of the late Prof. and Mrs. J. X. Plante of Texarkana, Texas.

He is a graduate of Wiley university, Marshall, Texas, where he received the degree Bachelor of Science, cum laude. At that time his ambition was to enter a medical school to become a specialist in diseases of children; taking singing as his avocation. His early voice training was under the tutorship of Prof. Norton E. Dennis, dean of music at the Chicago Musical college.

Mr. Plante's first professional work was done with the internationally known Williams World's Famous Singers of Chicago. It was with this company that he received most of his experience, having toured the U. S. several times. After studying voice in Chicago, for five seasons under Prof. Alexander Nakutin of Kimball Hall, Mr. Plante was offered the position of Baritone singer and announcer with the Ford Motor Co., Octette, from which he resigned several weeks ago.

At the present time he is a student of Dr. Wm. Howland of the Detroit Institute of Musical Art. However, he gives his talented wife, Nelle Dobson Plante much of the credit for his vocal technique and

ESTELLE ANDREWS,
Coloratura Soprano,

graduate of the Detroit Foundation School of Music and a former pupil of Yolande Maddox. Mrs. Andrews has a sweet, clear voice. She is well known as a pleasing concert singer and also has experience in choir directing. She is a former member of the Detroit Negro Opera.

———Also on the

BENJAMIN WAILES,
Tenor,

received his training at Southern and Wilberforce Universities and also studied in New York under Wm. Herman, Metropolitan Opera coach. He starred in Max Gordon's production "Sing Out the News," in New York and was an understudy in the "Hot Mikado"; he was also soloist with the Fisk Jubilee Singers. He is singing with the Ford Dixie Eight at present.

histrionic ability.

Brace Beamer of Radio station WXYZ is quoted as saying, "Plante has a great voice, and a natural gift for acting."

Mr. Plante recently has been asked to audition for a role in a well known New York stage attraction. He is a member of Omega Psi Phi Fraternity.

LOUIS MITCHELL,
Pianist and Composer,

former accompanist of Ford Dixie Eight, has studied extensively under Arthur Traver Granfield and Minor E. White of the Detroit Institute of Music. He was coached under the European conductor, Albert to Ziarko and has many compositions to his credit. He will play two Liszt compositions.   ..

———On the Program are———

DOROTHY STEGER,
· Contralto.

She began her studies in voice at the age of 14 under Mrs. Allen Minor in Battle Creek where she was reared. Coming to Detroit in 1921 she studied under Archibald Jackson and graduated from the Detroit Conservatory in 1925. She then took post-graduate work under Thaddeus Wronski, former director of the Detroit Civic Opera Co. Later she continued her studies in New York under Ward Stephens, Florence Botsford and Katherine Bxed, taking course in voice, teaching and choral directing. Her voice has a wide range, as she sings in the mezzo and lyric register, as well as the contralto. She is also a good pianist. For several years she has done choral work in the department of recreation and is now choral director and public relations director at the Brewster Recreation Center.

These five talented artists will furnish an unusually enjoyable evening's entertainment, so don't miss this musical treat.

PATRON'S TICKETS 50c   GENERAL ADMISSION 35c

Detroit Tribune, March 7, 1942

- In 1943, Steger taught classes for choral singing and piano instruction at the G.A.R. (Grand Army of the Republic) Building at 1942 Grand River Avenue in Detroit. She was also a teacher at Cass Technical High School.[34]

On January 26th, she sang as a soloist at a Department of Parks and Recreation sponsored benefit musicale for the crusade against infantile paralysis.[35]

On March 20th, the second "All-Star Musicale" took place in the large auditorium of Detroit's St. John Presbyterian Church. "Mrs. Dorothy W. Steger was especially appealing as she sang Bohn's 'Claim is the Night' and 'Till I Wake' by Woodfolk-Finden, which were adequate to show the beauty of her sweet voice in the contralto register; she was equally pleasing in her soprano number sung as an encore, which displayed the wide range of her voice."[36]

Detroit's Top Talent Prepares For Annual 'Musicale Elaboretta'

THE DETROIT TRIBUNE, SATURDAY, MAY 20, 1944.

1045 St. Antoine Street, Corner Columbia—CLifford 2924

Recreation Group To Present Treat Of Season

Affair Will Be Held At Brewster On Friday, May 26

Bustles, hoop skirts, bandanas and other old-fashioned costuming will be very much in evidence when the curtain rises on the Musical Elaboretta to be presented at the Brewster Recreation center at 8:30 p.m., Friday, May 26.

Taking part will be choral groups and soloists trained by Mrs. Dorothy Steger, choral instructor for the Department of Parks and Recreation, who have been rehearsing diligently to provide this evening of musical entertainment for their friends.

This reporter visited a rehearsal in which all the groups participated and was very much impressed with the quality of the voices. That each group had been admirably trained by Mrs. Steger was evident in every number. Every soloist has a fine contribution to make and the numbers selected are of infinite variety. It will be a show you won't want to miss.

A particularly amusing number will be given by Mrs. Anna Murphy impersonating Mae West in a contralto solo: "The Man I Love." Miles Faison gives a stirring performance in "The Blind Plowman," a baritone solo.

To Give Skit

Miss Evelyn Francis is appealing in her solo: "My Sweet Little Alice Blue Gown." A hilarious touch is provided by Theopholic Danzy with the group from Sojourner Truth is a parody entitled "The Old-Fashioned Nightshirt."

When you hear 17-year-old Kathleen Miller render "Beautiful Dreamer" as a solo you will grant that she shows promise. The Miller group of teenagers join her in singing "The Lord's Prayer."

Soprano Charity Weeks of Brewster center will lead her group: John Hall will do that grand bass number, "Asleep in the Deep." Others who will make special contributions will be Elizabeth Lowman of Allen Temple; Dora Steele of St. Peter Claver; Elisabeth Ward and Marie Jones of Brewster; and Doris Smith of the Junior Association of Women's clubs. Carl Steger will furnish incidental music. Boy Scout Troop 114 will do the ushering.

Dorothy Steger as choral instructor for Detroit's Department of Parks and Recreation prepares choral groups and soloists for the city's annual 'Musicale Elaboretta.' Her son "Carl Steger will furnish incidental music."
Detroit Tribune,
May 20, 1944. Public Domain.

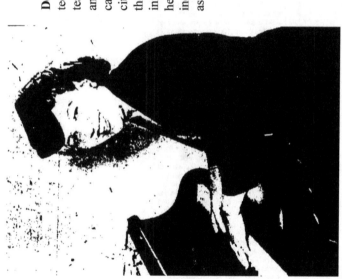

Dorothy Steger, an esteemed pianist, music teacher, choral director, and developer of musical programs for the city of Detroit between the 1930s and 1940s, influenced many during her illustrious career, including her son Carl as a musician.

Mrs. Dorothy Steger to Teach "Piano By Ear" Class

The Jewish Community Center announces a class in "Piano by Ear," conducted by the Department of Parks and Recreation.

This class will be instructed by Mrs. Dorothy Steger, who has had extensive experience in piano teaching. These classes will enable persons wishing to play for their own amusement or desiring to accompany group singing in their classes, or who already play by note, but who cannot play without music to become acquainted with the piano in a lesser or a greater degree without the technical details necessary for classic music execution. The first class will begin Oct. 30, at 8 p. m.

Detroit Jewish Chronicle, **October 20, 1944**

- In 1945, Steger's approximate work income from the Department of Parks and Recreation was $2,600. Between October 26th and 28th, she was the director of the community singing at the first annual Youth Leadership Training Conference of the Detroit Branch.[37]

- In 1946, Steger and her "York advertising agency" musical group participated in a "two-hour musical pageant" which traced "150 years of Detroit's history." A cast of 500 people, including other musical groups, took part in the event.[38]

According to Detroit historian Dr. Jiam Desjardins, "I knew her during certain social circles. She was very well spoken." "(She) sang in churches and in concerts for private clubs throughout the state. (She) was also an excellent whistler." In addition to playing the piano, Steger also "played the harp," according to an oral family history account.[39]

OFFER MUSIC CLASSES .

A summer course in "Music for Fun" will offer free classes in voice, piano instruction or both for talented children between 5 and 14 years of age, it was announced by the Department of Parks and Recreation. The course will start on July 11.

The course is intended to help develop the vocal or musical talents of youngsters who show aptitude and promise but who have not had any instruction.

Mrs. Dorothy Steger, musical specialist for the department will give the courses and she will audition the applicants and then enroll those who are sufficiently talented for the course.

Auditions will be given at 10 a. m. on Monday, July 7, and on Thursday, July 10, so that no time will be taken from the instruction periods on Friday. They will be held at the G.A.R. Recreation Center, corner of Cass and Grand River avenues.

In directing children's choral groups in various sections of the city, Mrs. Stegar has found many youngsters whose outstanding musical ability should be developed but in many cases it has not been possible for them to receive instruction. For this reason the course is being inaugurated as one of the public service features of the recreation division.

Detroit Tribune, July 5, 1947. Public Domain.

Sometime during her career, Steger became a member of the National Association of Negro Musicians.[40]

The National Association of Negro Musicians (NANM) is the "country's oldest organization dedicated to the preservation, encouragement, and advocacy of all genres of African American music."[41]

Established on May 3, 1919, in Washington D. C., the "NANM grew from concerns on the part of black artists, critics, and patrons that communal music traditions such as the spirituals were being corrupted by vaudeville and popular recordings from the early twentieth century. The association also championed the idea of innate artistic genius within the black race, making it an important advocate of African American contributions to national life and culture during an era of scientific racism and public derogation of blacks."[42]

Scholarship winners frequently achieved national and international prominence as did Marian Anderson, the first scholarship recipient (1921), composer and pianist Margaret Bonds, composer Julia Perry, mezzo-soprano Grace Bumbry, conductor James Frazier, and concert pianists Leon Bates and Awadagin Pratt.[43]

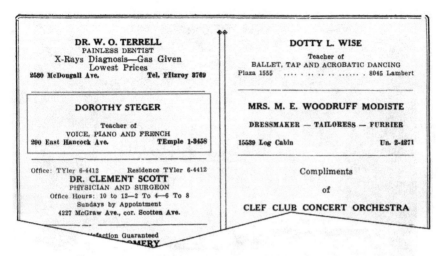

Dorothy Steger advertised her teaching abilities on a page of a National Association of Negro Musicians booklet. ca. 1936. Courtesy of the Burton Historical Collection.

Steger, educated in music and voice, worked for Detroit's Department of Recreation for over 17 years. She was a pianist, teacher, choral director, and play leader. "She had been credited with the development of a city-wide music appreciation program which included thousands of adults and children, both White and Negro, throughout the city. She originated the annual Christmas Carol programs at the City Hall."[44]

On December 14, 1947, Steger died of a cerebral embolus, a p.o. (post operation) hysterectomy and possibly pneumonia at Detroit's St. Mary's Hospital.[45] Her funeral service was held at the Plymouth Congregational Church on Garfield and Beaubien Streets. She was interred at the Reese Cemetery on Three Mile and Dickman Roads in Springfield, Michigan.[46]

Dorothy Steger's 1902–1947 headstone in the Reese Cemetery in Springfield, Michigan. Photographed by AMBS. ca 2016. Public Domain.

Dies in Detroit — Mrs. Dorothy Steger, 44, a former Battle Creek resident, died at 7 p. m. Saturday, in Detroit, where she resided following her marriage to Gordon W. Steger in 1919. Mrs. Steger was born in Detroit in 1903, the daughter of Mr. and Mrs. Robert Williams, moving to Battle Creek with her family as a child. Mr. Steger died Aug. 31, 1945. She taught piano and voice in Detroit. Mrs. Steger is survived by her father, residing at 38 West Rittenhouse avenue; a son, Carl Steger now with the air forces; and a brother, Arley Williams of Detroit.

Battle Creek Enquirer, December 15, 1947

28—THE DETROIT NEWS
TUESDAY, DECEMBER 16, 1947

New York State's poultry population averages about 12,000,000 birds. Chickens are found on approximately 107,000 farms in the state.

LAMP SHADES

In Time for Christmas Delivery

★ CLEANED   ★ RELINED   ★ RECOVERED

Faultless

HO 1010

IT'S O.K.

IT'S O'Keefe's

IMPORTED *Ale*

Obituaries

PERCY O. LATHAM

Services for Percy O. Latham, brother of Detroit's assistant postmaster, William R. Latham, will be held Thursday in Los Angeles, Calif., where he died Sunday. Burial will be in Los Angeles. Mr. Latham, who was 58, was born in Windsor and came to Detroit when seven months old. He was employed by the City Motor Transport Service until 11 years ago when he moved to California. A veteran of World War I, Mr. Latham was one of the founders of the John Faust Post of the American Legion. He was a past commander of the post. His wife, Elizabeth, of Los Angeles; three brothers, William, Arthur, of Whitmore, Mich., and Cal, of California, and a sister, Mrs. Kathleen Smith, of Seattle, Wash., survive.

MRS. DOROTHY STEGER

Services for Mrs. Dorothy Steger, 45, teacher of choral singing and piano for the Department of Parks and Recreation, will be held at 10:30 a. m. Wednesday at the Plymouth Congregational Church, Garfield avenue and Beaubien street. Burial will be at Battle Creek. Mrs. Steger, an employe of the parks and recreation department for nearly 19 years, died Saturday at St. Mary's Hospital. The classes in choral singing and piano instruction which she taught at the GAR Building and at Cass Technical High School have been canceled, the recreation department announced. A son, Pvt. Gordon Carl, Jr., of the Army Air Force, survives. Mrs. Steger's husband died Aug. 31, 1945.

Dorothy's obituary in *The Detroit News* references her son as "Pvt. Gordon Carl, Jr."

2-YR. OLD BABY BURNED TO DEATH

Hit Patient, Orderly Is Fired

CHRONICLE
MICHIGAN
RELIABLE — INDEPENDENT

MAIN OFFICE: 242 ELIOT ST. — TELEPHONE TEMPLE 1-4877

VOLUME 12   DETROIT, MICHIGAN, DECEMBER 20, 1947   NUMBER 39

BRADBY HEADS NAACP

BEATS HILL 205-33

The Rev. Robert L. Bradby, Jr., was overwhelmingly re-elected president of the Detroit Branch of the NAACP at a tumultous annual meeting last Sunday.

The Rev. Mr. Bradby, who defeated the Rev. Charles A. Hill last year for the top office, again defeated the Rev. Mr. Hill by a vote of 205 to 33.

The Rev. Mr. Hill was placed on the ballot by nominations from the floor by Coleman Young, leader of the block that "wants to make the NAACP more militant."

Young himself was a write-in candidate for secretary. He was defeated by a vote of 195 to 19.

Edward Turner was elected first vice president, Mrs. L.W. Tyrell, third vice president, Mrs. Celillus Morgan, Guerite Coar, assistant secretary, Mrs. W.A. Thompson, treasurer.

The 300 members present heard, President Robert L. Bradby and executive secretary, Edward Swan, summarized the activities of the branch during the past year. Samuel Gibbons, retiring treasurer, reported the condition of the finances of the organization.

The usual efforts of radical elements to question the election procedure and defeat candidates recommended by the nominating committee failed.

Twenty men and women representing business, professions, labor and church groups were elected to the executive committee.

RACE WORKER

Washington, D.C
Unemployment rates among colored workers are twice as high as they are for white

UNTRUE TALE!

Rebuked for telling a falsehood about mutual tickets found in her possession, Mildred Crown, 20, of 5426 Rivard, was fined $100, last week by Recorder's Judge Joseph A. Gillis.

Accused near Brush and Medbury the young woman told Gillis that she intended to play 41 bet slips taken from her.

When Gillis discovered the slips were all different, he accused her of falsifying in—

Housing Pinch Felt By Negroes

by Marilynn Howard

The question as to whether the segregated pattern will be applied to the units at Fort Wayne which were secured by the city last week, was brought into sharp focus by the case of Mrs. Amanda Wallace of 62 Canfield, who, with her 11 children faces eviction from her one-room apartment, this week.

Mrs. Wallace shares an apartment with her daughter, Mrs. Dorothy Wilson, who has two children. Another daughter has a child and takes care of the children while Mrs. Wallace, the sole provider, works at the Chrysler plant.

All water must be carried from a downstairs apartment. The laundry must be sent out and laundry for 15 people is no small task.

Mrs. Wallace is indicative of hundreds of Negro families, in the Detroit area.

WAS STRUCK WITH CHAIR HE SAYS

A Receiving hospital orderly was dismissed Saturday night following an outburst of violence in Ward 1 - 6 of the institution.

Cornell Cook, 3, of 8436 Brush, a part-time orderly, was dismissed from his job for taking part in an altercation with one of the patients, Ulysses Yarber, 3447 S. Bassett.

According to Yarber, the fight began after he and three patients returned to the ward from a hospital movie to hear Cook "cursing and berating" another patient, Allen Byrd.

"He asked him if it were necessary to use "such offensive language, especially since Byrd is an old man," Yarber said, "but he told us to mind our own damned business."

Patients who corroborated the story up to this point were Willie Bledsoe, 960 Mack; Samuel Kleckley, address unknown; and Byrd, who recently came here from the state of South Carolina.

Yarber said that Cook turned and hit him under the right eye when he protested the attack on Byrd.

The suspended orderly gave a different account of the altercation, stating that Yarber struck him two times with a chair before he tried to defend himself.

Early Deadline

Because of the Christmas Holidays The Michigan Chronicle will be published on Wednesday of next week.

All news intended for publication in that issue must be in this office by 5:00 p.m. Thursday, Dec. 18.

Newsboys are requested to call for their papers Wednesday morning 9 o'clock.

Lying in a Receiving hospital bed with a bruised and swollen left eye is Ulysses Yarber, 3447 S. Bassett, who figured in an altercation with Orderly Cornell Cook, 8436 Brush. Cook was dismissed from his duties Saturday night.

Mrs. Dorothy Steger, of 438 Hague, who died in St. Mary's hospital last Sunday night following an illness of four days. Mrs. Steger was choral director for the Department of Parks and Recreation.

DEATH TAKES MRS. STEGER

Funeral services were held Wednesday for Mrs. Dorothy Steger, 45, of 438 Hague, who died last Sunday night in St. Mary's Hospital.

Mrs. Steger, in the hospital since last Wednesday, had been ill for some time, according to her family. Cause of death was given as heart ailment and complications of the blood.

She worked in the Detroit Department of Parks and Recreation for more than 17 years, and in later years was choral director for the department.

She had been credited with the development of a city-wide music appreciation program which included thousands of adults and children, both White and Negro, throughout the city. She originated the annual Christmas Carol programs at the City Hall.

Mrs. Steger was educated in the public schools of Battle Creek and in Detroit, graduating from Northwestern High school and the Detroit Conservatory of Music. She also studied music and voice in New York.

She is survived by her son Carl, now in the Army Air Corps, Eglin Field, Fla.; her father, Arley Williams, of 655 Alger.

Interment was scheduled for Battle Creek.

Free Hubby In Suicide Of Spouse

Hiner Walker, 34, of 877 Erskine was released to the custody of his attorney pending a hearing on a writ in Recorder's Court this week.

Walker had been in custody as police probed the death of his wife, Geneva 32, two weeks ago.

Walker told police that when he returned home from a nearby store, his wife had shot herself in the breast and left arm. The gun was in the palm of her right hand.

According to Det. Lieut. Harry Williams, all evidence tends to show that the young wife committed suicide.

Boost Housed

For-Washington

Commissioner

WASHINGTON — A full-fledged campaign has been launched here urging President Truman to appoint Charles H. Houston, nationally-known attorney, to the District of Columbia Board of Commissioners.

W
T

T
for t
day

Hu
Mothe
rescu
lives
John

Rich
old
"Batt
a pi
sed
baske
paper
ted
and
over

He
Richa
uttie
aperte
pair e
torre
sista
Loui

He
"Neig
anful
didn'
many
home
the s
Bepha
espec

He
to tal
into t
other
could
the Se
John's
Payne...

Heart
have o
the ne
connur
colore
employ
Chrysle
where
for F
lected
Frida

Als
told
that of
company
then
ing a c
a hom

TANN
ADJON

Exam
Hensle
of 223
with p
illegal
a 15 y
Oct. 22
Friday
Judge C
Stein

Ta
allegad
Carpent
bond, T
and Hist
$5,000

Vets

Wash
The Amer
commit
called

On December 20, 1947, **Dorothy Steger** was honored with a tribute and memorialized after her death on the front page of the noted Detroit black-owned newspaper *Michigan Chronicle*. A closer view of her obituary is on the following page. Public Domain.

DEATH TAKES MRS. STEGER

Funeral services were held Wednesday for Mrs. Dorothy Steger, 45, of 438 Hague, who died last Sunday night in St. Mary's Hospital.

Mrs. Steger, in the hospital since last Wednesday, had been ill for some time, according to her family. Cause of death was given as heart ailment and complications of the blood.

She worked in the Detroit Department of Parks and Recreation for more than 17 years, and in later years was choral director for the department.

She had been credited with the development of a city-wide music appreciation program which included thousands of adults and children, both White and Negro, throughout the city. She originated the annual Christmas Carol programs at the City Hall.

Mrs. Steger was educated in the public schools of Battle Creek and Detroit, graduating from Northwestern High school and the Detroit Conservatory of Music. She also studied music and voice in New York.

She is survived by her son Carl, now in the Army Air Corps, Eglin Field, Fla.; her father, Arley Williams, of 655 Alger.

Interment was scheduled for Battle Creek.

Odds And Ends

—BY—

FRED HART WILLIAMS

Passing of Mrs. Dorothy Steger Mourned by Author Who Well Remembers Her Youthful Aspirations and Efforts

A late telephone message Saturday night that aroused the writer from a deep sleep, shocked us into an awakening with the news of the unexpected passing of a long-time and valued friend, Dorothy Steger.

It seems but a short while ago, as we were leaving Lucy Thurman YWCA, during a noonday hour, we met Mrs. Steger on her way into the dining hall, there to lunch. The usual friendly greetings were exchanged between us.

We noticed though that our friend did not seem in the same high and happy spirit as was her wont. Questioned brought forth the statement that she expected to enter a hospital for a major operation. As is customary in situations of this nature, we attempted to cheer Dorothy with some advice as to "keep up your chin" and "you will come out of it all right."

Wishing her good luck, we went our respective ways. Neither of us were aware then that this was to be our final meeting and parting.

We knew Dorothy when as a young girl, she carried high within her an intense desire to become a great vocalist, aspiring for the concert stage.

She studied hard and long to achieve this ambition. Not only here but in New York City and under the best voice teachers available. Fate somehow decreed otherwise shaping Dorothy's life along paths musical possibly of greater worth than if she had accomplished a concert career.

Mrs. Steger although not achieving her desire to mount the musical rungs that would acclaim her an artist, carried on with her studies both in voice and piano and latterly, with choral work and directing. Her lamentable passing at a comparatively young age, will long be felt throughout the community where she has held an excellent reputation as one of the major characters with the Detroit Parks and Recreation Department of Music.

For the past several years no large scale pageant that provided a musical background and in which the Recreation Department was in-terested, was without the efficient and expert service of Mrs. Steger. Whether the performances took place in the vast confines of Detroit's Olympia, on the broad and green acreage of Belle Isle or in widely scattered auditoriums of the department she represented, or those of other organizations whether sacred or secular Dorothy could always be found directing choral numbers and individual musical offerings that brought expressions of pleasure and praise from performers and audiences, with appreciative spontaniety.

Mrs. Steger's work and individual efforts extended into all groups and areas regardless of creed, color or race, she gave of her talents willingly and happily. That she will be greatly missed goes without saying.

The Department of Parks and Recreation and the community have suffered a great loss with the succumbing of Dorothy Steger.

Dorothy Steger was memorialized by noted journalist, author, historian, and patrons of the arts Fred Hart Williams in the *Detroit Tribune*, December 20, 1947. Courtesy of the Library of Congress. Public Domain.

Fred Hart Williams, born on February 2, 1882, and educated within Detroit from high school to law school, "dedicated his life to the collection, preservation, and interpretation of historical materials about African Americans."

Williams donated materials to the main Detroit Public Library to establish the E. Azalia Hackley Collection which honors blacks in the performing arts. His personal family history papers are also included in the collection.

Williams died on August 14, 1961. Named in his honor, the Fred Hart Williams Genealogical Society was created in 1979 in Detroit. As the first black genealogical society in the state of Michigan, it's committed "to research and preserve African

American family histories for future generations. It also collects, preserves, and makes available to the public, manuscripts, documents, genealogical records, and historical materials.[47]

> *"God has given us music, perhaps His greatest gift.*
> *The more we know of it the more we know of Him."*
> —Dorothy Steger

Dorothy Steger wrote and released an instructional booklet in 1938 titled *Singing Simplified* which is displayed below and on the following five pages.

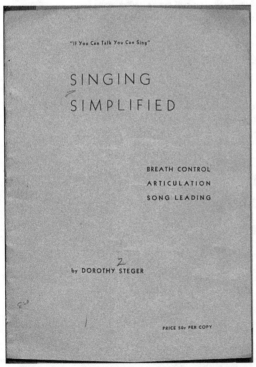

Singing Simplified.
ca. 1938.
Courtesy of the Library of Congress. Public Domain.

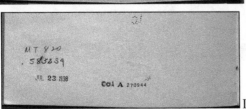

Inside the front cover.

My Dear Mrs. Steger:

I have read over your pamphlet "Singing Simplified" and I feel that it should prove very useful to anyone interested in singing, especially the untrained voice. Your explanation seems very clear and simple and in your work I feel you have given a fine contribution to the public.

A. C. Jackson

ARCHIBALD C. JACKSON, teacher of Voice at the Detroit Institute of Musical Art, has one of the largest classes of private students in Detroit. He is the director of the music at the Church of Our Father and the Northwestern Baptist Church. Mr. Jackson has toured the principal cities of the United States and Europe as baritone soloist.

"If you can talk you can sing"

SINGING SIMPLIFIED

BREATH CONTROL	ARTICULATION	SONG LEADING

by Dorothy Steger

Dedicated to The Girl Scouts and Boy Scouts of America

For you who wish to sing "for your own amusement," for you who find it expedient to know something of singing, and for you who think you cannot sing; this little book was written.

FOREWORD

The basic principle of singing is so simple it may be expressed in a few words. It is taking a breath properly and releasing it into tone.

Singing is as easy as talking when one knows, by instinct or acquirement, the fundamentals of the action. Explained and demonstrated, it becomes as much a definite process as is tap-dancing or geometry, and therefore can be satisfactorily self taught.

Although great voices are inborn, the person with an even less than average voice can learn to sing pleasingly well.

Breath control is the foundation of singing. Ultimate development would result in an ability to take in, and smoothly release, just the necessary amount of breath for any particular word or phrase.

The process of learning to sing, for man, woman, or child, is a gradual acquisition of breath control plus the important details of articulation, expression and delivery.

PART I.

BREATH CONTROL

The lungs is the one place in the body specifically for retaining breath. A deep breath is taken by expanding the ribs out (not up) and inhaling, thereby causing the lungs to fill with air. Permitting the ribs to sink causes a release of this air. A slow sinking releases a small amount of breath gradually (for soft singing), a rapid or instant sinking releases a large amount of breath (for loud singing).

Practice in the following manner. Place the widely spread finger tips high up under the arms and firmly against the ribs. Expand the ribs, slowly inhaling, pressing out hard against the fingers. Hold this breath a second, then jerkily, very slowly, count aloud to ten letting out a little breath at each number you speak. Let there be a gradual sinking of the ribs, until at ten all breath is expelled, the ribs as flat as possible. Expand the ribs again, in-haling as much as you can, then yet a little more and repeat the counting process.

If you become dizzy, do not be alarmed. You are simply getting more oxygen into the body than it is used to.

Now take a breath (expanding the ribs) and sing the numbers instead of talking them, letting the ribs, by sinking, press the air gradually out. When singing a song, follow the same procedure, letting out a small amount of breath for soft singing, and a lot of breath for loud singing.

Copyright 1938 by Dorothy Steger

Exercise daily to establish breath control. Blowing at a curtain is good practice. Stand just far enough back to move it slightly with a slow steady stream of air.

Say "ah," making the sound last as long as possible by letting out breath gradually. Now sing ah softly holding it by letting tone out through a gradual release of breath. Do this for weeks if necessary until a soft, smooth, steady tone can be held indefinitely.

Sing softly, do re me re do, as many times as possible in one breath. Do this smiling, several times daily. Remember that the ribs sink as you sing.

Hum any song you know, then softly sing it with an ee sound instead of words, smiling all the while and letting breath out gradually.

Most faults of the voice may be corrected through breath control and soft singing with a smiling mouth position.

The tremolo (wobble) is a serious fault. Spinning the voice out along an imaginary straight line will help.

Slurring, dragging notes up and down, is also bad. Sing your note and leave it where you place it.

A nasal toned voice may be improved by a smiling mouth position and soft singing.

While learning breath control one may also be studying articulation. When there is a general understanding of both, sing, and learn to sing by singing. Keep three things in mind: breathe quietly, release breath smoothly, keep the mouth open in a smiling position.

There is an instructive exercise book one should have, called "68 Exercises in the Synthetic Method" by Root. Most singing books are too technical for beginners, but this one is excellent.

PART II.
ARTICULATION

Singing differs from any other form of music, in that there are words, which need to be understood, else one might as well be playing a violin or trombone.

Breath control, relaxation, proper mouth position, and certain changes in pronunciation, may gradually bring about clear enunciation and flawless diction.

Relaxation and proper mouth position is easiest obtained by smiling. A great big exaggerated smile should be practiced until an easy, natural, smiling, singing position is attained.

A change in pronunciation is sometimes necessary to facilitate clear utterance. Here are listed a few such changes as well as other important factors relating to beautiful, natural, easily understood, singing.

Words ending in er; change er to ar, to get an open tone. Ex. mother, mothar.

EE sounding words on high notes must be changed to A. Ex. sea, say; steal, stale.

Words ending in y, pronounce y, ee. Ex. lovely, lovelee; every, everee.

Words like look, should, could; pronounce with an oo sound. Ex. look, luke; should, shoode.

When the first word of a phrase begins with a vowel, place a slight h in front of it. This will prevent a harsh attack. Ex. ah, hah; into, hinto.

The, coming before a vowel must be pronounced thee.

A, alone, should always be pronounced as the u in nut.

When a word is on two notes, one of which is high, place an h in the middle of the word. Ex. moon, moohoon; deer, deeheer.

Hold a tone, not by holding the breath but by letting out breath while singing the vowel sound of the word. Ex. cold, coold.

The higher you sing the wider you should open your mouth, lips back in a big, big, smile.

Never take a breath in the middle of a word. Breathe at commas, periods and natural stops. Read a song through aloud, before singing, to get the expression.

Hold one word until you are ready to say the next one. A consonant ending may be slightly carried over to a vowel. Ex. but only, but tonly; make out, make kout.

Ending consonants may be practiced this way. Take any four lines of a song, and read them aloud, tacking an a, at the end of each word. Ex. Mya countrya tiszofa theea, sweeta landofa libertya. Repeat, whispering the a sound (u in nut). Now sing the words with just a suggestion of the a. Always sing so, to be sure your words are complete.

The beginning and ending consonants are important but should not be over-emphasized. Get to the vowel sound of the word as quickly as possible. Ex. from, froom, not ffrrromm.

Breathe easily. Correct breathing is quiet breathing.

REMEMBERS . . . . .

You can't pour water out of a bottle which has the top covered; you can't sing through closed lips. Endeavor to keep the mouth open, lips back. Let the breath have free passage out into song.

Soft singing requires more control than loud, and incidentally develops the voice.

A loud tone should be soft first. Never hit a tone. Attack softly, instantly expelling a lot of breath if you want a loud tone. The difference in loud and soft tones is the greater or lesser amount of breath released.

Let there be a continuity in your singing, broken only by breaths or staccato passages. A train of cars might illustrate. They are separated, yet intact by the coupling-pins. So let your words connect; the vowel the car, the consonant the coupling-pin.

Don't push and strain; don't make yourself sing; let yourself sing.

Operatic arias are for trained voices. Don't attempt songs which are too difficult.

You can best sing what you can best envision. Don't sing words. If the song has no meaning for you, skip it.

Make it a rule not to sing a song that does not fit you and the occasion. Never sing a song you do not like or do not know well.

Stand easily, one foot slightly in advance of the other, body weight thrown forward on the balls of the feet. Hands should be held loosely at sides, or in front with one laid loosely in the other, and held at or below the waist line.

Naturalness and ease are conducive to beautiful singing.

An elevator goes up and down in the building. The building doesn't move. So let the voice go up and down without a lot of body and facial movements.

Singing is a splendid foundation for speaking. Public speaking courses should contain some singing.

Singing develops one, physically and mentally; brings about better posture, more poise, and a graciousness of manner; improves the health through all these things and through the increased oxygen supply which deeper breathing gives.

It is well to study a few books on singing. Here are the names of three. They are excellent, and not too technical.

Singing ....Witherspoon
Plain Words on Singing ....Shakespeare
Clearcut Speech in Song ....Rogers

If by now you are deeply interested in singing, or you find you have an excellent voice you were not aware of, seek out a good vocal teacher. Whether you intend to sing for your own "amusement" or wish to enter the professional field, you will not find the time spent perfecting your voice, wasted. God has given us music, perhaps His greatest gift. The more we know of it the more we know of Him.

PART III.
SONG LEADING

Recreational or group singing, which is very difinitely singing just to be singing, is becoming of greater importance each year. Group singing is increasingly popular in club-meetings, recreation groups and camps, churches, scout troops, political meetings, etcetera. Its value lies in its democracy, and in the fact that oftimes quartets, trios, glee clubs and choral groups, result from the music consciousness created in the group.

As trained leaders are rarely available to such groups, some person in the group should be chosen to lead singing as is desired. That leader, probably selected because of an ability to play the piano, or the possession of a good voice or a pleasing personality, no one of which signifies an ability to lead a group in singing, may be at a loss.

He should know, however, that ordinary song leading, not requiring the comprehensive knowledge of singing, choral directing necessitates, is comparatively simple. A little study of singing and of songs will set him aright. Then, if he has a well developed sense of rhythm and plenty of self confidence, he should make a very successful song leader. Here are a few suggestions as to things he should pay particular attention to.

FOR THE SONG LEADER

Use only songs you know well yourself.

The selection of songs should be guided by the ability, age, and sex of the person or group to sing them, and the occasion.

Do not bother your group with technicalities. Remember they want to sing, not learn to sing.

Sing softly as you direct.

Do not direct formally. Use as few movements as possible; only enough to indicate the rhythm of the song. Formal directing of recreational music is as out of place as evening dress in the morning.

Have your group begin together, and stop together. The right hand upheld may mean ready; a dropping of it should be the signal to start. Both hands held out high can mean, hold the tone. The left hand may indicate soft, with a shushing movement open palm toward the group, and loud with a lifting motion of the hand palm upwards. The stop can be easily indicated by a finishing, dropping, movement of both hands, or a swing-ing, cut-off, movement of the right hand.

Select songs for their strongly marked rhythms (such as march or waltz time) or for their beauty. They should be neither cheap nor silly. Much of the music of the great masters is simple and can be adapted to ordinary use. Folk songs are excellent, being simple and singable. Some popular music should be carefully chosen and used. Have song sheets at least, song books, or octavo copies, if possible.

Start out with songs whose melody is familiar, (have copies of the words), then grad-ually work into two and three part harmony, and finally into four part. For adults, un-trained, three part harmony is perhaps easiest and most effective; soprano, tenor and alto the same an octave apart, and baritone and bass the same.

If your group is small or very informal, tell them how to breathe, and to let breath out while singing. On difficult high notes, call attention casually to the change in pro-nounciation which will make them easier and also to the necessity of a wide open mouth. Tell them to breathe together, at the same places, (commas, periods, etc.) and to complete-ly finish words, holding them out fully when necessary.

Tell or stress the meaning of the song. If it is unfamiliar, give a brief history when possible. Also, go over any particularly difficult or tricky parts and have your group talk it through first, in the rhythm of the music, all before singing the song.

Smile, and repeatedly remind everyone to smile while singing.

Stress the beauty of soft, lovely, controlled, tone.

Know that singing is fun. Make your group love the singing period through your own love for it.

FINIS

CHAPTER 4

The Conversion

"When he received his military ID badge, his race was listed as 'White.' "

—Gerald Steger reminiscing with a chuckle after his cousin Carl Steger showed him his United States Army military service badge.[1]

"My mother would say, 'I wonder if he's still working there?' as Carl's 3rd cousin Patricia Taylor reflected back on her memory of him.

"Carl used to work at a restaurant not too far from Northland [Mall Shopping Center in Southfield, Michigan]. The people that worked there thought he was white. I used to catch the bus with my mother [Oreatha Steger]. I was a kid—about ten years old. We be on the bus going to Northland and we pass the restaurant where he worked at. I said, 'Let's go there.' She said, 'No, some other time.' "[2]

CARL STEGER

Registered Address : 3704 MUNDY RIDGE DR
SARASOTA FL 34233

FVRS Voter-ID: 100056178

Registered: 11-09-1983 Status: Active Total Items: 19

```
3016 AB          08/30/2016 PRIMARY
0414 AB          11/04/2014 GENERAL
0612 EARLYNPA    11/06/2012 GENERAL
0210 EARLYNPA    11/02/2010 2010 GENERAL
2410 EARLYNPA    08/24/2010 2010 PRIMARY
0408 EARLYNPA    11/04/2008 GENERAL
2908 EARLYNPA    01/29/2008 PRES PREF PRIMARY
0607 EARLYNPA    11/06/2007 VENICE GENERAL CO SUR TAX
1107 EARLYNPA    11/07/2006 2006 GENERAL ELECTION
0905 EARLYNPA    09/05/2006 2006 PRIMARY ELECTION
0204 AB          11/02/2004 GENERAL
0502 AB          11/05/2002 GENERAL
1002 POLL        09/10/2002 PRIMARY
1902 POLL        03/19/2002 SCHOOL REF
0700 POLL        11/07/2000 GENERAL
0398 POLL        11/03/1998 GENERAL
0696 POLL        11/05/1996 GENERAL ELECTION
0392 EARLY       11/03/1992 GENERAL ELECTION
0888 EARLY       11/08/1988 GENERAL ELECTION
```

State of FLORIDA
County of SARASOTA

    I, KATHY DENT, Supervisor of Elections, hereby certify
the foregoing to be a true and correct copy of the voting record
of CARL STEGER as it appears on record in my office.
Witness my hand and seal on September 26, 2016.

                        KATHY DENT
                        Supervisor of Elections

                    By: _Michelle Tuffland_____
                            Deputy

Carl Steger's voting record is referenced in a two-page *Sarasota County Supervisor of Elections Voting History Report* (1988–2016) above and on the following page. Courtesy of the Sarasota County Supervisor of Elections Voting History Report for Carl Steger, Michelle Tuffland, Deputy, 09-26-2016.

```
      Voter ID: 07217719
  FVRSIDNumber: 100056178

       Name    : STEGER, CARL
       Status  : A
       Address : 3704 MUNDY RIDGE DR

       City  : SARASOTA     Zip : 34233

     Precinct : 231 -0
Register Date : 11-09-1983
          Sex : M
         Race : W
Date Of Birth : 01-01-1926
        Party : NPA

     Military : NO
     Overseas : NO
 Out of Cnty  : NO
     Asst Req : NO
       Shutin : NO
     Homeless : NO
     Withheld : NO
     Disabled : NO
    Mail Reg. : NO


     Last Activity: 08/30/2016
     Last Card Req:
     Last Voted: 08/30/2016
     Last Change: 07/25/2012 23:02:19:00
     Pollworker: NO

Voter's Districts:
             CD16      16TH CONGRESS DIST
             CO02      CNTY COMM DIST 2
             HBC       HOSPITAL BOARD CENTRAL
             SD04      SCHOOL DIST 4
             SS23      SS23
             SH72      STATE HOUSE DIST 72
```

Note that **Carl's race is listed as "W" for White** on the second page of his Florida voting history report.

Judaism: A Culture, Religion, Nationality, and More

"He converted to Judaism during his first marriage."[3] Some may question why a man who decided to pass as "white" would convert to a faith that is mainly held by a tribe of people who have also consistently felt the sting of ethnic racism over a multitude of generations.

To get a better understanding of Judaism, I met and interviewed Rabbi Aaron Bergman on August 29, 2016, in his spacious office at the Adat Shalom Synagogue, located on a vast and beautiful campus in the city of Farmington Hills, Michigan, almost nine and a half miles northwest of Detroit. Rabbi Bergman, a Detroit native, raised in Oak Park, Michigan, and one of two presiding Conservative Jewish rabbis at the synagogue, is the founding Director of Jewish Studies at Frankel Jewish Academy and has been an instructor in the Melton Adult Education program. As I sat waiting for our interview to commence, I surveyed the area and enjoyed from a distance the numerous paintings of Jewish-related subject matter and books that aligned his office walls. In addition to being a writer, I characterize myself as a visual artist of realist drawings and abstract paintings.[4]

"And so it would be interesting to have him passing as white joining a group that was also to some extent also trying to pass in some ways too."

Author: The premise behind the book is to honor Carl, but also, it's a discussion of race and racism, and my speculation of why he decided to pass as a white Jewish man. It also includes other perspectives from his black and white families and former associates. And that's where you come in, concerning his conversion into Judaism and the need to know more about the faith.

RAB: That's interesting because a lot of Jews have tried to pass as non-Jewish. The issue of passing—that's why it was interesting. You know people have changed their names. And so, it would be interesting to have him passing as white, joining a group that was also to some extent also trying to pass in some ways too. So, there's a lot of interesting intersections where he probably maybe felt more at home with people who also didn't feel at home.

Author: Right. Exactly. Although there was anti-Semitism back during that time as well—it was great, but being African American or black, it was even—

RAB: Yeah. Well, thanks to Father Coughlin it was pretty awful—true. And it's getting worse again by a lot, but that's a whole other story. But yeah, that church on 12 [Mile Road] and Woodward—broadcast nationally. It was very pro-Nazi—anti-Semitism.

> Father Charles E. Coughlin, born in 1891 in Hamilton, Ontario, Canada, was ordained as a Catholic priest in 1916. His ideologies were influenced by the Catholic teachings of conservative clerical activism and the Basilian Order. The Basilians "believed that the Church should return to its theological roots and, among other issues, restore the prohibition against usury" which was "the main source of the ills that afflicted modern society." After leaving the Basilian Order in 1918, Coughlin became a priest under the diocese of Detroit.[5]

> In 1926, Coughlin established a new parish named the Shrine of the Little Flower in Royal Oak, Michigan. Broadcasting nationally from the church, Coughlin's early subject matters pertained to teaching children about catechism, "religious services with political overtones" and championing the working class. But with the onset of World War II, his audience escalated

along with his rhetoric "into anti-Semitism when he blamed bankers, who he said were Jewish, for the economic collapse and said Jews were responsible for the rise of communism in Russia."[6]

According to some historians, Coughlin's speeches, writings, and associations appear to attribute him with having "had significant anti-Semitic sentiment throughout his career."[7]

Author: And it didn't help with Henry Ford and his views as well.

RAB: Yeah. It probably wasn't until—easily the late '60s—the Jews started feeling more comfortable. Yeah. That ghost lasted a long time. Even now if you raise his name—people [who] grew up in that era, they'll just—it's a tough subject. It's interesting that all the things that connect and that. Yeah. I'd be curious why—if he converted for religious reasons—for social reasons?

"It's not really a pure faith—it's cultural."

The problem is Judaism isn't really a useful word because there's a religious aspect, but you can be an atheist and still be Jewish. It's not really a pure faith—it's cultural. In fact, we call ourselves a tribe.

We talk about each other, asking each other, 'Is that person a member of the tribe?' as opposed to a member of the faith. We tend to get put together like Jewish-Christian-Muslim, but it's not really. You know in America you divide out kind of by religious things. But it's more complicated than that and also because there's no central control. Every synagogue is independent—it hires and fires. So, every place in town—you can go to every different synagogue in town but you'll get some overlap. So, were there specific things you wanted to know or specific questions or—?

Author: Some of the things that I've obtained from the Internet—from one perspective is:

> "...rabbis make it clear that unless the person follows the precepts of the Torah and accepts the 'Thirteen Principles of Faith' of Maimonides, he cannot be a Jew. Although this person may be a 'biological' Jew, he has no real connection to Judaism."[8]

RAB: Yeah. None of that's true [Slight laughter]. Ah, you're still Jewish. Just like if you were born in America and you don't memorize the *Constitution*, you're still American. The problem is that just about every website you get if you put the word "Jew" in, it's Nazi and anti-Semitic and written by them. If you put the word "Jewish"—I would suggest a good place to go which has a lot of good information is called *My Jewish Learning*. And they're a pretty reliable website. Most of the stuff written online is by neo-Nazis and Klansmen and haters. In fact, if you put the word "Jew" into Google, you'll get an apology saying most of what you're going to see is anti-Semitic. If you use the word "Jewish," you'll be okay. But I say, MyJewishLearning.com is a really good place and it'll take you around, and it will give you a broader perspective on things. That one's pretty reliable.

If you're Jewish, you are Jewish, and it has nothing to do with faith. I mean it doesn't hurt. But if you are born into the Jewish people, it doesn't matter what you do; you're Jewish and you can convert into the Jewish people as well. Like Hitler tried to call us a race, but it can't be a race if people can convert into it [Laughter]. You know, it's kinda by definition [Laughter]. Yeah! I find a lot of the stuff on the Internet absolutely makes me cringe. But yeah, the MyJewishLearning is a good place in there. That's probably the most reliable and the least hate-filled of any of them. Some of the stuff that's out there is unbelievable. I mean I'm sure you can believe it.

Author: Exactly.

RAB: If you're going to research anything on race and religion, you're going to get a lot of ugly—

Author: Exactly.

RAB: Yeah. We don't decide whether someone's Jewish or not. If someone converts, there are kinda like standards and stuff. Once they convert, they convert. Rabbis don't have an elevated—we don't have any elevated powers in Judaism. Like in Catholicism, the priest—what the priest actually gives the house makes them married—performs the thing. Our job is to make sure it gets done properly. So, in Judaism, a couple marries each other. I don't marry them. I'm just there to make sure it all happens. Any lay person can lead services. It doesn't have to be the rabbi. So, it's a different—it's philosophically a different approach. But yeah, but that's part of the issue . . .

I'd be interested in who Carl worked with to do his conversion. That would be fascinating to me. What process he went through? What rabbi he worked with? Even what denomination?

Author: Years ago, I contacted Temple Beth El [a known Detroit Synagogue] to see if he was possibly recorded within their records and they couldn't find anything there. But I would be interested in it.

RAB: Or if he did Reform or Orthodox—Conservative?

Author: Orthodox, Conservative, Reform, Reconstructionist, and Humanistic. The correlation would be like the various denominations in Christianity—would you say?

"Like we think of ourselves in terms of 'peoplehood' and that religion is an aspect of being a part of the people—culture is an aspect of people and things like that."

RAB: Well, the difference is that in Judaism, you can belong to several different denominations at once and you don't convert between denominations. Like if you're Jewish—you're Jewish. So, we have people who actually belong to Conservative, Reform, Orthodox all at the same time. So, it's not like going from Catholic to Protestant or Lutheran to Methodist. There's no conversion process within Judaism. So, if you're Jewish, you're part of the entire tribe, but the tribe is broken down into different units and subdivisions and stuff. But it's all still the same. Like we think of ourselves in terms of 'peoplehood' and that religion is an aspect of being a part of the people. Culture is an aspect of people and things like that. But if someone's Conservative and they say, 'Oh, I want to go to an Orthodox place,' great—just go. Like, there's no—

Author: There's no allegiance?

RAB: Right. Exactly. Yeah. And you can go to in one weekend as many denominations as you want. So, it's kinda part of that not being part of any central control saying 'okay this is...' Now, there are guys who think they're central control and there are people who think they are the—but they are not [*Laughter*]. You don't have to listen. In fact, you can start your own denomination and if people like it, and they come—great. It's a very democratic process.

All the learning is available to everybody. As a rabbi, I don't have access to like just rabbi stuff. I have more time to learn it and maybe I have a little more formal training. But every single Jewish person has access to the exact same texts and learning as rabbis do. So, I think that that part is important—it's more of a meritocracy. Are you going to put in the time to learn it? Are you going to try to be a decent person? But it's not that like being ordained gives you a special status. But again, there are people that think that, but it's—we all got ego issues [*Laughter*]. We wouldn't be in this business if we didn't have it. Just how much do you want to own your ego issue [*Laughter*]?

Author: And it's the same as Christianity.

RAB: Exactly. Yeah. The guys that tell me they don't have any ego issues—yeah, you do [*Laughter*]. You do. Just how does it manifest itself? You can't get up in front of a thousand people and talk to them if you didn't have some kind of—ego. Ego management is part of the thing.

Author: Some other information that I referenced—if you don't mind me reading it—

RAB: Yeah, sure.

Author: 'So, what is it that Jews believe, and what are the basic precepts of Judaism? There are five main forms or sects of Judaism in the world today. They are Orthodox, Conservative, Reformed, Reconstructionist, and

Humanistic. The beliefs and requirements in each group differ dramatically; however, a short list of the traditional beliefs of Judaism would include the following:

- God is the creator of all that exists; He is one, incorporeal (without a body), and He alone is to be worshipped as absolute ruler of the universe.

- The first five books of the Hebrew Bible were revealed to Moses by God. They will not be changed or augmented in the future.

- God has communicated to the Jewish people through prophets.

- God monitors the activities of humans; He rewards individuals for good deeds and punishes evil."[9]

RAB: Yeah. That one is—those last couple are problematic. We believe though the prophecy ended in the third century B.C.E—that Malachi was the last prophet. So, we don't believe—like if someone since then said they're a prophet—basically that once the Bible was given, that God doesn't even get to interfere with that. Because you can't run a community if every now and then a guy pops up, 'No, no, God told me you're—.' No, we got the rules. We can take it from there.

"...all people are created in God's image."

The rewarding good and punishing the wicked—that's been problematic for a long time because, first of all, it's not true. A lot of good people suffer. So even the last couple thousand years they're trying to figure out why good people suffer—why bad people are rewarded. So, there are some disagreements on that.

There is this one theory that if a good person is punished, it means that they may have done something wrong so all the punishments they're ever have in this world are now, and then they'll go to heaven free and clear. And the wicked person may have done something good in their lifetime, so they get a reward for that now and then nothing. But what we try to do is let God do God's job and our job is to take care of each other. But I would say that probably the biggest one is—it sort of flows over that—is that all people are created in God's image.

"Because we're not salvation based, we don't see any need for everyone to be Jewish."

In Judaism, we don't believe you have to be Jewish to be saved. I mean, we are not a salvational religion. We just try to be a good person—treat people with some kindness and dignity, and you're in. So, we don't actively look for converts in a sense that it's not necessary. People who look for converts are trying to save their souls. Because I get this all the time—I get letters all the time from preachers trying to save my soul. It's like, really? I mean I appreciate the thought, but I'm good. So, because we're not salvation based, we don't see any need for everyone to be Jewish.

And we don't think of ourselves as better either. I mean I hate this phrasing of what they say, 'You people call yourself The Chosen.' That's a whole thing in and of itself. But there's no Jewish heaven and then non-Jewish heaven. It's not that Jews are more beloved than anyone else. If everyone's in God's image, everyone—even the cousin you don't like—that one's still in God's image too. The people are, 'Oh! Everyone's in God's image?' Oh yeah! Of course, everyone is. Yeah, even your niece. Oh, her too [*Laughter*]? You know in the general [sense], everyone's on board. But when you get specific, you know that's where it kinda breaks down for people. But even they are created in God's image. Yes, so those are, I say philosophically, some of the big ideals. But there's a lot of things in terms of lifecycle events—holidays, things like—I mean there are things that are distinctive I think to Judaism.

So, I would say in general we believe that if you are a good person you go to heaven the same way as anyone else. But there are a number of rituals that we have that I think keep us as a people. And I think that part of our success as a people even though there are a few of us on earth—I think maybe 13 million, 14 million on the entire planet. So, we're not even big enough to be a statistical anomaly. You know you see on the census it says plus or minus two or three percent?

Author: Right.

"...we think in the ideal of community and setting of communal institutions and trying to help each other."

RAB: We're not even big enough for that. We're a very small people and even Israel's a very small country. It can fit inside the state of Michigan five times—the entire country. So, it's a small place—it's a small people. But we've been around a long time because I think part of it is that we have—we think in the ideal of community, and setting of communal institutions, and trying to help each other. Even when we don't like each other, we try to help each other—which is important. Because if you only help the people you like . . . You know I tell people, 'If there's no one difficult in your family, it's you [*Laughter*].' But also, we believe that you have to help your neighbor too. So, we've been very involved in social justice issues and things like that because if everyone's created in God's image, it means everyone's created in God's image. So, it's always trying to balance off the tribal versus the general.

> *"...if you're talking to your average Jewish person on the street, 'What are those moments that matter the most?' It would be lifecycles and holidays."*

But I would say that our lifecycle events tend to be based on transitional moments like the celebrations and things or the . . . I say the rituals that are around transitions like birth—there are a lot of rituals, then adolescence—we have rituals and marriage and divorce. We have a relatively positive view of divorce. We don't have this ideal of 'Who God has brought together, let no man rend asunder.' If it didn't work, it must not have been God who brought you together. So, we actually tell a couple 'congratulations' at the divorce because you now get your life back. So, a divorce doesn't bring a change in status religiously. You can just sort of go on and remarry or not or whatever it is. And then they're rituals of illness and death and . . .

So, all transitions in your life, that's when we try to get the community together. And then the holidays are just—the cycle of the holidays goes from the ideal of helplessness and liberation which is Passover. Like God takes the people out all the way through the holiday cycle. Okay, now you're independent and responsible for yourself. So even the calendar sends a message. So, on My Jewish Learning [website], they'll have all those things. But I would look up 'lifecycles' and 'holidays.' Because I would say that for Jewish people, those are the two most important things. Like if you're talking to your average Jewish person on the street, 'What are those moments that matter the most?' It would be lifecycles and holidays. My guess is that's probably what grabbed Carl too.

Author: Okay. When you say 'lifecycles,' marriage—?

RAB: Bar mitzvahs, marriage, like the circumcision, and all those sorta things.

Author: Okay, various stages of—

RAB: Every time you have a change in your life, we try to get the community together to help you into that next piece which is very comforting. So, even if you're not a religious person, per se, you go through changes. And also, it's a recognition—it's a change for everyone. Like, if you have a kid who gets married, that's a change for the kid, it's a change for you—so helping everyone along. We're actually looking at developing something for kids who get their driver's license—a prayer for the parents we have now because that's a big change.

Author: Right. Definitely.

RAB: I have four drivers and I remember when each of them [Whew] . . . Part of its good because you don't have to do carpool and part of it's like that's your car they're driving off with.

Author: Right [Laughter].

RAB: 'Oh Daddy! You don't have to worry about me.' Like, 'Yeah, I do.' I worry professionally. Yes, that's what I do. But I would say that in general, those sorta things. And like the home rituals—like lighting the lights and Passover things, those are significant.

It's interesting even just the terminology. It's like when people talk about, 'Are you a Jew now?' It's gonna be derogatory. Like we call each other 'The Jews' or something like that. But if you see—even like *The New York Times* they'll say now we don't use the word 'Jew' anymore. We always talk about a Jewish person because there's so many derogatory things involved with the word 'Jew.' So, if in your research, you go by Jewish— which is why it's called *My Jewish Learning* instead of learning about Jews—it's asking to be run by the Arian Nations. There is some really scary stuff, really scary. And I don't know where you fit politically, but Trump [the 2016 United States Republican Presidential Nominee Donald Trump] has just brought these dudes to life like I've never seen.

Author: Right.

RAB: Yeah. I've never been this worried.

Sadly, Rabbi Bergman's worries concerning an increase in anti-Semitic slander and violence would be realized when on October 27, 2018, 46-year-old Robert Bowers entered the Tree of Life Synagogue in Pittsburgh, Pennsylvania, and murdered 11 Jewish worshippers and wounded six others including four police officers. After being injured during the exchange of gunfire with police, Bowers was reported to have talked about how "all these Jews need to die," and then he surrendered and was taken into custody. A 97-year-old woman, a husband and wife, and two brothers were among those killed in the worst massacre against the Jewish community in United States history.[10]

Also "alarmingly higher rates than normal" of increased anti-Semitic Google searches in the United States were discovered after the Pittsburgh synagogue attack and the April 2019 attack in Poway, California, according to a year-long study by the cable network news company CNN. "The Anti-Defamation League (ADL) said anti-Semitic incidents in America rose for the third year in a row, hitting near-historic highs. There were 1,879 documented attacks against Jews and Jewish institutions across the country in 2018."[11]

Author: Yeah. I don't like either of them as far as the policies, but especially Trump because he has put himself out there even as far as the anti-black rhetoric—not just the Jewish . . .

*"I don't want you to love me.
I want you to treat me according to the law of the land
and what I'm entitled to."*

RAB: Oh, it's horrible! I don't know if it's just horrifying and embarrassing or what it is. But what he basically said is that every African American lives in poverty, is afraid of getting shot, and all your schools are . . . And he's saying this to a white audience and I'm like—really?

Author: Exactly.

RAB: I'm sitting there watching this and I'm like, 'How does this even . . .' He has created more of an us versus them.

Author: Exactly.

RAB: Now if he gets up and says, 'We have to make our schools better, our communities better.' Great! But you're going to be the president and you're still talking about 'your [*Laughter*]?' Who is he going to be the president of?

Author: Right. He's supposed to be the president of everyone—the free nation.

RAB: And no one is a hater of just one minority. No one says, 'I'm fine with the rest of you, but you Dutch guys.' You ever see Austin Power's *Goldmember* [Hollywood film]?

Author: Yeah.

RAB: I love it when Michael [actor Michael Myers' portrayal as the film's lead character Austin Powers] goes, 'Yeah. There's two kinds of people I hate, those intolerant and the Dutch [*Laughter*].' I love that [*Laughter*].

Yeah. But that's how I feel like these guys, 'Oh yeah. We love everybody.' I don't want you to love me. I want you to treat me according to the law of the land and what I'm entitled to. I got friends who love me. I don't need you to love me. Because as soon as—I hear this from religious people too, 'Oh, we love you—we want to save . . .' I'm like, you don't love me. You don't love me as much—my mother doesn't love me as much as you say that you love me. I want you to treat me by the law of the land. That's all I want out of you [*Laughter*].

"Either give me corrupt or useful
or give me clean and not so great, but don't give me
corrupt and hateful—and inefficient."

Yeah. So, I'm horrified. I have never. . . Yeah. And it's, 'I can't be an anti-Semite. Yeah. My daughter's a Jew.' Oh really? Oh, that solves it then. Good, good [Laughter].

Yeah. I just found out that Herman Goebbels ["Joseph" Goebbels], the director of propaganda for the Nazis, his father-in-law was Jewish.

Author: Oh really?

RAB: Yeah! And he had him executed anyway—during the holocaust. That's all this coming up. His secretary [Brunhilde Pomsel] is still alive! She's 105 years old![12]

Author: Oh really? Wow!

RAB: Yeah. And they interviewed her, and she said, 'Yeah. We had no idea what was going on.' Like, you're his secretary! My secretary knows more about me than I do! You know—really [Laughter]? Like, really? You didn't know [Laughter]? So, the fact that we're still living in this world—still having these conversations, I'm just— just horrified. I mean, I don't love Hillary [the 2016 United States Democratic Presidential Nominee Hillary Clinton] at all, but I think she's your good old-fashioned corrupt awful human being. Like great, I know what to do with that [Laughter]. I'm fine—I can negotiate through that. But yeah, she's easily one of the most corrupt people we've ever had. But in comparison to Trump?

Author: Yeah. There are differences.

RAB: Yeah. It's been a long time. I would say maybe Gerald Ford [the 38th president of the United States] was the only one I really liked because he really took one for the team [Laughter]. You know [he] threw his entire career away because he thought it would be better for the country. Like, I appreciate that.[13] But Hillary, she'll be fine. She'll lie and cheat, but she'll . . . If you're corrupt but you do the job, I can live with that. Either give me corrupt or useful or give me clean and not so great, but don't give me corrupt and hateful—and inefficient.

Author: As far as Trump is concerned, the only positive aspect is he's speaking his ideology and it's not hidden.

RAB: Exactly. Kinda bringing the cockroaches out on the ledge. Yeah. I can't even—I can't even believe it. Yeah. Yeah. We're in bizarro world. But all of these things that are still floating around and still an issue. Yeah. It kills me.

Author: Would you happen to know about how many converted black Americans are practicing Judaism?

RAB: It's an interesting question on two levels. One would be when we do conversions, we don't mark race on the certificates.

Author: Okay.

RAB: So, you will have to kind of find out anecdotally. The other issue is you had a Black Israel movement that began in the 1800s where there were a group of African Americans who declared themselves to be the true Israel and they started their own synagogues and communities and things like that. Actually, Michelle Obama's cousin is a rabbi whose lineage was from the Black Hebrews and then he converted to become mainstream.

Author: Okay.

RAB: There's actually an organization—I'm pretty sure I have the right number—that is primarily concerned with issues of Jews of color. He's an amazing guy. I've talked to him a couple times. His name is Rabbi Capers Funnye. He's Michelle Obama's cousin and he's actually a great rabbi. He's based out of Chicago. He started with—his family was Black Hebrew and he eventually converted in the more mainstream community and had his synagogue convert more into the mainstream. It's called the Beth Shalom B'nai Zaken Ethiopian Hebrew Congregation.

Author: In reference to the various sects of Judaism, your synagogue practices which one?

RAB: We're Conservative. It's a pretty traditional service, but men and women participate equally, and women can be rabbis also. In fact, the other rabbi's a woman. I try not to call her the woman rabbi because I don't call myself the man rabbi [*Laughter*].

Author: Right. Have you ever heard of a particular case such as the one I presented—a black person passing—

RAB: No. This [is] actually the first one. I had a number of black people who wanted to become Jewish and some did, and some didn't. But no one that I was aware of. But also, I've only been a rabbi since 1991. So—I know it'll always be an issue, but I don't know if it's been as much the issue as it was and whether it will be again. It's depending where—yeah. It's a wonder if things do progress or do they kind of circular [or repeat] [*Slight laughter*].

> "[It's] never been a president ever that had to deal with that level of criticism just for his existence on earth."

What happen is the internet united all these crazy white supremacy groups. They were kinda fading—obviously. Like you got a group in Idaho, you got a group in Florida—they're all kind of isolated, and then all of a sudden, they're all networking with each other. Yeah! And they said they wished President Obama could be president eight more years. They said it's the best thing they ever had to their recruiting efforts.

Author: Wow! And there are those in the black community who wished that President Obama could have done more. Although, it would [have to] be a delicate balance. Being the president of everyone, which is the main objective, but still . . .

RAB: Yeah, exactly. I have always felt for him of how torn he must have felt constantly and how he negotiated here—there. It must have been just excruciating. I don't know that anyone could have imagined it any better being put in the middle.

Author: Right. That's true.

RAB: Yeah. Because he was the first one who was criticized just for who he was, not for what he was doing. [It's] never been a president ever that had to deal with that level of criticism just for his existence on earth. No president ever had his citizenship called into [question]—Trump still did—anyway. That whole birther thing.[14]

Author: Right! Exactly!

RAB: So, I can sorta see both sides. He must have been killed in the middle—on this. I try to read a variety of sources. I figure no one source has it right, but somewhere [Laughter] and just read them. And oh my god, how tough must it have been to—then trying to raise daughters knowing the hateful things people say. If I were to read about my daughters what he had to read about his daughters, I would go nuclear on those people. Like, I would make sure that they were audited [Laughter]—

that their identities were erased from the database. Like, you can say things about me—you say things about my daughters—I've got all daughters.

Author: Oh! Do you?

RAB: So, I take that very—

Author: I've got two daughters.

RAB: Oh! I got four daughters so I [*Laughter*]—

Author: And a female dog [*Laughter*].

RAB: Yeah. Okay.

Author: So, I'm the only male in the household.

RAB: We got a cat; it's male, but that doesn't count [*Laughter*]. It's still a cat [*Laughter*].

Author: True, true [*Laughter*].

RAB: But I think I probably felt the worst for him as the father of daughters.

Author: Right.

RAB: Because what they were—like they always say stupid stuff about the president's kids, but what they were saying about his daughters is a new low.

Author: Right. Exactly—daughters—his wife. That is a new low.

RAB: It was ah—it was stunning and now Trump is just saying what everyone's thought.

Author: Exactly. Thank you. Well, Rabbi Bergman, I really appreciate it.

RAB: Oh, my pleasure. This is fascinating for me. I appreciate you came in. Yeah!

Author: Okay. Yeah!

RAB: That's why I like to meet instead of doing stuff through email and text and stuff.[15]

The author Eric B. Willis (l) with the distinguished **Rabbi Aaron Bergman** on August 29, 2016, at the Adat Shalom Synagogue in Farmington Hills, Michigan. From the author's photograph collection.

According to the *My Jewish Learning* website:

"Judaism is the world's oldest monotheistic religion. According to the Bible, Abraham and Sarah were the first to recognize God, and they are considered the ancestors of all Jews today.

Some people think that Judaism is a culture, like being Irish or Indian. Others view it as a religion. Still others say that being Jewish is a nationality, and that the Jewish homeland is the Land of Israel. The truth is, being Jewish encompasses all these things—and a whole lot more. The entire span of Jewish life and knowledge is nearly impossible to define, yet exciting to explore.

Different groups of Jews believe different things. Judaism has three main denominations: Orthodox, Conservative, and Reform. Many other subgroups and philosophies exist within and beyond these including Reconstructionism, Hasidim, Jewish Renewal, and others. To some extent, all these groups regard the Torah—the Five Books of Moses—as the central book of Judaism. Some Jews value its stories. Others derive their beliefs and their customs and traditions from the Torah's laws.

Judaism has many practices and ethical teachings. Almost all Jews celebrate some form of Jewish holidays, from attending a Passover seder to lighting the candles on Hanukkah. Some Jews keep kosher and only eat certain foods or foods prepared in certain ways. Many Jews celebrate Shabbat every Friday night and Saturday and will attend synagogue and listen to the Torah being read, a different portion each week."[16]

Becoming a Jew is not just a one-time declaration of faith but rather an evolutionary process that culminates in the adoption of a new cultural, national, and even historical identity. Conversion to Judaism requires serious study, active participation in Jewish holiday and life cycle events, and finally, a commitment to

Jewish practice that is actualized by a rabbinically prescribed ritual.

The "birth" of a new Jew through conversion mirrors the process by which the Israelites became God's people and accepted God's covenant at Sinai: Circumcision, which male Israelites underwent before leaving Egypt, and immersion, which parallels the ritual cleansing performed by all Israelites at Sinai, are the *sine qua non* rituals of the conversion process. Full responsibility for every conversion rests in a three-person *beit din*, or rabbinic court, which searches out candidates' motivations, ascertains their knowledge of Judaism, and approves the conversions.[17]

Dr. Charles Domstein, a local educator and archivist, had the following to say about Rabbi Bergman during our brief interview on July 29, 2019.

"Rabbi Bergman is quite a known scholar in the community. I had the honor of having his girls—his children. I was the principal of the Akiva Hebrew Day School and I had his children there. Also, I used to teach at Oak Park High School and he's a graduate of that school. So, whenever I see him, it's like bringing up pleasant old memories. His wife, by the way—she's an educator and she's also very well noted in the Jewish community.

Rabbi Bergman will often take positions that are maybe non-traditional. He looks at things in many ways in a more modernistic way than perhaps somebody who might be more traditional. For that, plus the fact he has a terrific sense of humor, people respect him for that.

He's very active in the whole Jewish community. Often times he will participate in events and he will be asked to perform ceremonies of a religious nature—of a birth of a baby, marriage of a man and woman, and the passing of a loved one. That often will happen. We have in our community three funeral homes and often Rabbi Bergman and other rabbis will be asked to officiate at those ceremonies. What they do first is they sit down with the family and have the family pour out their love and affection for the loved one. And what they would then do is give anecdotes, and then Rabbi Bergman and others would give analogies at the funeral so that the people who attend the funeral would then know that person a little bit better and respect what they have done in their lives. As I said he is a very well-respected man and Adat Shalom is very prominent in our community."[18]

Carl may have also been influenced to convert to Judaism because of his close relationships with Jewish friends, including Arlyn Meyerson, whom he may have met sometime during the '50s. Arlyn "used to come over to the house," recalls Carl's daughter Kimberly Steger-Sherrill.

"Arlyn Meyerson was born deaf and grew up in Detroit, Michigan, where his father owned a restaurant business. When Arlyn was 14 years old, he started working for his father during wartime, for it was difficult to find restaurant help during that time. Arlyn started working as a busboy and cashier to help out, gaining experience by working his way up from the bottom. During the same time period, he also worked for Ford and Lincoln Motor Companies and Kaiser-Frazer. After graduating from Wilbur Wright High School, he trained to be a draftsman, and married his wife Hester Wayner, who is hard of hearing. The two have five children."[19]

In 1960, Arlyn and his hearing brother Gerald received a loan from the U.S. Small Business Administration (SBA) to start a new restaurant called Scotch 'n Sirloin. The restaurant was located in northwest Detroit on 20480 James Cousins—, east of Greenfield Road and south of Eight Mile Road.[20]

Opening a day after Labor Day, "it seated 175 people and employed 60 workers. Eight of them were deaf. Scotch 'n Sirloin became very successful from the time it opened."

"The building was close to the Northland Playhouse. Actors and actresses often came by to eat after their performances, and "well-known sports figures—two to three times a week."[21] Since 1965, Carl performed as a lounge singer and pianist at the restaurant.[22]

In 1975, the restaurant permanently closed its doors due to Meyerson's onset of financial problems after opening a larger second restaurant called Trio. After his retirement from working in the restaurant business after 55 years, Meyerson was asked in a 2000 interview by *Jewish Deaf Community Center* (JDCC) News if he had any regrets. He responded, "Yes, one regret was that we started too big from 175 seats at Scotch 'n Sirloin to 450 seats at Trio. That was too big of a jump."[23] On September 21, 2018, Meyerson, who lived in Commerce Township, Michigan, died at age 93.[24]

Carl's former friend and jazz pianist Charles Boles recollected about his own personal appearance at the club.

"I played there. Yeah. Now I vaguely remembered that Carl played there, but it was a really, really—It's still sittin there, I believe. Been vacant for years now. I played there when it was on its last legs. And it used to get—attract money. It was quite the money club."[25]

The **Scotch 'n Sirlion** restaurant where Carl Steger was employed for about ten years between 1965 and 1975. Dexter Natural Color Pub. by P.T. Olsen Photographic, Detroit, Michigan.

Interior views (above and on the following page) of the once famous **Scotch 'n Sirloin** restaurant in Detroit. Courtesy of Dexter Natural Color Pub. by P.T. Olsen Photographic, Detroit, Michigan.

This photograph shows the piano and microphone Carl used as tools for his profession to intimately entertain many customers at the restaurant.

TO SCOTCH 'N SIRLOIN in Detroit that actually began back in 1921 when the late Buddy Meyerson had a confectionery and soda shop on the corner of Oakland and Holbrook ... People enjoyed such pleasures as a stroll to the corner for a dish of ice cream and penny rock candy and licorice sticks for the kids.

Buddy's and Mary's three sons, Arlyn, Jerry and Aubrey each served boyhood apprenticeships at mom and dad's Buddy's Log Cabin Barbeque on the corner of 12th and Clairmount ... As young men, they decided to open their own eatery.

Detroit was enjoying the post-war boom and expanding into the suburbs ... When a location on the far northwest corner of the city became available, they were ready.

Result was the Scotch 'n Sirloin, which marked another milestone in the Meyerson family's long history of food service.

The Detroit Jewish News, February 6, 2004.

According to Arlyn Meyerson's son Mark about the restaurant and Carl:

"I managed the Scotch 'n Sirloin during the late '60s—early '70s. I was young when I first met him. When I started managing, I began to know Carl better. He played there about seventy percent of the time. He was quite the character.

Mark Meyerson, 26-year-old son of Arlyn and Laura Meyerson, is taking over for dad in a big way ... He's doing a fine job as night manager at "the Scotch" ... now on a full-time basis.

A news article referencing Mark Meyerson's newly acquired full-time management duties at the Scotch 'n Sirloin restaurant. *The Detroit Jewish News*, February 4, 1977.

He knew everybody [the customers] by name. He was personable. He made everyone feel warm. He would mention a person's name and where they were from. Carl came in at nine or ten at night to perform." After inquiring about his wife, Meyerson replied, "I saw his wife–she had blond hair. I don't know if it was his first wife."[26]

Harvey Leach

Harvey Leach was Carl's best friend. He owned a furniture business in Detroit. He had a "high strung personality —meticulous." "He was murdered by the mob."[27]

> The murder of Harvey Leach, a Jewish business owner, became one of Oakland County, Michigan's "most high-profile unsolved homicides of the 20th century."

> In 1971, Leach purchased a failing Robinson Furniture company and renamed it Joshua Doore. The company became successful and widely known for its advertising jingle that informed customers "You got an uncle in the furniture business—Joshua Doore, Joshua Doore."

> Several years later on March 16, 1974, Leach would also become known for becoming a victim of a possible mob hit. His body was discovered in the trunk of his car with his throat slashed in Southfield, Michigan, a suburban city northwest of the Detroit city limits. According to FBI informants, Leach reputedly mob-connected with his friend Leonard Schultz and Detroit's Mafia chief Anthony "Tony Jack" Giacalone to expand Joshua Doore through a loan. He "began butting heads" with Giacalone after he "got his hooks into the business" and "the company began incurring financial problems."

"One member of the Detroit underworld familiar with the Leach situation summed it up this way: 'The Giacalones were trying to bust out his business [mob slang for takeover and bilk] and the Jew bucked, not to mention the rumors that he was sleeping with a girlfriend of Billy's when Billy was away at school [prison]. That put things over the edge. At that point, he had no chance. He was the walking dead.'" Vito "Billy Jack" Giacalone, Anthony's younger brother, was "also a powerful mobster in the area and a decade-long capo [or mafia captain] and future underboss in the syndicate." He was released from behind bars in the months prior to Leach's untimely death.

Over a year later, Schultz and the infamous Giacalone brothers were also investigated and named as suspects involving the renowned disappearance of Jimmy Hoffa.[28]

A Mysterious Death

Everybody said Harvey Leach was a nice guy.

So police were mystified when Mr. Leach was found murdered on March 17, 1974.

Mr. Leach, chairman of the board of directors of Joshua Doore Inc., a furniture retailing chain, was discovered in the trunk of his Lincoln Continental in the parking lot of the Congress Building in Southfield. His death was caused by a heavy blow to the right side of his neck.

"We have absolutely no clues, no possible motive and no suspects," a spokesman for the Southfield Police said after the incident.

Today, the case remains unsolved.

Mr. Leach, who was 34 at the time of his death, is buried in Memorial Park South at Machpelah.

Harvey Leach was born May 18, 1939, in Detroit and lived on North Park Drive in Southfield at the time of his death. Associates described him as a brilliant businessman.

Mr. Leach joined Robinson Furniture in the mid-'60s and by 1971, he had taken control of the business with a partner. In 1972, he started Joshua Doore — whose famous logo was "You've got an uncle in the furniture business" — as a subsidiary of Robinson. It featured five large showrooms of furniture that patrons could purchase, and take home, on the spot. It didn't take long for Joshua Doore to advance, with Robinson Furniture becoming the subsidiary.

Yet Joshua Doore's financial status was questionable at the time of Mr. Leach's death. A *Detroit News* article about the case notes that profits had dropped dramatically — 44 percent — in the nine months ending Sept. 30, 1973. There was talk of organized crime involvement in the business.

Mr. Leach had last been seen early Saturday morning the day before his body was discovered. His fiancee, who also lived in Southfield, and several business partners reported that he had missed meetings.

Mr. Leach had been dead for 12 hours when police found his body. He had on the same coat, pants and brown shirt he had been seen wearing on Saturday morning. His car was locked and the keys were gone. There was no murder weapon.

Police believe the killer met up with Mr. Leach soon after 9:45 a.m. Saturday, when he left his fiancee's home for a meeting in Franklin. But their investigation ended there.

Joshua Doore Furniture Inc. is no longer in existence, though Robinson Furniture, under different ownership, continues to this day. It now advertises with its own uncle, "Uncle Robinson."

Mr. Leach was survived by his mother, his fiancee, two daughters and his brother.

Soon after Mr. Leach's death, his former associate at Joshua Doore told the *Detroit News* "I just can't believe anyone would do this to him. Everyone liked him. I don't think the guy had an enemy in the world." □

PHOTO BY THE DETROIT FREE PRESS

Harvey Leach:
He "didn't have an enemy in the world."

Carl's former friend **Harvey Leach** and his "mysterious death" is the subject of the above newspaper article. *Detroit Free Press,* January 27, 1995.

Jimmy Hoffa

"He [Carl Steger] was playing at the Machus Red Fox restaurant in Bloomfield, Michigan, when Hoffa disappeared from the parking lot." Carl was included among a long list of people to be interviewed by the FBI about the famous incident.[29] The Machus Red Fox restaurant was located seven miles north of the northern Detroit city limits. "That was a very mobster-gangster place," as recalled by Carl's former friend Charles Boles.[30]

The **Machus Red Fox** where Carl was performing on July 30, 1975, when Jimmy Hoffa disappeared from the restaurant's parking lot in Bloomfield Township, Michigan.

James Riddle Hoffa or "Jimmy Hoffa" was born on Valentine's Day, February 14, 1913, in Brazil, Indiana. During the 1930s, he became a member of the International Brotherhood of Teamsters. He eventually became the union's Detroit chapter president.

In 1952, Hoffa, an "ambitious and aggressive" labor organizer who expanded the union's membership roll and negotiated improved contacts for his constituents, was elected as the union's vice-president. In 1957, he became the president over the most powerful and richest labor union in the country.[31] Hoffa supported civil rights, Martin Luther King, Jr., and other activists. Concerning segregated local unions in the South, he said, "If they want segregation, we don't want them. We pride ourselves on the fact there are no Jim Crow locals in our union."[32]

In 1966, Hoffa was indicted and received a 13-year prison sentence for mail fraud and jury tampering. Nevertheless, in 1971 President Richard M. Nixon commuted his term after he'd served four and a half years and barred him from union activity until March 1980. Wanting to reclaim his position as Teamster president and being "optimistic about his chances for a favorable ruling by the U.S. Circuit Court of Appeals in Washington, D.C.," Hoffa sued to have the legal restriction removed.[33]

On July 30, 1975, Hoffa told his family he planned to meet with three men for lunch at a restaurant. At 2:00 P.M., he went to meet for a "peace conference" with Teamster associates and reputed Detroit crime syndicate and high-ranking Mafia figures Anthony (Tony Jack) Giacalone, Anthony (Tony Pro) Provenzano (described as a "capo" in the Vito Genevese mafia family in New Jersey) and Charles O'Brien, Hoffa's foster son. The restaurant was the Machus Red Fox on Telegraph Road, south of Maple Road in the wealthy suburb of Bloomfield Township, Michigan. According to other investigators, Giacalone's father, his brother William Vito, and Leonard Schultz, a Detroit labor consultant with an extensive criminal record and an association with the Teamsters, were to meet with Hoffa and Giacalone. Nonetheless, Hoffa disappeared and his car was found in the restaurant parking lot. As reported by a witness, he was last seen standing outside of Machus Red Fox.[34]

According to a 1978 national newspaper article, "Published reports have speculated that Hoffa's meeting was to be in the restaurant, but this was belied by his casual attire (it's a dressy place) and by his failure to go inside. The government theory–and it is only that—is that he knew he was going to be picked up at the restaurant and taken to a spot nearby and that he would have entered a car only with someone he knew intimately."[35]

Knowing that his wife Josephine was not in good health and was scheduled for surgery the month after his disappearance, Hoffa's family, friends, and associates believed that he would not voluntarily disappear with knowing the family circumstances.[36]

Several speculations exist as to the reason for Hoffa's disappearance and possible murder including the following:

- While serving federal prison sentences, Provenzano and Hoffa had a dispute involving the usage of Teamster union pension funds and Provenzano reportedly wanted to keep Hoffa from becoming the Teamsters Union president again during his quest for union power.[37]

- After his 1971 release from prison for jury tampering, conspiracy and fraud, and an attempt to resume control of the Teamsters, Hoffa sought to undermine Frank E. Fitzsimmons, his former friend and successor as union president with "the allegation that controlling positions in the union were filled with racketeers and convicted criminals." Hoffa said this would change if he was the president. The organization's crime figures no longer needed Mr. Hoffa and killed him for "rocking the boat . . . ." According to investigators, records of past evidence and background interviews showed that Hoffa previously obtained the presidency of the union with the inclusion of mobsters and their support and assistance.[38]

- The mob was opposed to Hoffa's ideology of restoring Teamster's authority back to central control. After Hoffa's conviction and resignation as president, the union's power became regionalized and local crime families had direct access to it.[39]

- Hoffa may have angered the Giacalone brothers, his longtime friends, because of his refusal to disclose what union records federal investigators had subpoenaed in connection with Anthony Giacalone's April 1975 indictment in Detroit for income tax evasion and a kickback scheme to defraud a Michigan Teamster member medical plan.[40]

- Hoffa "stood in the way of a loan from the Teamsters pension fund worth $900,000 in kickbacks to union and organized crime figures." The proposed nine-million-dollar loan to Fairfield, New Jersey, real estate developer Salvatore "San" Malfitano was reportedly discussed between Provenzano, the northern New Jersey Teamsters leader, and Hoffa—ten days before his disappearance.[41]

In 1999, Hoffa was posthumously inducted into the Labor's International Hall of Fame for his "devotion to the Teamsters" and for "bettering the lives of all working-class families." The James R. Hoffa Memorial Scholarship Fund was also established to award scholarship grants to the children of union members.[42]

The disappearance of Jimmy Hoffa remains one of America's most enduring and unsolved mysteries of the 20th century. "Many of those with links to the Hoffa case have taken secrets to their graves—Giacomo 'Black Jack' Tocco, Leonard Schultz, Vito 'Billy Jack' Giacalone, Anthony Giacalone, Tony Zerilli—the list goes on."[43]

A collage of newspaper headlines from across the U.S. in regard to the unsolved case involving the disappearance of the infamous and former Teamsters Union President Jimmy Hoffa, ca. 1975-2018.[44]

CHAPTER 5

"Guess Who's Coming to Dinner?"

After discovering Carl Steger's last known residential address in the rural township of Highland, Michigan, my wife Patricia and I decided to make an unannounced visit to his abode. It was on an early spring afternoon, May 1, 2005. There was an air of excitement, anticipation, and anxiety as we traveled almost an hour to his house from our home in the city of Southfield.

About a block from our destination, the neighborhood became visually unfamiliar to me—unlike any I've seen before in Michigan. It was as though we had driven into an east coast type community only to be seen in states such as Maine, Rhode Island, and Massachusetts. As we traveled over a small bridge and crossed a narrow canal, the road led us to a large lake that had an appearance of a perforated line, barely appearing from behind and in between the row of houses that appeared before us in the distance. The quaint area, along with its contemporary-styled and angular houses, appeared to be closed-off from the outside world. I remembered Carl's former friend Charles Boles once said that "you probably couldn't find a black person in Highland, Michigan, unless you rounded up the crew—rounded up all those usual suspects."[1]

*"He was an entertainer. He performed at night
and enjoyed the lake during the day."*

After locating the house, Patricia and I walked leisurely along the concrete stairway and I knocked on the front door. No answer. Again, I knocked. There was still no answer. "I guess no one's home," I muttered to Patricia with a slight tone of disappointment. As we began to turn away, we noticed a neighbor next door unloading groceries from the trunk of his car. The unidentified man asked as we began our approach, "Can I help you?"

I responded, "Do you know if Carl Steger lives here? I'm a genealogist and I'm researching my family history."

The neighbor said, "Oh, they've been gone years ago."

I asked, "Could you tell me about him?"

With a slight grin, the former neighbor said, "He was an entertainer. He enjoyed the lake during the day, and he worked at night." He pointed toward a house on the other side of the canal. "Carl's wife Carol has a cousin who lives over there."

I replied, "Thank you very much," and drove to its location.[2]

Upon our arrival, my wife and I observed a woman removing groceries from the back of a vehicle in the driveway of the home. *This must be the shopping day for the neighborhood,* I sarcastically thought. "Hi. My name is Eric Willis, and this is my wife Patricia. I'm a genealogist, I'm researching my family history, and I'm looking for a man named Carl Steger. I was told by your neighbor that Carl's wife Carol is your cousin."

The woman responded, "That's my husband Fred, but he's not home."

I asked, "Would you please ask him to call me whenever he has the opportunity? I would like to talk with him and ask him a few questions about Carl."

The woman graciously agreed, and we left for our journey back home.

At 8:31 P.M. that evening, the telephone rang.

Fred: Hello. May I speak to Eric Willis?

Author: Yes, I'm Eric Willis.

Fred: My name is Fred. My wife Wendy said you're researching your family history and you wanted to ask me some questions about Carl?

Author: Yes. Thank you for returning my telephone call. Would you please tell me about Carl? Is he alive?

Fred: Carl passed away two years ago.

Author: Oh really?

Fred: He moved to Florida. He played the piano, and he was a singer—always happy—complementary. He bought the house on Lakeview Street [in Highland, Michigan]. Carl took her [his wife Carol] in and her four kids. They moved out of the house about twenty years ago.

Author: Thank you very much for the information. Do you know of anyone else who may be able to provide me with some additional information about Carl?

Fred: Carol was married to Barbara's brother. Barbara is Carol's ex-sister-in-law.

Author: Do you have Barbara's telephone number?

Fred: No, but I have Lois'. Barbara and Lois are good friends. She would have her number.[3]

After calling and introducing myself to Lois, the following information was revealed.

"I was an acquaintance of Carl's—excellent musician. I met him at Scotch 'n Sirloin on Greenfield. He was very pleasant. He knew everybody. He knew politicians that came into the club and they knew him—nice, nice man."[4]

Afterward, I called Barbara. After informing her about being told of Carl's death about two years ago, she said, "Carl's not dead!" Now why was I surprised to hear her respond with that piece of vital information? By now and thus far on this journey, I should have come to the realization to "expect the unexpected."

Nevertheless, with a voice full of utter surprise and excitement, I said, "Carl's not dead?"

"No. He and Carol live in Sarasota, Florida."

I asked, "Could you tell me about Carl?"

She said, "They [Carl and Carol] met at Scotch 'n Sirloin. Carl—he has two daughters that live in Michigan."[5]

> *"He's paranoid and he doesn't want to*
> *talk with you and I don't know why."*

May 2, 2005, turned out to be another day filled with eye-openers. After engaging in several revealing telephone conversations with Carl's daughters Kimberly Steger-Sherrill and Dawn Steger-Davey about their dad and my familial connection to him, an extreme curiosity was thrust into the forefront. Kimberly revealed that her dad "didn't talk much about his parents because of the way they died." "He has his mother's piano," and "if he hadn't taken us in, I don't know what would have happened." In reference to Carl's former friend and employer Arlyn Meyerson, she said, "He didn't want Dad to marry my mother." Kimberly also said her dad was "paranoid and he doesn't want to talk with you, and I don't know why."

I replied, "I sound convincing to you, don't I?"

She said, "Yes, you do."[6]

Carl Steger's formal family residence in Highland, Michigan. April 2005.
The photographs are from the author's photograph collection.

The following day, Kimberly called me and said she talked with her father and that "he's not being cooperative." "I would like to meet with you for lunch along with my sister Dawn and to look over the information that you have. I would like to ask you not to contact him because I want to try to convince him this way."

I agreed and we decided to meet at a mutually agreed upon restaurant in the city of Pontiac, Michigan.[7]

May 21, 2005 was a sunny afternoon as I arrived for my meeting with the Steger sisters and walked with great anticipation through the doors of the musically filled restaurant. A woman with an eagerly sounding voice asked, "Are you Eric?" It was Carl's daughter Dawn seated off to the side in a booth.

I replied, "Yes, I am."

At that moment, it was as though the pivotal scene from the movie *Guess Who's Coming to Dinner?* was being played out before my eyes. The 1967 film starred Spencer Tracy, Katharine Hepburn, Katharine Grant, and Sidney Poitier. Poitier portrayed a black doctor who was engaged to a young white woman from a liberal upper-class family. His fiancé invited him over to her home to meet her parents and their expressions of surprise and shock at his ethnicity initially overwhelmed them.[8]

I walked over, sat in their booth, and salutations and introductions were exchanged. The group included Kimberly, Dawn, and Dawn's husband Ronald. I informed everyone that Carl was African American and that his mother Dorothy was a noted pianist and vocal teacher in the city of Detroit during the 1930s and '40s.

Kimberly, exhibiting a potpourri of facial expressions of confusion, shock, and amazement, found it, I believe, hard to accept that her stepfather was not ethnically a white Jewish man. She continued to question the surprising revelation. As I glanced into her sister's face, Dawn appeared to be amazed as well, but less disturbed. With my quick attempt to make some sense out of the matter for Kimberly, I said, "Even Sammy Davis, Jr. was a black Jewish man. He converted over to Judaism."

In support of my response, Dawn replied, "Yes. Sammy Davis was Jewish."[9]

The Other Black American Jewish Entertainer—
Sammy Davis, Jr.

"Once when I was playing golf with Jack Benny, he asked me what my handicap was. I couldn't resist kidding him. 'I'm a one-eyed Negro who's Jewish,' I said. People seem to appreciate a sense of humor on what all too often is a ticklish subject, so I guess that accounts for the wide circulation that crack has gained. Well, in a way my kids top me. Not only are they Negro, they are children of a racially mixed marriage, they are Jewish, and two of them—are adopted. Does this mean that they all have everything going to make them mixed-up children of a mixed marriage? Don't count on it, Charlie."

"We don't avoid the question of color, and we don't push it. We live it openly and honestly—with decency and dignity. What is so wonderful to me is that my children are completely comfortable with kids of any and every color. Children are not prejudiced unless prejudice exists at home or unless the children acquire it in the streets. However, if you're properly vaccinated in the home, you build up an immunity against being infected by almost everything you may encounter in the streets. I go with that old saying that 'the fruit does not fall far from the tree.' "

"What I want for my children is what I've always wanted for myself: I want my children to grow up to be healthy and live in a world that is healthy both spiritually and physically, not a world that is war-torn and hate-torn. I want my kids to have dignity, and I want them to greet their fellow men as they expect to be greeted. In other words, I don't want them to walk around with a chip on their shoulders because they are Negroes who feel prouder of their race than the next man feels of his. I want them to feel proud of the fact that they have what I consider the best of both races. And I think this doubles their chances of not turning into mixed up kids."

"We hope to raise our children as good Americans and as good Jews. If they are one, they can't help being the other."

—Sammy Davis, Jr., October 1966.[10]

Also known as an actor on film, television, and the Broadway stage, and as a comedian, Davis lost his left eye in a near fatal automobile accident in 1954. While recuperating in the hospital, his friend Eddie Cantor—a noted white Jewish performer on stage, screen, radio and television—"enlightened him on the

Sammy Davis, Jr. (center) poses with singer-pianist **Jo Thompson** and singer Billy Daniels at the **Meyersons' Scotch 'n Sirloin** restaurant in Detroit sometime during the 1960s. *The Detroit Jewish News*, September 24, 1999.

similarities between the Jewish and black cultures." After reading Abram Sachar's book *A History of the Jews* and studying Judaism, Davis converted over to the monotheistic Jewish faith, nationality and culture—"a peoplehood."[11]

"As an African American, his later affiliation with Judaism sometimes caused him personal anguish. The Jewish community never fully embraced him as a member." After his interracial marriage to Swedish actress May Britt in 1960, which was outlawed in 31 American states, and his endorsement of the 1972 United States Republican presidential nominee Richard Nixon, many within the black community ostracized him and called him a "sell-out." Nevertheless, Davis, as a civil rights activist, was a large financial supporter of the movement. In 1968 he was awarded the Spingarn Medal by the NAACP (National Association for the Advancement of Color People)—awarded for the highest or noblest achievement by an American Negro during the preceding year or years.[12]

As the conversation continued with Kimberly (KSS) and Dawn (DSD), Kimberly conveyed that she was going to go into her father's files during next year's visit with her parents in Florida. I immediately expressed my desire for her not to pursue such an action as to not to cause any possible divisions amongst themselves.[13]

DSD: I thoroughly believe it that he converted. Just because that time—of that time frame—

KSS: When I tried to say Dad he even knows—you know he even talked to some of the people that you knew. My dad [said], 'No. Those people gotta be eighty years old by now.' And I'm like go on. That's such a long time [*Laughter*]. There's just no talking to him about it. Just—you know.

Listen! Just like Wayne [Kimberly's husband] said, 'It's very unlike my Dad—very unlike him,' [in regard to his defiant behavior of not wanting to talk with me] but—

Author: I guess following his past until now—talking to musicians within the last month for the first time. I think I mentioned to you, there was a jazz pianist named Charles Boles who said he knew Carl really well and said Carl decided to play classical music as opposed to jazz because there was more money in it. And Boles kind of lost track of him as well, just like a lot of other people in the area.

DSD: Well, he was very [well]-respected in the area before he moved down to Florida.

KSS: A lot of newspaper articles [were] written about him and—

DSD: Yeah.

Author: Are there?

KSS: Yes—an awful lot.

Author: What newspapers? Because was I trying to look for—

DSD: Mostly in Southfield [Michigan] like *The Oakland Press* and such. He was in *The* [*Detroit*] *News* and the [*Detroit*] *Free Press*.

KSS: Because for most of the years he played in Southfield. He was at the Scotch 'n Sirloin for years and then at [Machus] Red Fox on Telegraph. And then he was at Excalibur for a while and then a restaurant called Jakks ["Place" or Jakks Restaurant and Lounge].

Author: I wish I would have known that before they tore it [Excalibur] down.

KSS: Yeah. And then a restaurant called Jakks.

Author: Jakks Place. Yeah. Well, I have these [showing her a newspaper reference of Carl performing at the lounge].

"...I have a real hard time believing he converted..."

KSS: I see you've done your research [*Laughter*]. Actually, Mom said the owner of the Scotch 'n Sirloin [Arlyn Meyerson and Carl's employer] told Dad that it was very bold to marry Mom and that he could go with her. And Mom says—[*Crosstalk*].

DSD: Well yeah. Because he's probably lookin' at it like I just married a widow with some kids.

KSS: There was a lot of strain with Dad's relationship with the owner and that was the biggest part of the reason why he left. He used to come to our home a lot.

Author: Oh, did he?

KSS: Yeah. The owner of the—yep.

Author: And he's deaf?

KSS: Um-hmm. Yes!

DSD: Oh my god!

KSS: Remember [while looking at Dawn]?

DSD: Oh my god! I knew there was more.

KSS: They would come over to the house all the time.

Author: I sent him a fax about a couple weeks ago—trying to track him down to get some more information about Carl.

KSS: Right.

DSD: Wow!

Author: And he never responded.

KSS: They would come to the house all the time which is another reason—[*Crosstalk*].

DSD: Which is not beyond the possibility—[*Crosstalk*].

KSS: Which is another reason why I have a real hard time believing he converted.

DSD: He converted.

KSS: Because certain number of different places where a lot of Dad's friends would come visit. I just can't believe—

> "*Most people who convert know more about their religion than the people who were born into.*"

DSD: Kim. You have to figure the timeframe—number one, and he didn't mind talking about that—

KSS: I know, and I understand that—

DSD: And you have to consider the errors of convention.

KSS: Right and I understand that, but I don't—

DSD: I think that very much is the case.

KSS: But if you talk to Dad that in-depth about this—I don't know.

DSD: I think if you ask your dad, he'll see your point.

KSS: Well, why don't you test that from Mom knowing that he—[*Crosstalk*].

Mom never mentioned he converted.

DSD: So, she never mentioned it to you! She never mentioned it to everyone else—

KSS: I gotta get drunk and find out what's really going on [*Laughter*].

DSD: Yeah. I know. I understand. Babe. Most people who convert know more about their religion than the people who were born into.

> *"If he's capable to call here, I'm going to call 911 and just hang right up on him."*

KSS: I know a lot of his friends from up here [Michigan] moved down to Sarasota.

Author: Oh yeah?

KSS: A lot of people from up North. Yes! [*Pause*] He keeps trying to get me to move down there and I'm like, 'I'm not!'

Author: Yeah. If he wasn't so hesitant and apprehensive, I wouldn't have minded going down there but—

KSS: I'm—you know what? I think he will.

DSD: If anybody can, she can or—

KSS: Like I said, my husband is going down there next month.

DSD: When he realizes that this is not going to be anything that's threatening to him, I think—

KSS: When he realizes that things are not— Right. And don't take this personal—maybe it's his age, but he said, 'If he's capable to call here, I'm gonna call 911 and just hang right up on him.' And I said, 'Dad [*Laughter*]!'

Author: Yeah. I don't have the number anyway.

KSS: Yeah, I know [*Laughter*].

DSD: 'And this person was,' and what he said to me was, 'In this day and age you don't know who's calling you for what and for what reason they're calling you because from day to day . . .' I'm like, 'Dad, look!' I said, 'The man is very sincere. I mean he—he means absolutely no ill-will towards you. He's very sincere.' I said, 'Look! You—you're not going to be that difficult to get a hold of if the man wants to go there.'

KSS: His number is on the internet. 'Then I'm changing it.' Then I'm like, 'Call the man, Dad [*Laughter*]!'

KSS,
DSD &
Ronald: [*Crosstalk*]

> *"I mean he knew everybody.*
> *Anyone who was a personality,*
> *a rich celebrity in Detroit—they knew him."*

DSD: Yeah! I got the pictures of everybody.

KSS: Right! If I can ever—yeah, I can find it.

Ronald: All of us—of Scott and Tom—all of us.

DSD: Better yet, if you can even get from Mom the pictures from the day they got married.

KSS: I have it at home. I'm telling you—my nights spent at Mom and Dad's [*Laughter*].

DSD: I know. You were able to go see 'em much more than I have, dear.

KSS: Yep. Their marriage certificate is in Oakland County.

DSD: At the courthouse. Yeah, they were married at the Oakland County Courthouse.

KSS: I should have brought them with me.

Author: They were married in Oakland [County]?

KSS: Yeah, they were married at the Oakland County Courthouse.

DSD: Like I said, it [marriage record] would be under Carol Richard or Carol Schwikert—

Author: Oh. Okay.

KSS: And Dad said the judge that performed it—the judge who performed the ceremony was a friend of my dad's too.

Author: Oh! Okay.

DSD: When during my kid's hey-day which is when we met during the early '70s, he knew everybody. I mean he knew everybody. Anyone who was a personality, a rich celebrity in Detroit—they knew him.

KSS: He did that jingle, remember? For that florist?

DSD: Yeah.

KSS: Yeah.

DSD: And he was really good friends with Ollie Fretter—owner of Fretter Appliance.[14]

KSS: Uh-hmm. He got free tickets for everywhere.

DSD: In fact, he has a framed million-dollar check from Ollie Fretter. He knew everybody and anybody who was— In fact, Bill Bonds,[15] the brother of his on White Lake in Highland Township [Michigan]—that's where we lived. And they were—he knew them all.

KSS: And I can think of the newspaper articles would be either in the [Detroit] Jewish News events or—

DSD: I bet there were quite a few.

KSS: Yeah.

Author: Yeah. I went onto the internet and only came across two references of your father [showing them the article reference]—or maybe one reference.

KSS: Scotch 'n Sirloin. Yep!

DSD: Oh, Scotch 'n Sirloin. Yeah.

KSS: Okay. And I think what happen why he left the Scotch's was because of what he [owner Arlyn Meyerson] said to Dad about getting married and he didn't have Mom until after they were married. He said I wouldn't have lived with you to begin with if you had kids.

DSD: Yeah. I'm sure the man wanted to help with the widower of kids that he'd known less than a year earlier.

KSS: Mae Meyerson—they were at our house a little bit over—

DSD: Yep. Oh yeah.

Author: Yeah. That's his wife. Yeah.

KSS &
DSD: Yeah.

Author: I don't think this exists anymore [showing a newspaper advertisement reference of Carl performing at Jakks Restaurant and Lounge].

KSS: No. I don't think it is anymore.

DSD: What's that?

KSS &
Author: Jakks Place.

DSD: Oh yeah! I don't think it's around either.

Author: Scotch 'n Sirloin . . .

DSD: Is that still around? I don't think so.

Author: No.

DSD: It was on Greenfield and—

Author: Not too far from 8 Mile.

KSS &
DSS: Right!

Author: I used to live walking distance from there. I don't
         remember the building, but my mother does.

DSD: I remember you could see it from one of the
         expressways.

Author: The Lodge [the M-10 John C. Lodge Expressway].

DSD: Yeah. You could see the sign from the expressway.

Author: Let me see what else I can reveal to you.

DSD: Oh. She died from a complication of surgery [after
         reading the newspaper obituary of Carl's mother
         Dorothy which was provided by the author].

Author: Yeah. From what I heard she had some kind of an
         illness—

DSD: She had a cerebral embolism. It says here either post-op.
         hysterectomy or pneumonia. She got a free roll embolus
         which is a blood clot that travels to the brain and that's
         what she died from.

Author: Yeah.

KSS: So, wait, that's his mom?

DSD: Yes.

KSS: So, she died—what?

DSD: Of a cerebral embolism which is a blood clot that travels to the brain.

KSS: Oh. So, I wonder why she was in surgery?

Author: And you said Carl, your dad, the only thing he has is that piano, huh? [which was previously owned by his mother].

DSD: Yeah!

Ronald: Yep! Yep!

KSS: Yeah, because—

DSD: Yeah! In his crate.

Author: Wow!

Ronald: And he still has it to this day. He wanted her to have it.

KSS: Yeah. And I definitely want it. I know it's important to him, but you know I can't tell Wayne that he gotta stuff a U-Haul and drive it home, you know— [*Crosstalk* and inaudible].

Ronald: Not ever [having] trouble gettin' it out of the house down there and movin' it.

KSS: Right.

Author: I have a question?

KSS: Yeah!

Author: Roughly what year or what period did Carl move into the North Park Towers in Southfield [Michigan]?

KSS: I have no idea. I know that it was before—

Author: Was it before they met?

KSS: Yeah.

DSD: He was living there up until '72. There was a time after they got married that they were living separately until after they could find a house to fit all of us. So, they lived apart for about three months after they got married until they found a house.

KSS: I didn't know that.

DSD: Huh?

KSS: I didn't know that.

DSD: You're kiddin' me?

Yeah. After they got married, even as a single person she stayed [on] her own until they found a house. Because they got married in June—we didn't move into the house until August.

Author: May I have the names of your siblings?

DSD: I'm the oldest. I'm Dawn Marie and then Todd.

KSS: Todd Richard Steger.

DSD &
KSS: Scott Allen, Kimberly Ann, Timothy Allen, and Ann Marie Elizabeth.

Author: I had a great-grandmother named Anna Marie.

DSD &
KSS: Oh really? I'll be dog.

KSS: Ann is for my middle name.

DSS: And my middle name. Right.

Author: You're the baby?

KSS: No, Ann is. I'm the middle.

Author: Oh! Okay! Kimberly Ann.

KSS: I'm the favorite [*Laughter*].

Author: Okay [*Laughter*].

DSD: You think she's joking, but she is.

KSS: Thank you.

> *"...we did the whole Hanukkah
> and Christmas holidays together."*

Author: Okay. [inaudible] such as Judaism. You said Judaism?

DSD: Yeah.

KSS: I don't agree with that? I really don't.

DSD: Honey?

KSS: No. I mean, if it is, it is? But I just have a hard time understanding that.

DSD: You know I agree. I honestly do because of the time of the season and the day and age that that was.

KSS: But then why wouldn't . . .? I don't know.

DSD: And like—Kimberly, you have to say—

KSS: I'mma get him drunk.

DSD: Kim?

KSS   And I already contemplated Ron's exit to Minnesota? [*Laughter*]

DSD: You have to understand that people—

Ronald: Now you know why she's the favorite one. She's a "sarcastor."

KSS &
Author: [*Laughter*]

DSD: You have to understand that people who choose to be Jewish know more about the religion than those who were born into it.

KSS: Then why would it have been you know, with him marrying Mom being Catholic?

DSD: It wasn't! Kim! It wasn't a big deal!

KSS: It was.

DSD: It was a big deal for Mom. It wasn't a big deal for him. It was a big deal for Mom. Mom was raised in a Catholic church and he let us do both things. We were—it was so boring because we did the whole Hanukkah and Christmas holidays together. It was so boring—

KSS: But you know what? Even so, why didn't he . . .? But even to this day he doesn't—he definitely doesn't like to have his name associated with the temple.

"I think he will come around. I really do."

DSD: There could be some other issues over there, Kim. But honestly, he converted. Kim, open up your mind and say he converted.

KSS: I am. No, I just find that hard to believe. I really do. And not for any other reason and not that there are any incidences or anything—just because.

DSD: Only because of the time period that I believe that it was. [*Pause*] Sammy Davis did it!

Author: Yeah.

Ronald: Yeah.

KSS: Yeah! Oh, that's true. Hmm!

DSD: So right now, it's time. Accept that.

Author: So, he never said anything about his family?

KSS: He has somewhat opened up. You know the last several years as far as saying he lived—his grandparents lived in a flat house from him.

Author: Okay. You said in Battle Creek?

KSS: I think in Battle Creek. I really don't know for certain.

Author: Who knows? He could have been living in Battle Creek in 1930.

KSS: Right! And he never talked about when he was in Alabama—ever.

I think he will come around. I really do.

Author: Yeah. I hope so.

DSD: I think it would be really nice.

KSS: Like I said I do too. I think that once he—

DSD: I think once he realizes that this is not anything for him to be afraid of and treat it with kid gloves and wait—

Ronald: Let me bring it in to him gradually.

Author: Okay.

DSD: Wait until he's not afraid, do a couple [of] tests, and he may come around.

KSS: Actually, Wayne might do that because Wayne and he are really close too, and Wayne may even be able to talk some sense to him.

DSD: Once he realizes that it's not anything for him to be afraid of, I mean you can—

KSS: I think once he realizes you are who you say you are—

DSD: Right.

KSS: And it is not anything you know thinking in depth or whatsoever.

DSD: I honestly believe that.

Ronald: You would think that at his age he would want to get it out automatically before he goes cause it's the same—

Author: Right!

DSD: I would want to either make peace with everything he's got.

> *"I truly don't believe that it has anything*
> *to do with him trying to hide any of this or*
> *trying to pass off being white."*

DSD: Even if so, I don't think that—

KSS: I don't think it is what it is.

DSD: Kim?

KSS: I just really—and I don't have any reason to feel that way. But I just really don't think that's what it is. Because of the type of person my dad is. He's such an open and honest person. You know what I mean? And what you see is what you get. I truly do not believe that his unwillingness to talk about it is because of us. I would be very, very surprised if that's what it is, and I don't know why.

DSD: Regardless if it's that or if—

KSS: No. I know. Mom thinks he had a nervous breakdown after both of his parents passed away.

Author: I heard from Charles Boles—this is another revelation—Mr. Boles said he had some emotional problems and that he heard he even tried to commit suicide several times.

DSD: Really? [Pause] Well, that could explain a lot.

KSS: Right! I think that that's what it is.

DSD: That could very well explain a lot.

KSS: I truly don't believe that it has anything to do with him trying to hide any of this or trying to pass off being white. And if it is, it is—but knowing Dad as well as I do—

DSD: Maybe it was a small combination of both.

KSS: I don't think so. I think knowing him as well as I do, I truly . . . And knowing because of the person he is, I truly don't believe that that's what it is. I think he has a great physical façade. I think that that is—

Author: And also, per my apprehension as well of initially meeting you all because of what I found out about his emotional state and wondering how he is, and also the other part about him [revelation of his passing]—

DSD: He's a very emotional man.

"But racism was just never an issue
in our home growing up—ever, never, ever, ever an
issue. Ever!"

KSS: This feeling of the type of person Dad is, I just truly do not believe that it's anything—

DSD: Yeah. It could be who he was. It could be very emotional.

KSS: Even when I met Wayne, you know he was like 'That was never talked about? Racism was never talked about?' And I said, 'No, it was never! It was never, ever—

DSD &
KSS: [*Crosstalk* and inaudible]

KSS: But racism was just never an issue in our home growing up—ever, never, ever, ever an issue. Ever!

DSD: No. It wasn't.

KSS: And so, I truly just knowing Dad and how he is, I just truly do not believe it has nothing to do with it.

DSD: It very well could be a very emotional—

KSS: He was just really scarred by what had happened. I don't know why.

DSD: Did someone tell you he was very emotional?

KSS: After they died or before?

'Don't leave any stones unturned—pursue it.'

Author: Well, this was the Charles Boles who knew him back in the '50s. He mentioned he knew Carl very well and that he even went over to his house. He mentioned the street [name] before I even revealed it to him, so I knew that he knew him.

KSS: Right.

Author: He told me they met through a mutual trumpet player. He added that Carl had some emotional problems at times, and he heard [that] he tried to commit suicide several times.

DSD: Really?

Author: I expressed to him as well that I had some concerns. He said, 'I was adopted myself.'

DSD &
KSS: Hmm!

Author: And he said, 'I went east to west looking for my family and found my biological family.' So, he said, 'Don't leave any stones unturned—pursue it.' So, he encouraged me and things like that. When I got into genealogy, I prayed for God to open up the doors for me.

KSS: Um-hmm!

Author: So, I saw the doors being opened.

DSD &
KSS: Right!

Author: Even finding you guys. Like I said there were some apprehensions as well. But, on the other hand, Carl is the only living relative who could provide me with more information about my great-grandfather and about his parents, and possibly about my 2nd great-grandfather [William Steger] who lived in Alabama. I located him and his family in the census record.

DSD &
KSS: Right!

KSS: When we visit, we're all up late at night talking and Dad has never ever given me the impression ever—and we've talked a lot. He's never given me the impression that he is—that he's ever trying to hide anything about his family—that he was embarrassed or that he was unwilling to talk about it.

So, I think once he gets past the whole [thing of] you are who you are—

DSD: You're not a member of the mafia.

KSS: You're not a bill collector.

Author: That would be great.

KSS: I really—I do! I think that he would enjoy talking to you. I don't think he'll be opposed to it at all.

DSD: I think it would be great.

Author: Yeah. That would be wonderful.

KSS: I really think so.

Author: I even spoke to some family members on my mother's side—my aunts. I've got a cousin [Denise Kimball] who currently lives in New York. We're pretty close. [*Crosstalk*] And I even shared it with her, and she said, 'Well, if it was twenty—thirty years ago it may have been an issue, but this is who—'

DSD: Now do any of the people that you talked to, do they remember my dad as a kid?

Author: No.

DSD: Not really?

Author: There is a cousin in his early seventies, and he knew Carl. He's the only one. There're other cousins around that age who remember hearing about Carl.

DSD: Okay.

Author: This other cousin—his name is Gerald [Steger]. He said he remembers Carl working as a waiter and he said it was off 8 Mile [Road] somewhere. That's what he heard.

KSS: Wasn't his dad a bell boy?

Author: Yeah, back in the twenties and thirties.

KSS: Yes, Dad even told me that before.

DSD: It could easily be what you say. Now if you think about it you can get some stuff out of Mom about her family.

KSS: Right! I think it could have been the same way.

DSD: My grandfather, I met twice.

Author: And sometimes even through the journey in regard to some of my relatives, it was like pulling teeth trying to get information from them. I currently have a second great aunt on my father's side when I was researching my father's side of the family—she's currently 95—and she told me a couple of years ago 'To concentrate on the living and not the dead.'

KSS: Right! And see that's the thing.

DSD: It could very well be that is that—

KSS: I think that that's from when that time . . . and plus he's getting older. I think he's very protective and very, you know . . . I said, 'Remember Dad, it's not like when you were growing up!'

Author: Right!

KSS: You were very fortunate to have your grandparents living above you. But you knew your family history. It's not that way anymore. We all just don't have it. So why marry? Here's your daughters—I'm your daughter at night talking to you.

DSD: Right! I saw my grandfather on my mother's side four times in my whole life. And my uncle Jim, the last time I saw him I was six years old. He died a few years ago and I never saw him since. So, it could very easily be one of those things, and the same things with Mom.

KSS: Right! I think that that's what it is. I think that—I really think that once Dad sees all this, he will more than—I think that he'll get a kick out of it.

DSD: Do you have a picture of that?

KSS: Yes. I think he really [will]. Do you want my email address?

Author: Sure!

KSS: I think he'll get a kick out of it. I really do. I think he would. He'll be overwhelmed.

DSD: I think it's great!

KSS: Yes.

[BREAK]

KSS: Hey listen, I just—I don't know. I just find—

DSD: Keep your mind up.

KSS: Hmm?

DSD: Don't worry about that.

KSS: What?

DSD: Dad converted.

KSS: I don't—I, I want to know. You know. I don't—I think Dad's very open about—

DSD: Oh! I think he is too!

KSS: I think that he can be very honest about talking about things, but I don't . . .but if it is, it is. But I have just a hard time believing it.

DSD: I really hope that—I really honestly hope that he looks at this for what it is.

KSS: I think so.

DSD: It could be really cool.

KSS: I really think he will.

Ronald: Got all of your questions there?

Author: Your family moved to Highland, Michigan—roughly when—the mid-'70s?

DSD: 1974.

Author: Was it [during] the summer?

DSD: It would be August '74 when we moved down there.

KSS: We moved to Florida 1984, October, the middle of my senior year [*Laughter*].

Author: You moved to Sarasota, Florida?

KSS: Yep. Sarasota, Florida. Yep.

Author: Do you have any newspaper clippings of Scotch 'n Sirloin or—

KSS: Ummm, you know, I don't. I have tried to find some of those ones. You know I may take time off. I need to go down and—

Ronald: [*The*] *Oakland Press* or *The* [*Detroit*] *Jewish News*.

KSS: Yeah. I know Dad has—I know he should have—
[*Crosstalk*].

DSD: I know there's a couple in *The* [*Detroit*] *Jewish News*.

KSS: Do you know what? The last time we were down there—

DSD: And I know there was something in *The* [*Detroit*] *Jewish News* since he's been down in Sarasota.

KSS: I think Mom has an article or a book that has all of the—
[*Crosstalk*]. I know they said that it has *The Oakland Press* and stuff.

DSD: There was something either in *The* [*Detroit*] *Jewish News*—[*Crosstalk* and inaudible].

KSS: A lot of them go down there. Who was the couple that owns the um—who was lost at sea that owns—?

Ronald: Muer! Chuck Muer!

DSD: Chuck Muer! Yeah! They were very good friends. Yeah.

KSS: They come down all the time visiting Mom and Dad for the summer.

DSD: And they visited the house quite a bit.

"This is the kind of music
that I really wish I could play."

Author: Oh. Wow. The Red Cedars—is that another place that your father performed at?

KSS &
DSD: Yeah!

Author: Okay. Because I got that information from the [Detroit Musician's] union. Where was it located?

KSS: You know I don't particularly know. But it definitely—

DSD: Wasn't that in Union Lake?

KSS: Yes. It was.

DSD: It was in Union Lake?

KSS: It was a very, very short time.

DSD: Yeah!

Author: Oh.

DSD: That was in between when he got out of Jakks [Place] and [Machus] Red Fox.

KSS: Red Fox Machus.

DSD: Because if I'm not mistaken, the owners had an interest in Red Cedars and that was in Union Lake.

KSS: Right! Right!

Author: Okay. So, he performed at Jakks Place after or prior to—

KSS &
DSD: After Red Cedars. That was the last place he worked before we left Michigan.

DSD: Right. And then I think before Jakks, it was Red Cedars. And then before the Red Cedars, it was the Machus Red Fox.

KSS &
DSD: And then Excalibur and then Scotch 'n Sirloin.

DSD: I don't believe the Red Cedars did well at the beginning. I don't think they did well.

KSS: They even thought about buying that restaurant but— [*Crosstalk*].

DSD: They thought about— Yeah. Seriously, they thought about buying it for a good portion of time and then that didn't go through, and that's when he got a job at Jakks.

KSS: Right!

DSD: That was right there near the water in Union Lake.

Author: And then . . . Okay. You said the family moved to Sarasota, Florida in October '84?

KSS: Um-hmm!

Author: And they met at Scotch 'n Sirloin?

KSS: On Mom's birthday. Right?

DSD: I believe so.

KSS: And actually, one of the songs on the CD [*Sarasota: Carl Steger Live at Café L'Europe*] is her song—Roberta [Flack]. And 'The first time ever I saw your face.' That was what he was singing when she first walked in: 'The first time ever I saw your face.'

Author: Oh! Did he?

KSS: Um-hmm!

DSD: And anybody he talked to—he talked to anybody who knew every single style throughout the years—was making sure that he knew the audience and bringing the audience with it. If there was someone who walked in that he knew, he made an issue of recognizing them while he was singing right into the microphone.

KSS: I even have it at home, I think it was right when the CD was done when Café L'Europe had the big news thing and all the newspapers were there—there's a big press conference. I have it on tape.

Author: Oh! Wow!

DSD: And to say that he knew everybody—he just knew everybody.

KSS: Greg Wilson was from ACDC [a noted rock and roll musical group] who helped him produce the CD.

DSD: Yeah. I remember him talkin' about it.

KSS: And he would come in to see Dad all the time at Café L'Europe and [he] would say, 'This is the kind of music that I really wish that I could play.' And he helped Dad to produce it.

DSD: What was the name of the guy whose house we went to in Southfield when he went to record a record when they were still up here? Remember we went to his house and the guy had a studio?

KSS: I do. I don't know his name.

DSD: I can't remember what his name was.

KSS: I think it was that whole flowers jingle thing because—

DSD: Yes. That could have been it.

KSS: Something could be [*Laughter*]?

DSD: I think [a] part of the flower jingle was he was doing a lot of lollygagging in some studios to keep his name on some records that he didn't sell. That's when he was working in jazz.

Author: Oh! Okay. And you said your parents met at Scotch 'n Sirloin on your Mom's birthday?

KSS: Yep!

Author: What was the month and day?

DSD: I think they met in '73. They were married in '74. I think they met in '73.

Author: Okay. And you mentioned about his childhood memories as far as him living down below his grandparents?

KSS: Right! Right! And that was completely known. Like I said, since he stopped working, they really talked to him quite a bit. He had a wonderful childhood and that it's unfortunate things aren't, you know, the way they are now—that he had a wonderful family—very close, [*Pause*] really enjoyed um—[*Crosstalk*]. Just that it was a really neat place to grow up and that he talked a lot about his mom—not so much about his dad—a lot about his mom, and his musical ability and stuff. You know he doesn't have any muscles [inaudible] in his fingers.

Author: Oh!

DSD: Yeah!

Author: Due to the years of playing?

KSS: No. He was born that way.

Author: Oh!

KSS: He never had any.

DSD: Yeah, and in each of his index fingers.

KSS: And so, he has that ability to play the piano.

DSD: Yes. He would [inaudible] he would always plant like this and his fingers would literally go into his palms when he plays.

KSS: Right! But wonderful—you've couldn't have asked for a better person honestly.

Author: That's great.

DSD: Yeah. I think we can count on our hands how many times he raised his voice—very mild-mannered man. Like I said I think that the first time I ever heard the man swear to me [inaudible]. That's the first time I ever heard him swear. But he's just very, very mild-mannered. And, like I said, he married the widow of six kids. He adopted all of us so . . .

Author: Right. [*Pause*] Okay. Well.

KSS: Well. I think that um . . . [inaudible].

DSD: If anybody can do it, she can.

Author: Well. Okay.

KSS: I think so. I'll put him up to it. I really will.

Author: Alright. Well, it was a tremendous pleasure meeting you all.

KSS: [*Crosstalk* and inaudible]

DSD: It was good. Like I said, I'm really glad that we were able to do this. It was really interesting. From the first time I heard from you [and] talked to Kim about it, I just thought if nothing else, if we can't get him past you know whatever, and I spoke to him, and he's really, really unhappy . . . . We even thought it was really neat. It was very cool.

Author: Right.

KSS: But then again, I think a lot of it is the fact that people of that age are just very skeptical and very protective—

DSD: Oh. I'm sure [inaudible].

KSS: But I know—and honestly Mom has an album that has all of the newspaper clippings about Dad.

DSD: I'm sure she does and there's gotta be something with Sarasota papers, Kim.

KSS: Yeah, there is. Well I was online this morning and you know Café L'Europe is still using those advertisements of him [inaudible].

DSD: Are they really?

KSS: Mom [was] like, 'What are you going to do about it?'

DSD: [*Laughter*]

KSS: 'That's what I thought.'

DSD: Exactly.

KSS: [*Laughter*]

DSD: Ridiculous. What would be the cut for us?

Ronald: Yes, the attorneys from up north?

KSS: Yeah [*Laughter*].

> *"You know he's an absolute incredible person."*
> *"Yeah, he really is."*

DSD: And like I said unfortunately he can get real emotional about every little thing. So, which is unfortunately—it's like, 'Would you? Would you?'

Author: Oh. Okay.

KSS: Every 15 minutes.

DSD: Yeah. He gets emotional about every little thing and he seems to get more and more as he gets older. But that was like a major deal with us when we were kids and stuff. He be yelling around the house. Because he just, you know—

The best picture that I have of him in the spring or in the fall and [inaudible] outside the house, and he'd have his waders on and his winter coat, and he be all about getting this done. We're like, you know what? There's something that we forgot to pick up that we really need to have. If you go to the hardware store, Dad, we'll be all set. Because we knew that once he got up there, he be up there forever because he has to ask every saleswoman if this was what he was supposed to get. He would be there forever, and by the time he came back it would be done and over with and the ordeal would be over.

KSS: Remember the year there was a tornado and we were up in town.

DSD: Oh my god. He was on my youngest brother's bike riding around the island looking for all of us because there was a tornado warning. And then they're living in Sarasota, Florida where they have hurricane warnings and hurricanes.

KSS: You know he's an absolute incredible person.

DSD: Yeah, he really is.

KSS: Oh yeah.

DSD: He really is.

KSS: Really.

DSD: He really is a great guy.

Everyone began to review the nostalgic photographs of Carl and his young children.

DSD: I think that this alone does . . .

Author: It brings back a lot of memories.

KSS &
DSD: Yeah.

I shared with them a copy of a *Michigan Chronicle* newspaper which included a photograph of Carl's mother Dorothy and her obituary on the front page. We all compared it to one of several photographs of their dad which they provided to me as a gift.

DSD: I can't get over how much alike they look.

Ronald: Yeah, especially when you put—[*Crosstalk*].

KSS: Yep.

Author: Yeah, side by side.

Ronald: Side by side. Now you can tell that's her son right there.

Author: Around the eyes. Right—exactly.

KSS: And I know that that's why he always said that he doesn't
       miss his kids because he didn't have anybody who was there.

DSS: Yep. I gotta go. I got four children at home.

KSS: I got a 15-year-old.[16]

Author: Okay.

After my meeting with Carl Steger's adopted daughters **Dawn Steger-Davey** (l) and **Kimberly Steger-Sherrill** (r), they graciously agreed to pose for a photograph outside of a Pontiac, Michigan restaurant on May 21, 2005. The photographs above and on the following page are from the author's photograph collection.

Carl's daughters and Eric B. Willis.

CHAPTER 6

Racial Passing: The Dark Secret in Whiteface

"Racial Passing is a practice where light-skinned African Americans passed as white—meaning that they present themselves as white. And the reason why they chose to do this was that particularly during the Jim Crow era of racial segregation, it was very advantageous to be white in American society rather than being black. So it meant that often you can get a better job—you can live in a better neighborhood."

"Most of the people who passed as white did not want to be found. You know they didn't want to leave any record, any trace of the fact that they had passed."

"The history of passing is fascinating, and intriguing, and quite tragic. African Americans who passed really lost in terms of their family relationships, in terms of their connections to their community."

–Allyson Hobbs, Stanford University History Professor
and author of *A Chosen Exile: A History of Racial
Passing in American Life*

I also define racial passing as *the dark secret in whiteface*. The expression of "whiteface" was derived from "blackface." Blackface, which began in the United States during the mid-19th century, is a demeaning and racist mockery of black people through entertainment—distorting their appearance and behavior. White actors would mock enslaved Africans and free blacks by painting their faces black with shoe polish and burnt cork and sing and dance in minstrel shows before audiences, resulting in negative racial stereotypes of perceived stupidity and foolery.[1] Also racially offensive, the whiteface performance began around the late 19th century with Lew Dockstader, a white American vaudeville actor.[2]

However, for the purposes of racial passing, "whiteface" has been redefined not as a racist parody of white people, but as an overall illusion of light-skinned blacks posing as Caucasians existing in two clandestine and unparalleled worlds like the dissimilar black and white colored keys on Carl Steger's piano.

There were many advantages of passing as a white person before and during Carl's generation, and the practice continues today. However, Carl's reasons to pass as "white" are not exactly known. Nevertheless, the reasons documented below may have impacted his decision.

- Being a family of color during the early to mid-20th century, Carl and his parents most likely observed and may have endured a pervasiveness of racial prejudice and discrimination during their lives, as did many other people within the black population of Detroit and other cities and rural areas across the country. White supremacy continued to be enforced through legislation, intimidation, and physical violence.

- Raised as an only child, Carl's parents died when he was a young adult. He was 17 when his father Gordon died in August 1945. Two years later, his mother Dorothy died suddenly due to complications after surgery. It's unknown if Carl had any strong familial ties with his remaining living relatives outside of his immediate family, but with the sudden deaths of those nearest to him and after coming home from completing his military service, he may have felt alone in the world and his world may have been thrust abruptly into a state of depression.[3]

  Depression behaviors vary from person to person and include social withdrawal or isolation, rumination or "dwelling and brooding about themes like loss and failure..." and negative thinking.[4]

Carl may have also believed that since he no longer had much of a close-knit family, there was no shame to be attributed to those left behind and that the odds were in his favor to pass, therefore, resulting in a loss of kinship.

Carl's father **Gordon William Steger** is listed above in the "Death Notices" section of the September 2, 1945 edition of the *Detroit Free Press* newspaper. His aunt and Leroy Steger, Sr.'s mother Sarah Bradley is also listed amongst the related survivors.[5]

- Carl, with his very fair skin and wavy hair, may have felt isolated from some people in the black community because of his appearance as a white-looking man, affecting his decision to morph into a white society, and allowing other blacks to believe that he may have wanted to be white. Nevertheless, among some others within his race, his color may have afforded him some advantages that were not available to dark-skinned black people due to the practice of colorism.

"Colorism," a term believed to be conceived in 1983 by the noted black author Alice Walker, is the "prejudicial or preferential treatment of same-race people based solely on their color."[6] "Colorism, like all forms of racism, rationalizes color inequities with racist ideas, by claiming the inequities between dark and light-skinned people are not due to discrimination against dark-skinned people, but the inferiorities of dark-skinned people."[7] Colorism still exists within today's society through employment opportunities involving

media, marketing, and entertainment industries—
newscasters, television and magazine advertisements,
and the role selection processes of Hollywood actors
and actresses in film and in music videos.[8]

The presence of skin color discrimination within the black race
has its origin during this nation's period of slavery when
preferential treatment by slave owners was given to light-skinned
blacks—often the owner's offspring—rather than their darker
complected counterparts, thereby creating animosity in the slave
community. The practice continued during Reconstruction, and
thereafter with the creation of the Blue Vein Societies and into
the 20th century with the "Brown Paper Bag Test."

The Blue Vein Societies were mainly regarded as private
social clubs that were organized throughout the United
States and admitted only middle class and upwardly
mobile blacks whose skins were light enough to see their
blue veins.[9] However, Charles Waddell Chesnutt, an
influential black short-story author, educator, and
attorney around the turn of the twentieth century,
disagrees. His works periodically scrutinized the
sociological and psychological effects of Jim Crow laws
and practices and the nation's false claim of racial social
equality while sanctioning systems of segregation. He
documented the following about the earliest organization
in one of his fictional narratives.

"The original Blue Veins purpose was to
establish and maintain correct social standards
among a people whose social condition
presented almost unlimited room for
improvement" and "...character and culture were
the only things considered; and that if most of
their members were light-colored, it was because

such persons, as a rule, had better opportunities to qualify themselves for membership."[10]

Was Chesnutt's account of the Blue Vein Society a historical truth because of his awareness within the social circles of his environment in the North? Being very fair and having a strong appearance as a white man himself, Chesnutt's paternal and maternal grandfathers were white.[11]

WASHINGTON COLORED SO-CIETY.

HOW THEY DISCRIMINATE. WHY SOME DO NOT RECEIVE NEW YEAR'S DAY. THE SUPPOSED MONEYED PEOPLE.

Washington being a cosmopolitan city and the citizens being congenial, all new comers of any notoriety are admitted to the social circle. People in good standing from the states, are often surprised on arriving in the city to find some folks, from the states r town in which they live who are not anything at home, taking the lead in the colored society. The persons who are attempting to run society would no doubt like to establish a blue vein society in this city as a certain class had in certain parts of Ohio. The white people of superior intelligence condemn this class of Negroes. Social entertainments given by the better class of colored people in this city are cosmopolitan in their character, except a narrow contracted class whose prejudices are greater than their intelligence. The Monday night literary is a cast organization. There is more intelligence excluded than there is in the association. Some few doctors who belong to it, receive their support from the poorer class of Negroes. There are a few holding clerkships who belong to the Monday night literary. Messengers, watchmen and laborers are excluded. It is on the order of the Lotus club.

An amusing incident happened one time at one of the meetings of this club, which is very ludicrous A gentleman, who has a white lady for his wife and a doctor by profession, escorted a lady to one of these meetings and he says that he was insulted by the host because he asked for cream the second time. There are a few who will

NOT RECEIVE

on New Year's day, because they have no desire to meet a few objectionable upstarts. There is another class that society has made fools of and another that has made a fool of society. Parties, card parties and receptions are often given by some to gain admission to society. Another class of people are made to believe that, unless a person is always invited out he is not of a society class. This is often among the more ignorant class of the Washington society or a class that has been admitted to the social circle by sufferance.

DRESS

is a great object among a certain class. This class will dress if they have to go without eating. The greatest fuss and empty show will be found among that class of people who claim superiority over another class and who come from the lowest elements of society. It is this class that does so much discrimination, it is this class that has caused so many social scandals. Ex-register

B. K. BRUCE

never was the man to practice discrimination. He is generous to a fault. He is a man of honor and not one to forget his friends. All classes were welcomed by Mr. and Mrs. Bruce, while he was Senator afterwhich Register of the Treasury. Mr. Bruce has the respect and confidence of all classes of people. He is respected wherever he goes. Mr. and Mrs.

O'HARA

are very quiet, they crave less for social notoriety than any of our representative class. Mrs. O'Hara has a very gentle disposition and a lady of force and character.

The supposed moneyed men are, Recorder Douglass, Wormley brothers, Wm. Syphax, Richard Francis, John and Geo. Cook, R. J. Collins and many others. Mr. John A. Gray has been a very liberal man in his times. He kept one of the finest houses in the city. He first opened it for white people and was having a success until the Negroes kept clamoring for a respectable place to go. He opened his house to the high toned colored people and less than a year they broke him up.

A perspective of the **Blue Vein Society** was given above in the white-owned *The Washington Bee* newspaper, July 31, 1886. (Washington, D.C.)

A Blue Vein society is being organized by the colored people of Phœnix. Frank Shirley, of the Fashion barber shop, is at the head of the movement, and all the barbers in his employ, except Messrs. Thomas and Polk, will be admitted. All who have white blood are eligible to membership.

The Blue Vein Society is preparing a great fishing party for the early days of August. Say, boys, We wish you much pleasure, but stay out of "them water melon patches," along the river bank.

The Arizona Republican,
December 20, 1893 (white-owned)

The Richmond Planet, July 29, 1905
(white-owned)
Note the racist quote associated with the society.

The "Brown Paper Bag Test" was used as a visual tool to discriminate against black people whose skin complexions were darker than a brown paper bag. The racial bias disallowed their admittance into numerous American "upper class" black social organizations including churches, fraternities, and other civic groups. According to the scholar and historian Henry Louis Gates, Jr. as he recalled during the late '60s as a Yale University undergraduate student, "Some of the brothers who came from New Orleans held a *bag party.* As a classmate explained it to me, a bag party was a New Orleans custom wherein a brown paper bag was stuck on the door. Anyone darker than the bag was denied entrance."[12]

As reported in 2014 by Dr. David Pilgrim, another black historian, "I cannot say for sure, but I do not believe that the brown bag test is still being used, at least not in such a brazen manner. However, the attitudes that supported the use of a brown paper bag have not completely disappeared. It is clear that light skin is still favored over dark skin in this culture and that is true whether we are looking through the eyes of whites, light-skinned African Americans, or dark-skinned African Americans. This is part of the legacy of slavery and Jim Crow."[13]

A brown paper bag was sometimes used as a test and as a racist tool of discriminatory measurement for light-skinned and dark-skinned blacks for entry into certain upper-class black social organizations. If a black person's complexion was darker than a brown paper bag, the person failed the "test" and was not permitted to participate in the organizations of the lighter complected black aristocracy.

According to a 19-year-old black former Detroit resident living in the Black Bottom community in 1924:

"When I came to town, the people I lived with went to Bethel A.M.E. Church, which was located on Hastings and Napoleon. It's all torn down now, just expressway. I went there temporary. I was looking for pretty girls and what we called the 'high-yellow' gals—almost white. Mostly went to St. Matthew's where the pretty girls were. We had some friends at Second Baptist, so I'd go there occasionally, but I didn't belong. Everybody was looking for pretty girls. They were half-white or mixed and had pretty hair and all that stuff. That was quite the quite."[14]

The jazz pianist Charles Boles, his wife, and I engaged in a related discussion during my 2015 interview.

Mrs.
Boles: It's so important to know who your folks are.

Author: Exactly.

CB: I agree. I agree with that. You know it's like all my kids, now I got, as a result of being adopted myself, I adopted three kids.

Author: Okay. Wow. That's wonderful.

CB: So, when you tell people you have eight kids, it's enamored. 'You have anything else to do?' But you know I only had three biological children. I got eight kids. I got three biologicals, adopted three and two nat babies. But you know each one of those kids, they know who their dad is. You know and there ain't no need of tryin' to sugar coat nothing.

I give a man a lot of credit if he got enough balls to pass. But you have to be walking on pins and needles all the time because somebody can walk up from your past, man, and confute.

Author: Then you're losing out on your black community—your black side of your family. You're just tossing that away. Like you said the community is lost.

CB: I don't, man . . . You know what? All of this is a result of the white man's tyranny. I hate to say it that way. It's his tyranny that has brought us the 'if I'm light enough maybe I could pass and enjoy some of the advantages that that sucker is getting.' Because you know if you're black, I don't care how light you are. And some of the most confusing people in the world are people that are very light and just light enough where they could go either way. They go through hell because I remember being in high school back in the '40s, man, and some of the real light skin—they call them 'siddity girls'—

Mrs.
Boles: Elites.

CB: They're elites. They were too light for the brothers. 'Well she's too light, she's too white, she's too white for me. I don't want her.' You know. So, they caught hell and the real dark-skinned sisters would catch hell because she wasn't pretty enough. 'She's too black. I don't want her if she's too black. She's not black enough.' So, it was one excuse after another.

Author: And they had the brown paper bag test. Have you heard of that?

CB: I don't know.

Mrs.
Boles: What is it?

Author: If you weren't—

CB: Light as a paper bag?—

Author: Or lighter.

CB: You weren't going on at all.

Author: Right.

CB: Isn't that somethin'?

Author: So, there was prejudice within our own race as well as prejudice outside of it.

CB: Well, it still exists today.

Author: Exactly.

Mrs.
Boles: One more thing I like to say is we had some grandchildren and two of my little girls came over. And when they got ready to leave, I gave one of them a doll— the other too. But she didn't want the black doll.

Author: Ahhh!

CB: Sho didn't.

Mrs.
Boles: The black doll was just the rag doll. The white doll was all dressed up and everything. I tried my best to give her

that black doll. So that kinda hurt. And she didn't want it.

Author: Wow!

CB: She wouldn't take it. She had brought out two dolls, a black and white doll. She left the black doll laying right there on that sofa.

Mrs.
Boles: She didn't want no black doll and that hurt me so bad.

CB: She wouldn't take it.

Author: Yeah. They [doctors] did a study concerning that psychological mindset—

Mrs.
Boles: Yeah.[15]

"The Doll Tests"

In the 1940s, a series of experiments known as "the doll tests" were designed and conducted by psychologists Kenneth and Mamie Clark to study the effects of segregation on black children.

To examine the children's perception on race, the tests consisted of the use of four identical looking diaper-clad dolls except in color. The Clark doctors asked the selected children, between the ages of three and seven, "to identify the race of the dolls and which color they preferred. A majority of the children preferred the white doll and assigned positive characteristics to it." The doctors determined that the black children's self-esteem was damaged by "prejudice, discrimination, and segregation" which, in turn, created a feeling of inferiority.

"In a particularly memorable episode while Dr. Clark was conducting experiments in rural Arkansas, he asked a black child which doll was most like him. The child responded by smiling and pointing to the brown doll: 'That's a nigger. I'm a nigger.' Dr. Clark described this experience 'as disturbing, or more disturbing, than the children in Massachusetts who would refuse to answer the question or who would cry and run out of the room.' "[16]

Fourteen years later, lawyers from the N.A.A.C.P. learned of the results from "The Doll Tests" and decided to incorporate it as a part of their arguments against the unconstitutionality of racial segregation in public schools during the noted *Brown v. Board of Education of Topeka* lawsuit.

In the United States Supreme Court's unanimous decision in the *Brown* case that racial segregation in public schools was unconstitutional, "Chief Justice Earl Warren specifically cited Dr. Kenneth Clark's summary of all the social science testimony—on topics including the doll test —presented at trial."

"To separate them [children in grade and high schools] from others of similar age and qualifications solely because of their race generates a feeling of inferiority as to their status in the community that may affect their hearts and minds in a way unlikely to ever be undone." . . . "Whatever may have been the extent of psychological knowledge at the time of *Plessy v.*

Ferguson, this finding is amply supported by modern authority . . ."

"According to Dr. Kenneth Clark's analysis, the doll studies were relevant in that they showed how racial segregation interfered with students' personality development."[17]

CB: But you know what? Subliminal messages are being sent every day on the TV and most of us are too stupid or too dense to recognize them. But they're being sent all the time. It's just like I'm telling you this. Why would this man not know that I was smart enough to know he was making fun of me or tried to be demeaning when he's asking me to play 'Chattanooga Shoeshine Boy' or You know how to play 'Shine?'

Author: Right.[18]

As a teenager, I remembered seeing my grandmother Lilly Steger sometimes wearing a foundational make-up that was too light for her beautiful brown facial skin color. It was somewhat odd-looking. But I didn't fully understand what she must have felt inside—the associated insecurities resulting from the general population's perpetual and negative stigma against darker-skinned blacks, spanning from generations of psychological and physiological abuse, and socialization before, during, and after slavery within the United States.

Product advertisements and articles involving skin bleaching or lightening while sometimes loathing dark skin appeared periodically during the 19th century and increased with frequency during the 20th century in white-owned and black-owned newspapers throughout the country including the ones displayed on the following pages. Unfortunately, the practice of skin brightening or "browning" within America's black population as a symbol of privilege or access continues today and even more so throughout the world. In 2016, approximately $600 million worth of skin "brightening" and "anti-dark spot" products were sold in the United States.[19] Despite the potential dangers, "it's projected that global profits will reach $31.2 billion" by 2024.[20]

My grandmother Lilly Steger (c) and l-r, my mother Brenda (Steger) Willis and aunts Jacqueline (Steger) Brown, Barbara (Steger) Williams, and Carolyn (Steger) Kimball. ca. late 1960s. From the Brenda Willis photograph collection.

> *There is a slave woman at Worcester, Md., who is turning white, by the absorption of the coloring matter of the skin. She is nearly bleached out, with the exception of spots varying in size from a dime to a half dime.*

Ashtabula Weekly Telegraph, July 24, 1858   Ashtabula, Ohio (white-owned)

BLEACHING A BLACK WOMAN.

Her Skin Turned White by the Use of Medicine Prescribed by a Physician.

Special to Chicago Times.

There is a colored lady in Cincinnati who, after having been for some time under a peculiar medical treatment, is gradually, from the effect of the drug administered, being changed to white. The physician having charge of the case was found, and after some hesitation volunteered to accompany the reporter to see his patient. The lady is the wife of a mulatto man, at one time a photographer, in the city, but now keeping a stationery store, and both are well known. Mrs. Ball was born in Fredericksburg, Va., and is at present about 67 years old. Three years ago, after suffering about seventeen years with an ovarian tumor, she called on the doctor. Upon examination he found that the tumor was calcareous, and that to remove it in the usual way would sacrifice life. The only course in his opinion, was to follow a method of treatment that would give relief from the intense physical suffering which the woman experienced. With this in view he began the administration of a certain drug, the name of which he withholds for the present until he has completed the study of the case, and is ready to give the facts in detail, with theories and deductions to the medical profession, and through them to the public. Shortly after the treatment was begun, he noticed white blotches appearing upon the skin, which gradually enlarged and extended over the face, body, and limbs. Just at this time, too, the woman began experiencing relief from her excrutiating pains, and from that day to this has improved in health, until she is now better than for twenty-five years. As though in progress with her health, the blotches increased in size until one-half her body is as white as the purest Caucasian. She was originally a very dark mulatto. The portions of skin still retaining their original color are cold and clammy, while the whitened parts are warm and animated. The change has been very slow, as it has been going on for nearly three years, and the transformation is only half completed. The drug at one time peculiarly affected her e es, for, as she said; "When I looked up-street once, I saw things red." There was a time when the doctor, in the study of the case, asked himself if this might not be a transformation peculiar to this woman's case. Therefore, when a young colored boy came under his treatment for an ailment which called for the use of the same drug in connection with others, he administered it alone, and found to his gratification and satisfaction that the white blotches began to appear in a very short time, and he had to stop using the drug alone, and restored it to its combination. He thus feels confident that he has discovered a process by which possibly in every instance the Ethiopian skin can be changed. He was found just on the eve of his departure for the south. When he returns in about two weeks he will apply himself exclusively to the preparation of a statement of this case for the profession.

Weekly Chillicothe Crisis, June 1, 1882   Chillicothe, Missouri (white-owned)

A BLACK SKIN REMOVER.

The Negro Need Not Complain Any Longer of Black Skin.

This preparation, if used as directed, will turn the skin of a black person four or five shades whiter, and that of mulattoes perfectly white. It also removes wrinkles from the face and makes the skin beautiful. Any person using it can see the result in forty-eight hours.

It does not turn the skin in spots, but bleaches out white. It is a very good thing for weak eyes if allowed to get in the eye while washing the face.

One box of this powder is all that is required, if used as directed, the skin remaining beautiful without continual use, and is perfectly harmless.

Direction and preparation will be sent to any address on receipt of $2.00 or C. O. D.

G. Simms,
Broad Street, Richmond, Va.

The Richmond Planet, January 1, 1898   Richmond, Virginia (white-owned) Public Domain.

Colored People Delighted With New Discovery To Bleach The Skin

Atlanta, Ga.—Says that recent tests have proven without doubt that swarthy or sallow complexions can be made light by a new treatment recently discovered by a man in Atlanta. Just ask your druggist or Cocotone Skin Whitener. People who have used it are amazed at its wonderful effect. Rid your face of that awful dark color or greasy appearance in a few minutes. It costs so little that you can't afford to be without it. Just think how much prettier you would look with that old dark skin gone and new soft, light skin in its place. Men and women today must care for their complexions to enter society.

If your druggist will not supply you with Cocotone Skin Whitener, send 25c for a large package to Cocotone Co., Atlanta, Ga.

The Morgan City Daily Review, October 26, 1917   Morgan City, Louisiana (white-owned) Public Domain.

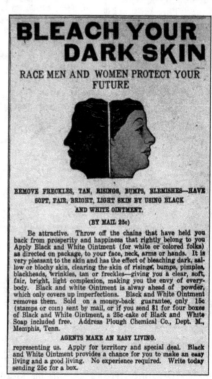

BLEACH YOUR DARK SKIN

RACE MEN AND WOMEN PROTECT YOUR FUTURE

REMOVE FRECKLES, TAN, RISINGS, BUMPS, BLEMISHES—HAVE SOFT, FAIR, BRIGHT, LIGHT SKIN BY USING BLACK AND WHITE OINTMENT.

(BY MAIL 25c)

Be attractive. Throw off the chains that have held you back from prosperity and happiness that rightly belong to you Apply Black and White Ointment (for white or colored folks) as directed on package, to your face, neck, arms or hands. It is very pleasant to the skin and has the effect of bleaching dark, sallow or blochy skin, clearing the skin of risings, bumps, pimples, blackheads, wrinkles, tan or freckles—giving you a clear, soft, fair, bright, light complexion, making you the envy of everybody. Black and white Ointment is alway ahead of powder, which only covers up imperfections. Black and White Ointment removes them. Sold on a money-back guarantee, only 15c (stamps or coin) sent by mail, or if you send $1 for four boxes of Black and White Ointment, a 25c cake of Black and White Soap included free. Address Plough Chemical Co., Dept. M., Memphis, Tenn.

AGENTS MAKE AN EASY LIVING.

representing us. Apply for territory and special deal. Black and White Ointment provides a chance for you to make an easy living and a good living. No experience required. Write today sending 25c for a box.

Nashville Globe, August 23, 1918
Nashville, Tennessee (black-owned) Public Domain.

Detroit Tribune, editions October 11, 1941 and September 25, 1942
(black-owned) Public Domain.

My mother Brenda and maternal Aunt Carolyn Kimball, two light-skinned black women, recalled the following conversation between their darker brown-skinned mother Lilly and her coworker while visiting her in a Detroit hospital where she was employed as a nurse many years ago.

"When Momma was working at Mount Carmel Hospital, me and Carolyn went to see her in the cafeteria. One of her coworkers asked, 'Oh, are these your daughters? They have pretty colored-skin.' Momma said [with a sarcastic grin], 'Yeah! I married a white man.'"

Afterward, I asked Aunt Carolyn for the racial identity of the woman who posed the question to Grandmother Lilly. She said she was "white."[21]

"Racist ideas are not all the same because black people are not all the same. There are many types of racist ideas demeaning the different types of black people, including black women and black men, and light-skinned and dark-skinned people. That a light skin is beautiful because of the striking resemblance to beautiful white people is a different type of racist idea than a dark skin is ugly because the striking dissemblance from beautiful white people."[22]

Nevertheless, Carl's physical appearance may have allowed him to benefit from colorism, but was his potential for greater success achievable by passing into a white society?

- Passing is more than a person's skin color and physical features. It allowed a key of access through the door of the "white" world and the establishment of associations and relationships economically, socially, politically, and institutionally. According to Carl's former friend and fellow pianist Charles Boles, "He played a lot of classical piano. He played jazz, but he could not make as much money at it." Also, "...one of the statements he made to me was, "Well, if I only depended on jazz, I wouldn't make a living."[23]

- The subject of passing was not obscure during Carl's youth and young adult life during the '30s, '40s, and '50s. Passing-related news appeared on the front pages of the national newspapers *The New York Times* and the black-owned *Atlanta World* in 1932; featured in *Life* magazine photographs in the '40s; and in Hollywood films such as *Imitation of Life* (1934 and 1959), *Lost Boundaries* (1949), *Pinky* (1949), and *I Passed for White* (1960).[24]

  > Pauline Green, a cousin within my paternal lineage and an advertisement and fashion model from Chicago during the 1950s and 1960s, was considered for the leading role in the 1960 Hollywood film *I Passed for White*.

  > According to Fred Wilcox, the film's producer, "I knew it was hopeless to look on the coast because we have very few Negro actors there. There are many in New York, but of course I need a girl who is colored and yet almost white.

I hear several who won't even come to me because they are actually passing for white in real life." Wilcox refused to cast a white girl in the role as was done with several prior movies. "It would deprive the film of the kind of realism I am looking for. If I can't get the right girl, I won't do it at all."[25]

My paternal cousin **Pauline Green** was considered for a role in the Hollywood movie *I Passed for White.*

My great-grandfather Leroy Steger, Sr. was close to Carl's father Gordon—biologically and relationship-wise. They were first cousins and possibly half-brothers—whose mothers were sisters and were possibly fathered by the same white man. According to various records, he was identified as "William Steger." As teenaged boys, they were raised by their grandmother Nicey and step-grandfather Nicholas Bohanan and worked on a farm in Huntsville, Alabama. Later as young men, Leroy and Gordon migrated from the South, temporarily taking up residence in one or two areas before eventually settling in Detroit around 1917.[26]

Leroy, as a mixed-race man, had a very fair complexion along with prominent Caucasian features. Perhaps to some, he was a white man and was afforded some privileges. However, there was no historical evidence uncovered through family interviews or documentation that Leroy ever identified himself other than as a black man. "He used to walk into the front door of [a] White Castle"—a fast-food restaurant known for its greasy and small-sized hamburgers. "He didn't know that black people had to go up to the (outside) window (to order their food)."[27] I knew through observed documentation, Carl's parents Gordon and Dorothy also made no effort to hide their racial identities.

"Even though there is absolute certainty that the chances of success are greater for a colored person who forswears his race than for the same individual, if he remains loyal to it, the vast majority do not yield to the temptation of passing for white."[28]

–Mary Church Terrell

As a black man, Leroy had no toleration for racial discrimination and he sometimes fought against it—at times literarily.

While living in Tennessee around 1916, "Leroy was sitting down and eating at a restaurant when a black man came in. The restaurant personnel told the man that he would have to wait and could not be seated. When the black man left, a white man in the restaurant said, 'I couldn't believe they let that nigger in here!' Leroy could barely swallow his food and in minutes, he got up and left the restaurant."[29]

Around 1917, Leroy "heard a white man call a black man a 'nigger' from his place or hotel window." Afterward, he jumped out of the window and cut the man. Fearing negative repercussions, he left the state on the run for Detroit. Thereafter, he sent for his wife Susie and their infant daughter Oreatha.[30]

Around 1923, Leroy worked as a chauffeur and Susie as a domestic for white businessman Charles E. Allinger and his family in their large two-story home on the west side of Detroit. Allinger worked in downtown Detroit as one of the principal officers, i.e., secretary and treasurer, for The Charles A. Strellinger Company, the largest machine and tool supply company in Michigan. One day, according to the oral family history, Leroy was engaged in conversation with Susie when Allinger called for Leroy "to go bring the car around." A short time later after seeing Leroy without the automobile, "Mr. Allinger said, 'You didn't hear me call you?' Leroy replied, 'Yes, I did.' Allenger said, 'When you hear me call you, you come running.' Leroy said,

'If you see me running toward you, you better start running.' After that, he [Allinger] didn't say anything else and they never had a problem."[31]

A photograph of **Leroy Steger, Sr.** ca. 1930s. Photographer unknown.
From the Linda Scandrick photograph collection.

"...he would come around."

Carl's daughters Kimberly and Dawn may not have understood why their father "was paranoid" and refused to have any discussions with me, his long-lost cousin. Nonetheless, at the conclusion of our enlightening meeting in 2005, they were assured and certain that "he would come around."

After several telephone conversations, a gathering, and the exchange of irrefutable evidence which included my extensive research, the obituary and photograph of Carl's mother Dorothy Steger, Carl's music CD, and the similar facial features in the images of Carl and Dorothy, Carl's daughters were convinced that I was not a person prowling upon the elderly, a mysterious mafia hitman from the past, or an FBI agent seeking to pepper him with additional questions concerning Jimmy Hoffa's disappearance. Also, if Carl was concerned about a "hired gun" from his past attempting to establish a connection with his present, his willingness to continue to perform publicly until the '90s seemed to contradict that train of thought.

The Last Letter Sent

"...to reestablish his black identity
through racial reconciliation while
assisting me with my genealogical exploration."

On March 27, 2006, I mailed a package to Carl which consisted of a typed letter and several photographs of our family members: Leroy Steger, Sr., my grandparents Leroy Gordon Steger, Jr. (who was also given the name "Gordon" after Carl's dad) and Lilly Steger, and a family portrait of me, my siblings, and our children. This was another steadfast effort to provide him with the opportunity to reestablish his black identity through racial reconciliation, while also assisting me with my genealogical exploration.

To:	3/27/06
Mr. Carl Steger	

From:
Eric Willis

Hello Mr. Carl Steger,

My name is Eric Willis and I've been researching for five years, my maternal Steger family history (from Detroit back to Alabama). I am addressing this letter to you because I feel that you are my only living Steger relative who could provide with some additional information about my great-grandfather Leroy Steger.

My great-grandfather Leroy and your father Gordon Steger were first cousins. I had discovered this by dedicating many hours of research at the main Detroit Public Library's genealogy department (The Burton Historical Collection). The

"The Last Letter Sent" (above and on the following pages) was my last attempt to establish a familial connection with my cousin Carl Steger in 2006.

research involved my Steger family line from the present (in Detroit) back to the year 1870 (in Maysville and Huntsville, Alabama) through the use of United States census records and other records. In the 1910 census record, I found that my great-grandfather Leroy (age 16) and your father Gordon (age 15) were living in the household of their grandparents Nicey and Nicholas Bohanan in a rented farmhouse in Huntsville, Alabama. Actually, Nicholas Bohanan was their step-grandfather because Nicey had married Nicholas two years after her first husband Willis Steger died. In 1920, I found out that Gordon and Leroy lived together at the Napoleon Apartments on Napoleon Avenue between Beaubien and Brush Streets in Detroit. My great-grandmother Susie and their daughter Oreatha Mae Steger also lived in the apartment. Between 1921 and 1924, your father and my great-grandfather lived together on 6561 Harford Avenue in Detroit. They also worked as porters at a hotel.

On January 20, 1921, my great-grandparents Leroy and Susie had their second child, Leroy Steger Jr. My grandfather was later known as Leroy Gordon Steger and then Gordon Leroy Steger as an adult. He was named after your father. My Steger relatives said his mother Susie used to call him Junior. (I have provided you with a photograph of Leroy Gordon Steger Jr.) My grandfather had 5 children, 1 son and 4 girls. One of the girls is my mother Brenda Joyce Steger. She later married my father, Samuel Willis, Jr.

By researching old Detroit city directories, I found out that you and your parents lived on 438 Hague Avenue in Detroit. I also spoke to some of your musician friends of the past such as Charlie Boles, Alma Smith, Jo Thompson and Jiam Desjardins. Mr. Boles said he knew you very well and that you both were good friends. After I told him that I was trying to locate you because of my family history research and that I had been unsuccessful up to that point, he encouraged me to keep trying and to "leave no stone unturned." He also expressed to me that he had been adopted and that he looked for his biological family and eventually found them. I met Mr. Jiam Desjardins at the library while I was doing my research. He told me that he knew you as well. He said, "I met Carl in the late '40s—early '50s. He was a pianist. He used to play at private clubs such as the Fox and Hounds and the Book Cadillac. He played popular music at the supper clubs."

Our cousin Gerald Steger (age 73), the eldest child of Oreatha Steger, said he remembers you when he was in his younger years.

Although, I have gathered a lot of information going through records about my great-grandfather Leroy, your mother (Dorothy, a noted Detroit musician and teacher), and father (Gordon, a career hotel porter), I am missing that most important aspect of who they were from a personal point of view.

• What were they like?
• How well did you know my great-grandfather Leroy Steger?
• Do you recall my great-grandfather Leroy and your father talking about their childhood lives in Alabama?
• My family said that my great-grandfather Leroy's father was a white man. According to his 1942 death record, his father's name was William Steger. Do you recall hearing any discussions about his father?

- What did your father Gordon look like? His mother and father's names were Mary and William (according to records). Do you remember him ever discussing his parents?
- Is there any additional information that you could share with me about our Steger family? Was there any talk about our ancestors and slavery?
- Is there any information that you would like to share with me about yourself and your musical career?

I met your two daughters last year and they said you were concerned about my interest in wanting to contact you. If you are still apprehensive about responding to me via a letter or a telephone call after reading this letter and viewing my enclosed photographs, I will not make any additional attempts to contact you.

God Bless you Cousin Carl.

Sincerely,

Your cousin Eric Willis
Family Genealogist...
...leaving a legacy for our children.

By 2021, a decade and a half had passed and not a reply, a follow-up, or even a whisper was ever heard again from Carl's daughters or Carl. It appears he was successful in persuading his family to discontinue all their contact with me—no more telephone calls, no more meetings, and no more photographs. Perhaps the inadvertent damage may have already been done—the revelation of his true racial identity. I had already "opened the can of worms" and there was no turning back now, I suppose. Then again, I presume, being in trepidation, Carl's response to his family was a last concerted effort to maintain his "whiteness" during the remaining years of his long and—I assume—mostly prosperous life. An open discussion of family history would possibly result in his further embarrassment and shame. He was born black into a black middle-class family, reborn later in life, and acquired success as a "white" man in an upper middle-class white family. He was 80 years young when I sent him my appeal in the form of the letter, and on New Year's Day 2021, he was blessed with his 95th natal day.

Carl may have also been motivated by not wanting to reopen some of his possible past and familiar emotional wounds after the death of his parents—emotions of isolation, paranoia, guilt, self-hate, and a fear of being exposed. But these emotions are a part of the human condition of racial passing.[32]

Will Carl acknowledge his black identity while still among the living? Another celebrity, Hollywood's former Broadway musical and film sensation Carol Channing revealed in 2002 at age 81 that she passed since she was age 16.

> Carol Channing's father George Channing was "one-part Negro." His mother was black and his father was a son of German immigrants. Carol's maternal grandparents were also from Germany.

> At age 16 and before she went off to college, Channing learned about her multiracial identity from her mother. Her mother said, "I'm only telling you this because the Darwinian law shows that you could easily have a Black baby." According to Channing during a 2003 television interview, "I know it's true the moment I sing and dance. I'm proud as can be of [my black ancestry]. It's one of the great strains in show business. I'm so grateful. My father was a very dignified man and as white as I am."[33]

> Before his death in 1957, George Channing, whose original surname was Stucker, continued to pass as white and became a newspaper editor and Christian scientist in California.

> Channing's career began on the stage around 1941 and later on Broadway and films. "Had she revealed the story earlier, she would never have had the career she had. No Black woman would have been cast as Lorelei Lee in *Gentlemen Prefer Blondes* in the 1940s, let alone the role of Dolly Levi in *Hello, Dolly!* She wouldn't have worn those Bob Mackie dresses on the Great White Way[34], or been the subject of Al Hirschfeld cartoons, or made all those guest appearances on *Password* and *I've Got A Secret* and *What's My Line*. Black celebrities, back then, were marginalized, at best."[35]

During a 2010 television interview, Channing said, "I can sing and dance better than any white woman anywhere." During another interview with CNN's talk show host Larry King, Channing said, "My grandfather was Nordic German and my grandmother was in the dark. I got the greatest genes in show business." Carol Channing died 16 days before her 98th birthday on January 15, 2019.[36]

"The core issue of passing is not becoming what you pass for, but losing what you pass away from."

According to Allyson Hobbs, an African American Stanford University professor and historian on racial passing:

"The largely unexplored realms of African American family life reveal how everyday people made sense of their racial identities. A history of passing can be found in the private and innermost spaces of African American lives, in sources that were not organized or assembled around the theme of passing. Passing becomes as unintended and unmistakable subject throughout family histories, which offer firsthand accounts of the interruptions, gaps, and omissions that a relative's decision to pass created. Departing from narratives that portray passing as an individualistic and utilitarian enterprise or one reserved for a handful of black elites, family histories bring into focus the collective nature and communal politics of passing."[37]

I argue "it is possible to pass for something without becoming what it is that you pass for. Indeed, it is my contention that the core issue of passing is not becoming what you pass for but losing what you pass away from."[38]

"Passing was not an automatic response to racial proscription. Some African Americans used passing as a crucial channel leading to physical and personal freedom. They declared their rights as American citizens and insisted on their humanity. What they could not fully know until they had successfully passed was that the light of freedom was often overshadowed by the darkness of loss."[39]

In May 1958, Robert P. Stuckert, a professor in Ohio State University's Department of Sociology and Anthropology, completed a study titled *African Ancestry of the White American Population*. Its purpose "was to determine the validity of" "a concomitant belief that all whites are free of the presumed taint of Negro ancestry or 'blood.' A Negro is commonly defined as a person having any known trace of Negro ancestry or 'blood' regardless of how far back one must go to find it."[40]

However, Stuckert's research included that between 1941 and 1950, about 15,550 blacks passed as white annually or 155,500 in ten years. In addition, "approximately 21 percent" or 28 million (28,366,000) of the 135 million (134,942,000) "persons classified as white in 1950 have an African element in their inherited biological background." He also predicted that these numbers would increase in future decades.[41]

From an opposing viewpoint, Nathan Irvin Huggins, a notable twentieth century black American historian, author, and leading scholar of Afro-American studies, stated in the early 1970s that "Black people, it seems, don't 'pass' anymore."[42]

"'Passing' has been a product of the single consensus in American race relations: the promise of American life and the American Dream actually applied to white men only. Throughout American history to our own day, laws, customs, and brute force have compelled Afro-Americans to know that they were not citizens. To use political power, to hold office, to own property, to get ahead, to protect one's family, and to survive may have been presumptions of the white American's existence, but they were often impossibilities for black Americans. At best, these conditions of citizenship have been problematic. Since being white made all the differences in American life, who would not be white if he could? But such reasoning exacted a psychic penalty. The man who worked as white but kept alive relations with black family and friends knew the immediate fear of detection. On the other hand, he who tried to play it safe by moving to another place and 'disappearing' into the white world doubtless nurtured guilt because of deception and the abandonment of race and family. And the fact that Afro-Americans did 'pass' only served to deepen white anxieties about racial identification.

Nevertheless, until the 1960s most Americans would agree that, given the inconvenience of blackness, anyone who could be accepted as white would likely grasp the opportunity. Blacks might think it disloyal and unfortunate; whites might think it deceptive and dishonest, but both understood and expected it to happen. Some even fancied that the final solution to race problems would come when everybody looked more or less alike in color.

The Black Revolution may have had little effect on real power relationships between blacks and whites, improving the opportunities of advantaged blacks yet changing little in the circumstances of the desperate poor and deprived. But the Revolution's insistence on race identity, race consciousness, race pride, and race beauty has made anachronistic the game of hide-and-seek traditionally played by whites and blacks in America.

What I think has happened in recent years is that the assumptions of reasonableness have been undermined. True, it is still an inconvenience to be black in the United States, especially if you are poor. But being white and middle class is not as desirable as it once was. There has been a great turning away by American youth from what has traditionally stood as norms and models of lifestyle. To most black people, white Americans are emotionally ill and morally corrupt—from the President and Billy Graham to the 'hard hat.' To become white, therefore, means to take that sickness and corruption as part of the bargain.

It is for this reason, as well as the reassertion of race pride, that it has become important for Afro-Americans to be black, if nothing else. Lest there be any doubt, a wide assortment of symbols—

hairstyle, clothes, speech—are adopted to assert blackness. Those black Americans who might otherwise be taken for white, rather than 'pass,' are even more anxious than their darker brothers and sisters to remove all doubt as to their blackness.

"The change is not faddish, but profound and significant. Its importance will not be discerned in changes in power relationships, employment statistics, or institutional practices. But it is likely to bring white and black Americans to a healthier and more objective sense of who they are. Identity can be less burdened by guilt and fear. If that is so, the change will be well worth the trauma and hysteria that has so often marked it." "If indeed, appearances are real, we have witnessed the end of a phenomenon that has persisted throughout American history."

Also, of the same opinion, the contemporary and independent scholar Robert Fikes, Jr. stated in 2014:

"The controversy that regularly surfaced for centuries surrounding light-skinned African Americans who resort to 'passing,' that is to say, willfully concealing their African lineage to gain social and economic advantage by reinventing themselves, usually as Caucasian but also as Latino, Native American, and Asian, has become a relic of our nation's past. It was laid to rest by succeeding generations whose increasing interracial experiences mitigated prejudice. Triumphs of the Civil Rights Movement in the 1950s and 1960s, the institutionali-zation of affirmative action and equal opportunity in the workplace in the 1970s and 1980s, the economic vitality of a surging black middle class, and seismic demographic shifts in the population over the past half-century, including the growing numbers of non-white immigrants from Asia, Latin American, and to a lesser extent, Africa, have permanently altered white dominance. These changes have, in turn, contributed to greater acceptance of intermarriage and pride in one's biracial and multi-ethnic heritage. It has also refocused social mobility in terms of class rather than race. In this new multiracial landscape, passing as white loses much of its immediacy and relevance.

White privilege has not suddenly and dramatically diminished in recent years. Rather, economic and social circumstances have reduced the temptation for persons whose racial pedigree was ambiguous to deny or blur their racial heritage."[43]

It is undeniable that DNA testing has had a tremendous impact on the advancement of genealogical research. But what about its relationship to racial passing, and whites unknowingly with black ancestry and living as white? A 2014 study involving the creation of a genetic portrait of the United States was conducted by Katarzyna "Kasia" Bryc, a 23andMe population geneticist.

"About 3.5 percent of self-identified European Americans have at least 1 percent or more African ancestry. It's likely that many of these Americans, who describe themselves as white, may be unaware of their African ancestry, which in many cases goes back between five to ten generations. There are also differences regionally—with the highest levels in the South—so that in South Carolina, at least 13 percent of self-identified whites have 1 percent or more African ancestry, while in Louisiana the number is a little more than 12 percent.

In Georgia and Alabama, the number is about 9 percent. The differences perhaps point to different social and cultural histories within the South. Among black Americans, those with the highest percentage of African ancestry also live in southern states, especially South Carolina and Georgia. The percentage of the population who are African Americans are also highest in those states, but there are also differences among states with similar percentages of African Americans. That may also be due to the different histories of those states."[44]

Henry Louis Gates, Jr., a leading African American scholar of black literature, history, and culture, stated:

> "...the more we learn about the black, white and *browning* of our past, the more we can see how absurd, how arbitrary and grotesque the "one-drop rule" that defined the color line in America for decades and decades during its most painful chapters truly was. Back then, a white-enough black woman or man could pass for white; now, with Bryc's findings,[45] we realize that all along, there was a whole other layer in the color aristocracy that no one could see. And to shop owners, hotel clerks, railroad conductors and federal judges in those times, appearances were what mattered; in our time, thankfully, it is the truth that sets us free.

As a result, I can't help but wonder how many 'hidden' blacks sat at whites-only Woolworth's lunch counters in the South before the 'visible' and brave black students of the early 1960s did so. The same could be said for our nation's historically white colleges and universities, its movie theaters and hotels, its water fountains and bathrooms.

We know that in 1892 Homer Plessy could have passed for a white passenger on the Louisiana railroad that led to the constitutional doctrine of 'separate but equal' in the Supreme Court. But Plessy spoke up, as did many of what were once known as 'voluntary Negroes' (men and women like former NAACP leader Walter White who refused to pass). But how many others remained silent without ever revealing who they were? Would that railroad line have stayed in business—or any business for that matter—if they had tried to enforce the 'one-drop rule' down to its very letter in all cases? And were there any who might have hidden inside the white robes of the KKK, knowing they were about to lynch one of their own?

It's not the historian's job to engage in counterfactuals, of course, but I do think it's safe to say that the pseudo-scientific underpinnings of Jim Crow, which provided so much legal justification and comfort for cruelty in the years between the Civil War and the civil rights movement, would have faced a very different challenge in court had DNA science been around.

I embrace the positives in these amazing DNA discoveries— further proof that America is more of a melting pot than we had even assumed, which is why my goal is and remains for every American to trace her or his roots as far back as the paper trail and DNA science will allow."[46]

> Hypodescent or the "One Drop Rule" as Gates referenced above, "was a determinant racial marker exclusive to the United States by which racial identity was defined, and a person was considered 'black' if he or she had any African ancestry. This unique rule has been embraced by black and white Americans alike, both socially and legally. It began in the North and was enforced throughout the South during slavery."[47]

> The rule is also a colloquial term to describe a set of discriminatory laws that were passed by white supremacists in at least eighteen states between 1910 and 1931 to define mixed-raced Negroes as a part of the subordinate group, and to penalize blacks and whites involved in miscegenation in an attempt to maintain the purity of the white race and culture—especially in the South during the era of Jim Crow.[48]

> These laws were declared unconstitutional under the 14th Amendment of the United States Constitution in 1967 when the United States Supreme Court ruled on anti-miscegenation laws in the case of *Loving v. Virginia.*[49]

In June 1958, Richard and Mildred Loving, a white man and a black woman, married in Washington, D.C. to avoid being charged for violating Virginia's Racial Integrity Act of 1924, the state's anti-miscegenation law. After their return home to Virginia, they were arrested by the police. After being charged and pleading guilty, the Lovings were provided with two options: a one-year prison term or leave the state for 25 years. They moved back to the District of Columbia. In 1964, five years after their conviction, the Lovings wanted to return to Virginia, and sued the state. Being represented by the ACLU (American Civil Liberties Union), the Virginia Supreme Court modified the sentence but affirmed the convictions. Thereafter, the case was appealed and argued before the Supreme Court including Justice Earl Warren who "pointed out that the law did not criminalize marriage between persons of two non-white races," suggesting a "white supremacist motivation," and "it infringed upon the fundamental right of marriage."[50]

The noted black writer and poet Langston Hughes wrote the following passage in his 1940 memoir *The Big Sea: An Autobiography.*

"You see, unfortunately, I am not black. There are lots of different kinds of blood in our family. But here in the United States, the word 'Negro' is used to mean anyone who has any Negro blood at all in his veins. In Africa, the word is more pure. It means all Negro, therefore black. I am brown. My father was a darker brown. My mother, an olive-yellow. On my father's side, the white blood in his family came from a Jewish slave trader in Kentucky, Silas Cushenberry, of Clark County, who was his mother's father, and Sam Clay, a distiller of Scotch descent, living in Henry County, who was his father's father. So, on my father's side both male great-grandparents were white, and Sam Clay was said to be a relative of the great statesman Henry Clay, his contemporary."[51]

"A great many Negroes in America are daily engaged on slyly trimming off the biscuits of race prejudice."

"...because there are many things in this U.S.A. of ours which Negroes may achieve only by guile, I have great tolerance for persons of color who deliberately set out to fool our white folk. I remember the old slave story of the mistress who would not allow her house servants to have any biscuits. She was so particular on this point that she would cut the biscuits out herself and count them. But the cook went her one better. When the mistress left the kitchen, the cook would trim a narrow rim off every biscuit—with the result that the Negroes had in the end a pan of biscuits, too.

A great many Negroes in America are daily engaged on slyly trimming off the biscuits of race prejudice. Most Negroes feel that bigoted white persons deserve to be cheated and fooled since the way they behave toward us makes no moral sense at all. And many Negroes would be way behind the eight ball had they not devised surreptitious means of escape. For those who are able to do it, passing for white is, of course, the most common means of escaping color handicaps. Every large Negro section has many residents who pass for white by day but come home to their various Harlems at night. I know dozens of colored whites in downtown offices or shops. But at night they are colored again.

Then there are those Negroes who go white permanently. This is perhaps a more precarious game than occupational passing during work hours only. Some break down under the strain and go native again or go to pieces. But hundreds of others pass blithely into the third and fourth generations—entirely losing their dusky horizons by intermarriage." "A famous Negro educator told me recently of having lost track of one of his most brilliant students, only to be asked to address a large and wealthy congregation in the Midwest and to find as pastor of this church his long-lost colored graduate, now the 'white' shepherd of a white flock. The educator was delighted at his former student's ministerial success in fooling the white folks."[52]

Do these things—this memoir, the Hollywood celebrity Carol Channing, and the population geneticist Bryc's 2014 study involving the DNA testing results of self-identified European Americans—prove that racial passing is still relevant in today's society and not a vestige of the past? I believe so. Although Carl Steger was born and lived a part of his life during the Jim Crow period, how many other light-skinned blacks, both young and old, are still living their lives passing in what some in error would call a "post-racial" America in the post age of the nation's first black president Barack Obama?

I was further enlightened during my 2015 interview with the pianist Mr. Charles Boles and his wife as we talked about my cousin Carl and the subject of racial passing.

CB: I wonder if it was in that book? I don't know if it was in that book or not [Pause] Club 49—49 Club. It used to have a little sign set back there—49 Club.

Author: Oh. Okay. So, to give you a summary of what I discovered about Carl [which] might stir up some memories, and then I'll go into the information you provided to me back in 2005.

CB: [Laughter] I'm glad that you remember that.

Author: [Laughter] Yeah! I wrote—

CB: I sure don't.

"He was thin and very—
I could see where he could pass."
"He was the kind of guy you can look at and
there was no way that you can tell."

Author: What I did after seeking Carl out—

CB: Um-hmm. Have you ever seen this man [while observing photographs of Carl which I provided for his review]?

Author: In person? No.

CB: I'm surprised that he had gained that much weight. Because when I knew him, he was a thin man—very light-skinned brother.

Author: Oh. Okay.

CB: Thin—was not nearly as big as this. But these are later, later life pictures. Because when I knew him, he was young and thin—very handsome.

Author: Yeah. I was kind of thinner myself a few years back [*Laughter*].

CB: Did you ever see pictures of him when he was young?

Author: No.

CB: He was thin and very—I could see where he could pass.

Author: Oh. Okay.

CB: He was the kind of guy you can look at and there was no way that you can tell.

Author: Oh really?

CB: Yeah!

Author: Do you have any pictures of him?

CB: I doubt it.

Author: Oh. Okay.

CB: But you know what now, you didn't check in the Burton? *[the main Detroit Public Library's genealogical Burton Historical Collection]*.

Author: Uhhh!

CB: And the only other person—he just died. I'm trying to think . . . You know a lot of the old people that was around they're around 80, 90 years old and most of them are dead now.

The conversation continued after I discussed and provided Mr. Boles with a summary of my research up to that present day.

CB: There was a guy around that just died here this year named Dan Clisco. He was a bass player. He used to collect pictures. You couldn't play with him on a gig without him taking a picture.

Author: Oh. Really? Okay.

CB: And I don't know if a picture [of Carl] is in his collection. I'm not going to bet, but I would be willing to say that there's a picture of him around.

Author: That would be great to—

CB: These are the only people that I know that you could contact. He just died this year. He died at an early part of this year. And Alma Smith Foster—she passed away. She's dead and people like Ernie Swan. Ernie Swan was the same kind of a piano player like Carl—and Carlos Cortez. These people were piano players that played those kinds of clubs and mostly [for] rich white people.

Author: Okay.

CB: And I remember Carl playing in clubs, but mostly [for] rich white people. Club 49 is the one place I remember him playing that I could put my finger back on right now in my mental mind. All those people are dead. Another person who would have known him, Johnny Allen—he just died.

Author: I didn't know about him.

CB: He was older than Alma. You see Alma was ninety. Johnny Allen was ninety-nine. And he was playing around here in the thirties with us. You know right now, everybody is either—they're alive and my age or they're old and dead.

Author: Yeah.

CB: So you never did find out if he had any kids or not?

I provided Mr. Boles with the information that I did not know if Carl and his first wife had any children, but he adopted children during his current marriage. His adopted daughter Kimberly Steger-Sherill informed me by telephone that Carl had not talked much about his biological family including his parents, and she does not understand why he's "paranoid" about speaking to me.

CB: He was hiding. It's too bad you couldn't go directly to Sarasota, Florida, before he dies though because he's an old man now.

Author: Right! Right! I have his address and telephone number, but I don't—

CB: You know if you could go down there, I think . . . You know, let me tell you something about people that's passing.

Author: Yes, sir.

CB: They try to have an anonymous past because they don't want you digging in there. Cause if they're passing, they're passing, and the past is wiped away.

Author: Right. Actually, um . . .

CB: His daughter probably said that [about Carl being 'paranoid'] because he said, 'Ahhhh, maybe it's the government or something. I don't want them digging around in my business. He probably said something like that. But he's going to be very anonymous with her and more anonymous with you.

Author: Because there's more interesting things that occurred—

CB: See, if you confronted him face to face and here's your mother, I know your past, and I'm your cousin . . . Just like when I found out that my grandfather was a white man. His relatives contacted me, and they gave me all the information—they didn't want to be bothered. You can tell they didn't want to be bothered. So, after I got all of the information that I could out of them, I cut them loose.

Author: And that's kind of similar because I know that during this time [of our interview], I believe that she [Kimberly Steger-Sherill] didn't know that her father was black.

CB: I'll bet you any amount of money had you said, 'I'm doing an article on musicians,' and never mentioned that you were any kin to him, you would have got all the information you want.

Author: Yeah.

CB: Sometimes—I'm just thinking it. However, if he's been in Sarasota, Florida, you can find him.

Author: Oh, I know where he's at because—

CB: I'd go down there tomorrow.

Author: Well, let me provide you with this additional information and then I'll pose that question to you—if you would still pursue it?

After I gave Mr. Boles additional information about my telephone conversation with Kimberly and her self-assurance that I was not a predator seeking to pry upon the elderly, I provided further research which led me to believe that Carl was possibly passing as a white man. I related my meeting with his daughters, revelations of indirect mob connections, and the account of Carl's performance at the site of Jimmy Hoffa's disappearance and the ensuing FBI interviews. Our conversation continued.

Author: So, she said she thought that maybe [the indirect mob connections] could have had something to do with why he didn't want to ah—that he was paranoid.

CB: Naw. No. No. He was passing.

Author: Right.

CB: And he had done it so long and he didn't want to drudge up none of the b******* from the past. And trust me, it's very difficult to pass [*Slight pause*] because you don't know whose goin' show up.

Author: Exactly. She also said that Carl had a good friend who owned a furniture store, and he was 'rubbed out by the mob.' So, she was 'trying to put the pieces together.'

CB: Yeah, but anybody . . . Who in the mob is going to rub out a 90-year-old man? And if he was a gangster thirty years ago, they forgot all about that.

"He controls this planet.
And [Slight pause] it's always going to be that way
because until people of color realizes and band together,
we gone always be the outside looking in."

After responding to Mr. Boles' question of how I acquired the obituary of Carl's mother Dorothy by researching early black newspapers, I elaborated about another discovery.

Author: Also, one of the interesting things I saw were the ads involving bleach [or] lightening—a lot of blacks trying to brighten up their skin complexions.

CB: You know we're such a—I guess you can call it a distorted race of people because we had so much trauma in our lives caused by that dirty rotten white man. And I don't want to seem prejudice.

Author: No! I understand.

CB: But he's a dog. He's a dog—like no dog exists. There's no meaner dog than that. He's done a number not only on us, but I always remind people that here's a man that hypothetically looked out over the horizon of the world and we'll say hypothetically that there was a thousand of him. And he looked over there across the river Jordan, if you will, and he saw a million of them—meaning people of color. Not necessarily all dark and black, but some—Arabs, all of . . . But he's a minority on this planet. But when a man is a minority and can come along and control even the toilet paper that people wipe their a** in Africa. If you wipe your a** in Africa, you can bet your bottom dollar that a white man made the paper. If you shoot your brother in Africa, you can bet your bottom dollar that he made the bullet. He controls this planet. And [*Slight pause*] it's always going to be that way because until people of color realizes and band together, we gone always be the outside looking in.

"Although I got some of the greatest advantages of being a black piano player. I did very, very well. I didn't make a lot of money—[Chuckle], I mean, but I live good."

Mrs.
Boles: You know, did you tell him about this guy that we met in Macon-Americas who took us all through the–?

CB: Well, I told him about, I can't think of his name right now, but I was telling him that he was a historian—a very, very lovely man.

Mrs
Boles: He told us about everything. He snatched the covers off everything.

CB: He took us around, and he carried me around—he spent his whole day. Not to mention the lead-up to our meeting because he researched a whole bunch of stuff for me to find my people. And I found pretty much of what I wanted that the people alive could tell me. People are dead. Because hell, I'm 83 so you know anybody that would be involved is probably dead by now.

Author: Yeah.

CB: My mother died when I was like five.

You know it's just like my story—when I found out [about] a white undertaker in Americas, Georgia, in 1918—one with a black woman. And I went to the town in Americas and his house—I saw his house, and I went to where my grandmother would have lived. It was right across the track, the typical 'across the track.' And he had lived in an affluent area and he was [a] well-respected undertaker in town going with a teenaged 15 or 14-year-old black girl. And he gave her a baby. Now [*Slight pause*], this girl would have to fend for herself with this baby. And she ended up not raising the baby, and the baby came here. And then she was a victim of boyfriend abuse cause the boyfriend—the momma's boyfriend was livin'—she was livin' with this boyfriend, and the boyfriend took advantage of the daughter. Now here I am!

So, these white people—they knew the history. You know what they said? 'Well, we're not ashamed. It's not true, it's just . . . .' Well, they really didn't want to be bothered. So, they said, 'Well, here's all the information.' They gave me everything that I needed to know. But they were doing that so they can get rid of my a**, so they wouldn't have to be bothered with me anymore.

But this man—you know I can understand a man trying to pass because [*Slight pause*] the advantages. Although I got some of the greatest advantages of being a black piano player. I did very, very well. I didn't make a lot of money—[*Chuckle*], I mean, but I live good. I understand though—I understand Carl, if he was and all the indications appear that he was.

Author: And that's what one of the things I was—

CB: He probably wouldn't even talk to you if you saw him.

Author: That was one of the things I had talked about toward the end of the conversation [with Carl's daughters]. I brought my camera and I asked them if I could take a picture.

CB: If they can take a picture with you?

Author: Yes, I have pictures.

CB: Very interesting. I'm surprised they let you do that. So, they're not his biological daughters, so what the hell.

[I showed Mr. Boles the photographs.] Yeah. They're as white as can be.

Author: Yeah.

CB: He raised these girls?

Author: Yes, and three or four more.

"You don't know. A black gene don't die brother,
it just gets old."

CB: You know some people would rather die and go to hell—
would die and keep their secret. You know passing is a
hell. You know what? There's a many of, many of black
persons that have passed. You know the only thing is, if
he had any biological children, he might not even admit
to it. Because if they're dark—because it's one thing you
can't cover. I don't care how light you are, a baby . . .
Now, I'm not dark, but I'm not white either. Now my
grandfather was white. Now my first wife was very light.
My first biological daughter is darker than me. You don't
know. A black gene don't die brother, it just gets old.
Yeah. And babies—you don't know what the hell its gon'
come out lookin' like. You better be tellin' the truth
about that s***. If he had any biological children, he
probably wouldn't want anybody to know who they are.[53]

In regards to Mr. Boles' comment about "a black gene don't die," an
incident was documented in the following 1845 northern newspaper
article about a "white woman" who was married to a white man of
German ancestry and was sued for slander by a doctor for giving "...birth
to a mulatto child."

AN INTERESTING QUESTION OF LEGITIMACY—ACCU-
SATION AGAINST A SOUTHERN LADY.—We have seen
a very interesting case copied from the *Western Journal of Medicine*, the particulars of which are not less
useful in a medical point of view than of interest to
the general reader. The facts involve a question of
paternity in one of the Southern Courts, and may be
condensed as follows :

A white woman, the wife of a painter of wealth
and respectable connexions, gave birth to a male
child of so dark a complexion that unpleasant suspi-
cions were awakened among her acquaintances. Her
husband died subsequent to the birth of the child, and
after remaining a widow four or five years, she again
married. A doctor, it seems, in an evil hour, charged her with incontinence, alleging that "she had giv-
en birth to a mulatto child." Upon this an action
for slander has been brought, and is still pending, the
jury having failed, on the first trial, to agree on a
verdict. Nine doctors appeared as witnesses, who
expressed opinions widely variant touching the mer-
its of the case.

It was proved that the first husband, the alleged
father of the boy, was a man of fair complexion, being of German extraction, but that his mother and
two of his uncles were dark like the child, and that
his family in Germany were descended from the Gipsies. It was further stated in the trial, that during
the pregnancy of the mother with this child, she was
repeatedly frightened by reports of "negro insurrec-
tions."

The appearance of the boy is described as remarkable. His surface presents different shades of color,
the chest and axilla being nearly white, while the ab-
domen is dark, the change occurring abruptly, and
being marked by a well defined line.

The boy has been growing gradually whiter since
birth; "his hair is nearly straight—a little curled, but
not kinked; his feet and ankles present nothing of the
negro peculiarity; his whole appearance might suggest the thought that he was the "product of a white
woman and a mulatto man." Such is the description
of the boy's physiognomy.

It was proved by the defendant that the character
of the plaintiff had not been above suspicion.

Some of the questions upon which the medical witnesses differ are thus put :

"Is not a mulatto from a white woman darker than
one from a black woman ?

"Are there any anatomical or physiological signs
by which a negro blood might with certainty be de-
tected ?

"Is it not usual for mulattos to grow darker instead
of whiter ?

Indiana State Sentinel, July 19, 1845   Public Domain.

"Do you think it possible that a *nœvus materni* could cover nearly the whole body ?

"Do you think it possible for color to show itself in the third and fourth generation ?

"Do you know of any mode of bleaching by which the skin might be rendered white !" (See Hood's History on bleaching young Niggerlings.)

It seems that the boy has been growing whiter since his infancy ; that he is wanting in the characteristics of the negro race about the heel and ankle ; that he is descended of the Gipsies, in whom the dark complexion is a hereditary quality ; and that some of his ancestors were as black as himself. Still it must be admitted that these proofs are not conclusive of the purity of blood, and the question is one which it may be impossible to place beyond the reach of controversy. Nature, in her operations in this obscure walk, seems not to be governed by very settled laws. Thus we are told of an English woman married to a black man, of whom the offspring was quite black ; and of a similar case in which the child resembled the mother in fairness of features, the whole skin being white, "except some spots on the thigh, which were as black as the father." White, in his work on the Gradation of Man, mentions a more remarkable case—that of a negress who had twins by an Englishman, one being perfectly black, with short, woolly, curled hair; the other white, with hair resembling that of the European. Beck, in his Medical Jurisprudence, has more cases ; going to show the difficulty of establishing any universal rule on the subject.

Parental likeness, in the estimation of Lord Mansfied, is one of the strongest arguments in favor of legitimacy. In a case which came before him involving this question, he said, "I have always considered likeness as an argument of a child being the son of a parent, and the rather as the distinction between individuals in the human species is more discernible than between other animals. A man may survey ten thousand people before he sees two faces exactly alike, and in an army of ten thousand men every man may be known from the other. If there should be a likeness of feature, there may be a difference in the voice, gesture or other characters ; whereas, a family likeness runs generally through all of these ; for in every one there is a resemblance, as of feature, voice, attitude, and action." This test, we should suppose, might avail in the case under consideration.

But Lawrence, in his Lectures, cites many facts going to show that the above law of transmitted likeness is not without exceptions. He remarks : "Children do not always resemble their parents ; and hence we have occasionally persons produced in each race with characters approaching those of the other races. Among the white races of Europe, scattered instances of individuals with skins nearly as dark as those of Mongole or South Sea Islanders, are not unfrequent."

"And you know I can see the advantage in it,
but I just hate being untrue to myself."

Author: So, from your perspective, Mr. Boles, what are the pros and cons pertaining to racial passing? I know you told me some things.

CB: There's some advantages to it. You know it's a frame of mind. To me, I feel like I did okay without passing anywhere. Of course, I couldn't pass anyway. But I tell people that my grandfather was white.[54]

You really can't prove anything until you see him and talk to him. Although all signs point to the fact that he is passing. If you come from Brush Street in the '40s—in the '30s, you were black. If you come from Hague, and I went to his house when he lived on Hague, and at that time he looked so white that he could pass. But he was a very thin and frail man. He looked like he might have been sickly. So, when I saw that picture of him, it blows my mind with that beard that he had.

Author: Okay.

CB: And you know it's like people have said, I don't know if nobody spoke it, but Beethoven [the great German composer and pianist Ludwig van Beethoven] was of color.

Author: Right. Yeah. I've heard that as well.

CB: But you see it in some books and some books you don't see that. When you talk to a white man he'll say, 'Ah! That's just some stuff they made up on him—fine German man.' Just like they say Hitler's momma was Jewish.

Author: And like I said the trickling of clues such as—

CB: The clues are there, brother—every clue.

Author: His [Army] Air Corps badge. I have a cousin who's living now said that my cousin Carl enlisted into the [Army] Air Corps and when he got his badge back, it listed [his race as] 'white.'

CB: So, he was passing even then.

Author: Right.

CB: What year was that?

Author: He enlisted in 1946.

CB: So, then he must have been tryin' to pass when I met him then because I met him after '46.

Author: Right.

CB: Your mother is not alive, is she?

Author: Yes, both of my parents are alive.

CB: Does she remember Carl?

Author: No. My cousin Gerald, he's in his eighties. He's the only one who knew Carl. There are two others who heard about Carl but just in passing.

CB: Well, you know the big thing here is that Carl was distancing himself even then. If he went to the army in '46 and then pulled that off with that badge, it means he was thinking about it even long before that probably.

And you know I can see the advantage in it, but I just hate being untrue to myself.

Author: Exactly.

CB: I'm a black man and I'm proud of it.

Author: Well, I really appreciate it. I really enjoyed—

CB: Man, I'm sorry I wasn't able to help you more than—

Author: No! No! No! You've been really helpful.

CB: Carl is an interesting subject but as they say, 'I would be very, very careful when you write that story cause ah you go there [in a baby talking voice].

Author: [Laughter] Yeah.

CB: Especially if he's alive, man. You make sure that he's—

Mrs.
Boles: You can tell that he's not going to pervert the truth.

CB: Unless you get down there—

Author: Right. Well, again, I really appreciate your time and the information that you did provide [to] me and discussing—

CB: Well, yeah. I find it very interesting—fascinating.

Author: Un-hmm. Yes, sir.

CB: Fascinating, cause I went through it myself, man, when me and my sister—god, I don't want to go through it. I ain't got the guts no more to go through it.

According to Allyson Hobbs:

"But passing—the anxious decision to break with a sense of communication—upset the collective, 'congregative character' of African American life; it undermined the ability for traditions, stories, jokes, and songs to be shared across generations. Even the task of completing a family history became prickly, if not impossible. To be sure, not all family relationships represented were congenial, but once a relative decided to past, meaningful touchstones and common experiences were lost. The fragmentation of one's identity and ancestral memory and the scattering of family relationships represent only a handful of passing's most troubling dilemmas."[55]

On March 31, 2022, my cousin Carl Steger made another life-altering conversion—a passing into the afterlife and a reunion with our Steger ancestors, both black and white.[56] Being saddened by the news while also optimistic, I hoped that perhaps the future will result in a conversation with his white family about racial reconciliation and our shared family histories.

How many of us know the whole truth about our families? But I want to know more truth about my Steger family so I will continue in the research endeavor. Sometimes I can be described as analytical and detailed-oriented. I recalled as a college art student my teacher once described my pencil drawing as being "too detailed and over the top." Nevertheless, she wanted to photograph the work for an art book she was writing.

My genealogical journey began with my attempt to seek information from anyone who may have known my great-grandfather Leroy Steger, Sr. I traveled down an unfamiliar road full of expectations only to eventually come to expect the unexpected. It has alternated between a missing person's investigation, family and local histories, personal memoirs, race, racism, religion, familial secrets, politics, organized crime, and tributes. Although while one unexpected dark secret was discovered, the unanswered questions surrounding Leroy Steger's birth and his childhood and teenaged-years remain hidden from me—for now.

However, as a person of the Christian faith, I believe that all unsolved familial mysteries will be revealed, if not now then during God's final judgment. As a genealogist, I would like for those hidden revelations to overcome the hindrances of man and manifest themselves in the present.

Regarding the historical relationships between black and white Americans, a change in individual hearts is the solution—not mindset surface changes through racial and political legislations. Today, the races have become so polarized and politics unruly that any solution is non-existent. Politics have burned bridges by stroking the dehumanization and divided states of America. Many laws of the land have been passed since the 1500s when black slaves were brought to the Carolinas region of "The New World" called America, including civil rights acts, the Emancipation Proclamation, constitutional amendments, anti-discrimination and segregationist bills, executive orders, etc. Nevertheless, the struggle continues.

Princeton University professor and author Imani Perry believes that a cultural shift is required.

"Racial inequality is a national cultural practice. We are not just living with the impact of the past. We certainly are. Right. When you look at something like the wealth gap you see, well, that's the impact of 20th century policies that created wealth gaps across the lines of race. But the reality I saw over and over again [during my research] is that people disadvantaged others based upon their membership in racial groups. Most traumatically, black people are disadvantaged. But it's not exclusively white people— it includes a significant number of black people who do that disadvantaging of black people and put black people in various professions of various sorts.

So, it's not really about this question of individual attitudes. These are learned behaviors. We exist in a culture that teaches us that . . . white people matter more. Right. So, if you understand that it's a culture, then it becomes very clear why it's so hard to address it, why policy is insufficient because you need a cultural shift. We have to tell different kinds of stories. We have to be intentional about the process. One of the common places in our society is that people often think it's impossible, it's not nice, or it's uncomfortable to talk about race. But one thing that we know from research is that talking about race actually helps people behave in a less discriminatory fashion. It's evidenced. Right. And so that's a cultural shift that needs to happen. We can all participate in the transformation, but this is not a matter of a kind of individual attitudes or individual behaviors."[57]

As expressed by the noted civil rights activist and preacher Dr. Martin Luther King, Jr.:

"There is also need for leadership from the people of good will in the white South. I would not have you believe for one minute tonight that there are not white persons of good will in the South. I am absolutely convinced that there are hundreds and thousands, nay millions of white people of good will in the South, but most of them are silent today because of fear—fear of political, social, and economic reprisal. God grant that the people of good will will rise up with courage, take over the leadership, and open channels of communication between races, for I think that one of the tragedies of our whole struggle is that the South is still trying to live in monologue, rather than dialogue, and I am convinced that men hate each other because they fear each other. They fear each other because they don't know each other, and they don't know each other because they don't communicate with each other, and they don't communicate with each other because they are separated from each other. And God grant that something will happen to open channels of communication, that something will happen because men of good will rise to the level of leadership." "Courage faces fear and thereby masters it. Cowardice represses fear and is thereby mastered by it. Courageous men never lose the zest for living even though their life situation is zestless; cowardly men, overwhelmed by the uncertainties of life lose the will to live. We must constantly build dikes of courage to hold back the flood of fear."

"There comes a time when one must take a position that is neither safe, nor politic, nor popular, but he must take it because conscience tells him it is right." "Now is the time to make real the promises of democracy. Now is the time to rise from the dark and desolate valley of segregation to the sunlit path of racial justice. Now is the time to open the doors of opportunity to all of God's children. Now is the time to lift our nation from the quicksands of racial injustice to the solid rock of "The hope of a secure and livable world lies with disciplined nonconformists who are dedicated to justice, peace, and brotherhood."

"The crisis in race relations can be attributed to the fact that there are still too many of our white brothers who are concerned about the length of life rather than the breath of life—concerned about their economic or their preferred economic positions, their political power and dynasties, their social status, their so-called way of life. And if only they would substitute or rather add breath to length. If only they would add the other regarding dimension to the self-regarding dimension, we would be able to transform the jangling discords of our nation into a beautiful symphony of brotherhood. One day all men and women of this nation must come to see that God made all of us to live together as brothers. That somehow every man must respect the dignity and worth of human personality and ultimately a man must be judged not on the basis of the color of his skin but the content of his character. Somewhere we must discover the world over that we must learn to live together as brothers, or we will all perish together as fools."[58]

As with Professor Perry, I believe in a cultural shift—for the white and black races to get out of their comfort zones and talk about race. Dr. King also believed that a dialogue between blacks and whites and a spiritual solution or divine intervention would transform hearts and bring into subjection the foolishness of minds and souls. "One day we will learn that the heart can never be totally right when the head is totally wrong."[58] The mandate has been placed on the body of Christ to instruct and to lead by example. But overall, it has not been as proficient today as it should be. The focus should be going out to implement God's kingdom in the earth, not the "church" house, the local or state governments, or The White House.

During the time of creation, God made every one of us in his own image, and he did not designate any preferential treatment in terms of color when we were formed out of the earth. And when he reestablishes His kingdom on earth, it will exist as a place of wholeness and unity—consisting of unified hearts through the Holy Spirit—liberated from human eyes, minds, and souls that were once consumed by the divisional stench of race, racism, religion, politics, and violence.

CHAPTER 7

A Tribute and Historical Collage Through Newspaper Articles and Advertisements

The articles and advertisements on the following pages are from *The Detroit Jewish News* unless otherwise noted.

"*P*roducers now are ignoring all musical principles of the previous generations. It's a joke. That's not the way it works: You're supposed to use everything from the past. If you know where you come from, it's easier to get where you're going. You need to understand music to touch people and become the soundtrack to their lives."

—Quincy Jones, February 2018

"*T*he record companies encouraged creativity, whereas today, if you can do something, develop something for a couple of months, 'We'll put you out all over the world, son.' That's one of the reasons I started out playing the clarinet. It took me actually years to learn the instrument. Everybody was studying to master their craft. Record companies would encourage this. Everybody was into the creative thing. That's not encouraged today. Illusions are encouraged for some kind of reason."[1]

—Wendall R. Harrison

Brewster Notes

PARTY OF CHORAL-DRAMATIC GROUP

By ILA MAE BOYD

Tuesday, February 7, was the scene of a birthday party given at Brewster Center, the hostess being Mrs. Dorothy Steger, vivacious director of women and girls activities. Mrs. Steger's various groups, the West Side Congenial Singers, the Dream Trio, the Birdhurst Glee club and the Brewster Trillodians made up a most interesting program of tap dancing, solos, reading, and choral numbers.

An unusual harmonica solo was given by Master Carl Steger, the son of the hostess who seems to be very talented along musical lines also. After the program delightful refreshments were served and then all indulged in bridge or danced to the soothing music of Matthew Rucker and his Twelve Spirits of Swing. All had a pleasant time. Some of the guests were Pudge Rubiner, Fred G. Nagle, Gordon Steger, Perry Jacks, Henry Murphy, Mr. and Mrs. A. N. Lake, Mr. Jacobs, Mr. Marinovich, and Mr. and Mrs. Newman, Miss Willia Lacy, Mrs. A. M. Hunter, Mr. and Mrs. Chenevert, and the Brewster Sports club.

Carl Steger, age 13, and his parents Dorothy and Gordon were referenced in the **February 18, 1939**, edition of the *Michigan Chronicle* newspaper.[2]

Carl Blows Out 16 Candles

Mr. and Mrs. Gordon Steger gave a beautiful surprise dinner at their lovely Cevera apartment on New Year's Day in honor of their son, Carl's 16th birthday. He was the recipient of many fine gifts.

Those present were: Patricia and Charlita Whitby, Dorothy Priestly, Margaret Stevens, Jimmy Matney, Henry McCullough, Westley Mason, Dagwood Langford, Mr. and Mrs. Walter Johnson, and daughter, Joyce. After dinner Carl entertained his friends by playing piano numbers and selections on his clarinet.

Carl was honored with a dinner by his parents for his 16th birthday. *Detroit Tribune*, **January 17, 1942**.

NOW—*An Outstanding Young Pianist*

CARL STEGER

CLUB **49** nr. Whittier Hotel   9217 E. Jefferson   ED 1-9419

The Detroit Free Press, March 29, 1960[3]

the lounge 111 W. Mich.

Last Time TONIGHT
Piano & Vocal Sensation

EDDIE BLUE
At the
PIANO BAR

—COMING MONDAY—
●**CARL STEGER — PIANO & VOCALS**
FREE PARKING   At Allegan and Capitol Ave.
Have Ticket Stamped at Lounge
Delicious Food—Cocktails

The State Journal (Lansing, Michigan), July 16, 1960[4]

BOUCHE'
LOUNGE
8350 SECOND   TR 1-4544
Every Friday and Saturday
CARL STEGER TRIO
ENTERTAINMENT WED. thru SAT.
No Cover, No Minimum

CARL STEGER at the Scotch and Sirloin piano bar, has been doing a fine job eight years for the Meyerson brothers . . . developing an unusually close rapport with the likes and dislikes of the Scotch patrons . . . plus an uncanny memory for names, which he cleverly intermingles with patter to go with his piano and singing style.

The Detroit Free Press, October 7, 1960[5]   March 2, 1973

"Carl works six nights a week, five hours a night, without hardly getting up off his piano stool."

Some say they built the Pontchartrain around Ernie Swan's piano.

Carl Steger plays for the "gorgeous" at the Scotch and Sirloin.

Ernie Swan is an old hand at the piano bar business. He says he had a beard before they were popular. It was black when he began.

A legend has built up that Ernie started playing piano at One Washington Blvd. and the Gershensons built the Pontchartrain Hotel around him. Legend or no, it is true that Ernie has been in the Salamandre Bar since it opened eight years ago last September. He played at the Blue Note nine years before that and was in the Wonder Bar four years.

He sits right alongside the entrance to the room and greets friends as they come in. He'll scoff at an odd request, "Old Man River," and then he belts the daylights out of the Kern classic. The customer picks up his barside conversation and Ernie demands, "Hey, you gonna listen to this?"

When the last derisive chord has rung out, Ernie snorts, "That's what you get for requesting a number like that!" He goes back to pounding the scarred Steinway with its peace symbols and pasted-on promotion sticker for a show at the Top of the Pontch two years ago. Ernie, for the record, is original New Orleans jazz trombonist Kid Ory's brother-in-law.

Don Hill has been playing at the **Gold Key** a year and talks about buying the place. He owns three apartment buildings already and is buying the motel

would come as no surprise. He is another long-termer downtown. Played 16 years in the Book Bar on Michigan and 15 in the Dream Bar on Griswold. That doesn't add up to 31 years as it seems. Pianobar musicians often play two places in the same evening.

Don's music revolves around Broadway shows, Cole Porter and Gershwin. People, he says, don't listen like they did in the 30s and 40s.

Matt Michaels never was one to talk much and the night he had the Vineyards' owner Fred Graczyk, TV personality Bob Hynes and comic Soupy Sales all at his pianobar at the same time, he couldn't be heard when he did speak.

The Vineyards runs more to jazz than most pianobars. Bess Bonnier and Mario Capazzoli were there before they went to the Lion's Head. Bess's customers seem to have strange problems. One lady wanted a baby but couldn't have one. Another always wanted to play piano and repeatedly asked her escort to verify her desire. Bess has learned to greet her friends without mentioning any names in case the he's and she's have become shuffled since last meeting.

Carl Steger greets the girls with a query. "Are you 20th Century or MGM?" and he calls most of them "Gorgeous" because he believes everyone is gorgeous.

From 8pm to 9, hum to yourself.

**Tom King
4pm-8**

**Carl Steger
9pm-2am**

Before and after, you'll be entertained by our two
terrific entertainers…Tom King, from 4pm-8,
Monday through Friday, and Carl Steger, from 9pm-2am,
Monday through Saturday. Naturally, you may also hum
while they're playing.

MC·PERSONS
SCOTCH'N SIRLOIN

Greenfield, corner of Jas. Couzens Hwy. (1-696) 342-5660

December 21, 1973

September 12, 1975

DUAL BILLING Scotch 'n Sirloin doesn't mean Ronnie Phillips and Carl Steger are appearing there simultaneously . . . Ronnie is at the S &S piano bar Sundays and Mondays, while Carl holds sway · Tuesday through Saturday.

October 10, 1975

CARL STEGER, popular piano stylist whose northwest offerings have become somewhat of a going-out trademark, opens this Tuesday at Jakks Restaurant and Lounge piano bar.

December 3, 1976

The new accoustics at Jakks make quite a difference with attraction Carl Steger able to be heard all over the room . . . Carl at the large new piano bar can best display his very notable talents which heretofore have been hidden in other places . . . Carl's remembrances of names and steady patter has been a main forte, but it isn't his biggest asset . . . In the background previously have been his fine voice and excellent ability on the keyboard . . . Unlike before, with the new accoustics, Carl's every musical word and note can be heard above the sounds of many voices . . . It's like the real Carl Steger has finally been discovered!

December 24, 1976

4A ST. PETERSBURG TIMES ■ WEDNESDAY, JANUARY 5, 1977

people

The goober cut

Suburban Detroit hair stylist Frank Agosta, top, shows off his newest creation, the goober cut, modeled by Carl Steger. It is no accident that the new hair style appears to be shaped like a peanut. Agosta created the style in honor of peanut farmer Jimmy Carter's coming inauguration as president.

UPI

Carl Steger appeared in various newspapers across the United States including Florida's *St. Petersburg Times* on **January 5, 1977**. The new style's creator Frank Agosta, president of Creative Hair Replacements in Southfield, Michigan, said he "hopes it will set a nationwide fashion trend." "The 'Goober Cut' is not without precedence. Men throughout history have employed hair styles to express their political opinions." Agosta turned model Carl Steger into what he termed as "An American male who expresses his faith for the future in terms of commitment of the Carter administration."

THE CHARISMA of Sid Hudson was heartily welcomed last week when the ex-Detroiter came from Las Vegas for a visit . . . Places like Max's Deli, Chuck Joseph's Place For Steak, Larco's, Jakks, Topinka's etc. bore greetings of "Hi Sid" from the many folks who know and like him . . . Sid's favorite song, "You're My Everything" is one of the very few that Carl Steger, Jakks pianist, didn't have in his repertoire . . . but Carl's assurance that he'll know it when Sid returns is like a gilt guarantee.

March 18, 1977

"THIS GUY IS great! I'd like to open a place in Las Vegas for him!"...Sid Hudson was talking about Carl Steger at Jakks on Greenfield and 10 Mile Rd.

Carl had long since played on the piano and sang "You're My Everything" which is Sid's favorite song...and was still tickling away at the ivories and vocalizing with more talent than we had ever seen him display.

Being a Las-Vegas-ite for almost 25 years, since leaving Detroit, Sid has been living on the Strip at the Flamingo Hotel...directly amidst the world's greatest entertainment.

Sid has seen the best of them...and when he pays Carl Steger such a compliment, it means something!

April 29, 1977

UNIQUE ANNIVERSARY gift is that given every year to Carol and Carl Steger, pianist at Jakks, Greenfield at 10 Mile...Arthur Klein makes arrangements for them at a top restaurant, including wine...They can't even buy a tootkpick...Arthur takes care of everything...and leaves the two love birds alone to hold hands.

July 8, 1977

CARL STEGER, PIANIST at Jakks, Greenfield and 10 Mile, must do it with mirrors ... How he sees people coming in without looking at the door is a mystery ...

September 16, 1977

April 21, 1978

For Carl Steger at Jakks, Greenfield and 10 Mile, to be tired would be like asking a hungry man if he had enough to eat... Carl thrives on the 88 ivories and it seems to put renewed vigor in him as the time goes by... A night we were there recently, he saved his best for the last... and to do Duke Ellington properly, you can't be tired and you must be very capable... Carl did a couple of Ellingtons better than he's ever done before... especially singing and playing "I Got It Bad And That Ain't Good"... This was followed by "Do Nothing Til You Hear From Me."

Carl Steger is best noted for his own personal style of interweaving names and places within his songs... But not recognized by so many are his excellent talents playing the piano and singing while noises may abound all around him.

To appreciate Carl is to block out all other sounds and just listen to him... His piano styling is among the best.

March 2, 1979

... Carl Steger at Jakks playing piano with picture of family always in front of him... His is among the most unusual acts in town... a one-of-a-kind type ...

July 4, 1980

Trio in the 12 Mile-Northwestern area of Southfield was another restaurant casualty. One early mistake was the $10 menu which wasn't bad if you ordered steak but was a turnoff to those who had to pay the same price for chicken or fish. That situation was remedied, but the three-room eatery continued to operate beset with financial snags.

The restaurant finally went into Chapter 11 and has since been taken over by FTD. The Meyersons, who owned the Trio and invested a lot of green stuff into it, also closed the doors of its once popular Scotch & Sirloin on Northwestern Highway in Detroit.

"The "Scotch," where the elite met to eat, meet and be entertained in a gala, noisy atmosphere, is now Fogo's Seafood and Spirits. The restaurant features a raw bar and seafood prepared in a dozen different ways.

But we miss Carl Steger and his piano bar. Carl greeted the regulars by name, sang their favorite songs and generally livened up the "Scotch," contributing to its reputation as a fun place.

LET'S STOP all the talk going around ... Carl Steger is remaining at Jakks on Greenfield and 10 Mile Rd. ... Wednesdays through Saturdays.

Carl is considered one of the premier raconteur-songster-pianists in the metro Detroit area ... and his many followers will be glad to know that the mind-boggling gibber-gabber topic is definitely settled one way or another.

September 25, 1981

October 2, 1981

CARL STEGER ended six years, last week, at the piano bar of Jakks Lounge, Greenfield at 10 Mile, with a big cake for everyone from owners Dick and Aggie LaCombe.

September 17, 1982

CARL STEGER, fine piano songster and repartee artist, is at Frisco's on Orchard Lake Rd. 5 p.m. to 8 p.m. Tuesday-Friday ... and Monday and Tuesday evenings at Nifty Norman's in Walled Lake.

December 3, 1982

CARL STEGER returns to his favorite stomping grounds ... the northwest area, where his piano styling and name repartee is so well noted ... May 16 ... at Red Cedars ... Nine Mile and Telegraph ... Tuesdays through Saturdays.

April 29, 1983

CARL STEGER at Red Cedars, Telegraph and Nine Mile, is off the piano bar bit ... doing more singing and piano styling, both of which he is most proficient ... Piano bars have their place, but Carl is much more an overall entertainer than one restricted to a short number of seats ... Although not as much as before (Scotch 'n Sirloin, Jakks, etc.), Carl at Red Cedars still intermingles his audience repartee.

It is a tremendous credit to Carl's ability as an entertainer that he can adjust to any situation ... The wide expanse at Red Cedars gives his vocal and piano abilities a clearer sound ... especially, also, with two sound systems ... People who have never before heard him are enjoying Carl as he sings and plays oldies with much customer delight.

Carl's repertoire and extreme knowledge of songs, composers, years, movies, etc. are highly appreciated ... and it is a pleasure to hear him ... Folks enjoy dancing to Carl ... and there is not much doubt but what Red Cedars owners Lenore and Jack Freed can be nothing but highly pleased with him.

June 10, 1983

[COUPON]

½ OFF

PRESENT THIS AD WHEN BUYING A DINNER AT REGULAR PRICE AND GET A SECOND DINNER OF EQUAL OR LESSER VALUE AT ½ PRICE

Expires 8/5/83

BANQUET FACILITIES FOR ALL PARTIES Up To 120   LIVE ENTERTAINMENT & DANCING MON.-SAT.

RED CEDARS

CARL STEGER at the piano Tues.-Sat.

23055 TELEGRAPH AT 9 MILE RD.   353-5170

Since 1939

Lelli's INN

7618 Woodward Ave.   871-1590

Extends Its Quality To Special Parties Up To 200

Specializing In: Bar Mitzvahs, Sweet 16s,. Showers, Anniversaries, Retirement Parties, Birthdays, Weddings, Etc.

Special Appetizer Parties Available.

CALL ERNIE OR SCOTT . . . AND ASK ABOUT OUR LOW BANQUET RATES FOR ALL OCCASIONS.

Prime Rib Buffet... All You Can Eat!

Only $9⁹⁵ plus tax

EVERY FRIDAY & SATURDAY
6 p.m. to 10 p.m.

Buffet Includes:
• Prime Rib • Baked Potato • Corn on the Cob • Broccoli • Freshly Prepared Pasta • Over 17 Specialty Salads • Also our sweet shop featuring make-your-own sundaes $2.00 extra.

LIVE RAGTIME PIANO ENTERTAINMENT

No reservations accepted

Call 557-4800 for more information

Sheraton-Southfield Hotel
SHERATON HOTELS & INNS, WORLDWIDE
17017 WEST NINE MILE ROAD, SOUTHFIELD, 557-4800

The Best of Everything

(Continued from Page 30)

there . . . and friend Lenore Paxton capably filled in with her fine piano stylings . . . Bill Street plays Sunday, Monday, Wednesday and Saturday evenings . . . Henry Feinberg is Sunday 3 to 7 . . . and Daniel Borgers, Wednesday, Thursday and Friday 4 to 7.

Sunday brunch has gotten big at Rhinoceros . . . table service . . . and classical harp by Deborah Feld . . . $8.95 price includes a cocktail.

More about the "museum-like" decor of Rhinoceros . . . A chandelier in the Green Room was imported from Venice . . . originally made with candles instead of tiny bulbs . . . The parts of a Green Room chandelier were all hand blown.

In the Gray Room hangs a heavy crystal art nouveau chandelier that was in Michael's 35-room home when he lived at Golf Club Estates on W. Seven Mile Rd. between Livernois and Woodward (Detroit Golf Club) . . . It is from France . . . made and imported in the late 20s . . . with chrome used instead of sterling silver . . . since that was the art nouveau thing in those days.

This fall will be five years for The Rhinoceros . . . It's good to see owners who work . . . an almost sure sign of success . . . Michael Tarrow is an art expertise gent but not adverse to general painting or wall hanging . . . that is, when it comes to The Rhinoceros . . . Norman Schwartz is working his way back to the genial day host for which he is noted . . . recovering from a back operation at Beaumont Hospital.

The elegant uniqueness of Rhinoceros makes it a favorite of so many . . . Little wonder why.

INFORMAL MODELING by Boardwalk, Orchard Lake Rd., south of Maple, is every Thursday, 12 noon, at Stage & Co. restaurant . . . with Shayna's Place, Marni, Begadim, Sacchi, Peanuts and The Clothes Pin.

BEAR COCKTAIL lounge is no more at Dimitri's of Southfield, Southfield Rd. and 10 Mile . . . It's now a banquet room with seating for about 120 people . . . with privacy available by specially-designed doors that will "slip" onto brick . . . Glass covering on the small openings and Tivoli lighting will make it a most attractive room.

Plans are also already in the works for a large catering hall by Dimitris Syros . . . in the northwest area.

SAMMY DAVIS JR. sings, dances and clowns at Meadow Brook Music Festival, July 26 . . . and nostalgia flows when big band singers Frankie Laine and Teresa Brewer team up for an evening of distinctive

stylings July 29 . . . Andy Williams, who won 16 gold records since his 1963 "Days of Wine and Roses" album, is the July 30 attraction.

GARY HAIGHT has renamed his puppet from D. Duck to Dandy Duck . . . much better . . . His ventriloquism, acting and moderling have caught on with much gusto, but handsome Gary is also an expert meteorologist . . . accurately forecasting the weather as very few can . . . He's a climatology consultant for companies . . . and has saved farmers hundreds of thousands of dollars

Gary may soon become affiliated with a local television station which will no doubt be interested in his enthusiastic approach to giving the weather . . . While in California, Gary played bit parts in 13 movies.

DURING JULY, Fridays are added to Mondays and Wednesdays at P'Jazz

(Continued on Page 32)

THE CLOCK

24818 SOUTHFIELD AT 10 MILE   557-4324

— 7 DAYS A WEEK — 24 HOURS —

FRIED CHICKEN $2.99

FISH & CHIPS $3.99

Includes: Choice of Potato, Cole Slaw and Homemade Bread

OTHER 24-HOUR SPECIALS

BAKED ½ CHICKEN $2.99

BAR-B-Q ½ CHICKEN $2.99

Includes: Choice of pot., cole slaw and homemade bread

BREAKFAST SERVED 24 HOURS
FROM $1.09

• BREAKFAST • LUNCH • DINNER
SERVED
24 HOURS!

BIGGEST VALUES
ANYWHERE!

SEE WHY WE ARE NO. 1 IN METROPOLITAN DETROIT

IRVING'S

THE DELICIOUS ALL HOMEMADE

Restaurant - Delicatessen

OPEN TUES.-SUN. 6 a.m. to 9 p.m.

27167 GREENFIELD RD: 559-1380

1 Blk. N. of 11 MILE RD.   TRAY CATERING FOR ALL OCCASIONS

ULTRA SUPER BREAKFAST — JULY 22 THRU JULY 28

Tues.-Sat. 6 a.m.-11 a.m.   Sunday 6 a.m.-10 a.m.

• 2 EGGS (Any Style)
• 3 PIECES OF BACON OR SAUSAGE
• HOME FRIES
• BAGEL, ROLL OR TOAST

$1⁷⁸

No Carry-Out

CARRY-OUT SPECIALS — JULY 22 THRU JULY 28

GET SECOND POUND **FREE** WHEN YOU BUY ONE POUND

TURKEY BREAST $6²⁵ lb.

OUR OWN HOMEMADE POTATO SALAD
OR
COLE SLAW   78ᶜ lb.

LUNCHEON SPECIAL — JULY 22 THRU JULY 28

11 a.m.-2 p.m.   NO SUNDAYS

OUR OWN HOMEMADE

CHICKEN SALAD $1⁹⁸
Garnished
INCLUDES: BREAD BASKET

No Carry-Out

DINNER SPECIAL — JULY 22 THRU JULY 28

BREADED
VEAL CUTLETS $4⁹⁸

PURE VEAL—WE MAKE OUR OWN CUTLETS
INCLUDES: SOUP OR TOMATO JUICE, SALAD or COLE SLAW, VEG. OR POT. & BREAD BASKET

No Carry-Out

An interesting coincidence that Carl Steger and Sammy Davis, Jr.—two black and converted Jewish entertainers—are both listed on page 3 of the **July 22, 1983**, edition of *The Detroit Jewish News*

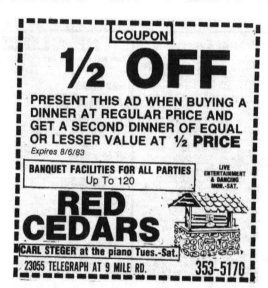

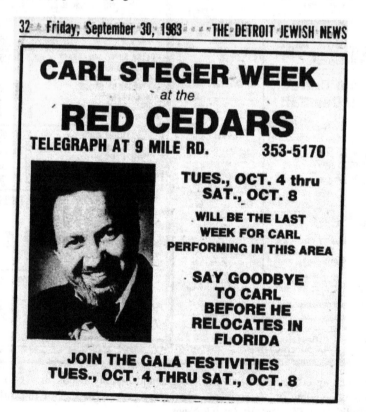

A closer view (above) of the Carl Steger and Sammy Davis, Jr. advertisements as shown on the previous page

Saint Georges

Restaurant   *Pianobar*

Finest in Gourmet Dining & Atmosphere

Memories of Europe...

...relive them once again with a visit to a wonderful gourmet restaurant in Sarasota.

Our Chefs and Crew are the finest Europe could offer.

AND NOW
St. Georges
Pianobar Presents
Carl Steger

for the first time in Florida a great artist and super entertainer.
He will perform at our unique Piano Bar every night (except Sunday) from 9 pm to 2 am.

Piano Bar with Late Night Menu and super entertainment

Lunch served 11:30-2:30 Mon. thru Fri.
Lounge & Dinner 5 p.m. to 11 p.m.
Late Night Menu 11 p.m. to 1:30 p.m.
Sunday Dinner 5 p.m. to 11 p.m.

For Reservations Call 365-9397

Located at Bay Plaza   1258 No. Palm Ave., Sarasota

Sarasota Herald Tribune, November 11, 1983, 4-D

MAIL DEPT. ...
"Sarasota is great and I have a good job. The weather is beautiful and the beaches gorgeous."
Carl Steger
(Carl is appearing at piano bar of St. George's Restaurant in Bay Plaza, N. Palm Ave., Sarasota, Monday through Saturday ... He'd really be thrilled to see folks from the home town visiting or living in Sarasota ... Carl and wife Carol's home phone is (813) 923-4051.)

December 23, 1983

"Thought I would drop you a note and thank you for informing me that 'home-towner' Carl Steger was now in my locale. I dropped in to see him at St. George's in Sarasota and needless to say, the performance was shades of the Scotch & Sirloin. It was wonderful seeing Carl and his hospitality to me was grand. For any other folks in the Tampa Bay area, Carl is appearing at St. George's, 1258 N. Palm Ave., Sarasota."

Dave Sterns
422 Evergreen Dr.
Oldsmar, Fla. 33557

January 6, 1984

ON THE MEND DEPT. . . . Sheldon Roth . . . recuperating after heart surgery . . . home from three months in Florida with wife Blanche.

They report an evening out at St. George Club in Sarasota, where long-time local favorite Carl Steger has been the dining room attraction since leaving Detroit area.

April 25, 1986

FROM FLORIDA, Phyllis Fishman sends info that Carl Steger, former pianist at Jakks and other spots, is now at Chez Sylvie Restaurant on Osprey Ave. S, Sarasota . . . "I found the only Charley's Crab restaurant on the west coast of Florida," writes Phyllis. "I ate there twice. It's on St. Armand's Key off the coast of Sarasota.

January 13, 1989

. . . Pianist Carl Steger, who left the Cafe St. Louie for a smaller, more intimate spot, is packing them in at Cafe L'Europe. The tables were turned on the musician the other night, though, when the entire cafe staff sang the birthday song to Carl, celebrating his 66th and sporting a new Mickey Mouse watch from his daughter.

Sarasota Herald Tribune,
January 14, 1992, 2E

. . . Memories were jolted back to the years when folks flocked to hear Carl Steger at Scotch 'n Sirloin and Jakks.

April 30, 1993

Who would have believed the Scotch 'N' Sirloin would close its doors?... Everything from the Shrimp Louis to the sirloin steak to the Dover sole was delicious. The place was always jumping with lunch, dinner and after-theater crowds and those who stood knee-deep around the piano bar listening to the songs of Carl Steger who knew most of the customers by name.

June 9, 1995

JAKK'S LOUNGE on Greenfield, between Nine and 10, was one of the area's more popular meeting places ... Carl Steger at the piano bar had a repartee that played on the egos of customers walking in as he mentioned their names ... The 165-foot parquet dance floor, with the likes of Billy Rose, always got a lot of action ... Owners Dick and Aggie LaCombe, who took over ownership from Jack Freedman in 1980, toyed with the thought of changing its name but thought better about monkeying around with success ... Those who frequented the local spot will tell you that if it could talk Jakk's would have had a lot of stories to tell. ☐

June 5, 1998

REMEMBERING ...Scotch 'n Sirloin on James Couzens and Greenfield, owned by the Meyerson family, had been there since 1950, continuing a tradition that started at Buddy's Barbeque on 12th Street and Clairmount in 1933 ... The many regulars were attracted by the modern decor and the fact that there was a pianist seven nights, from 9 p.m. to 2 a.m. ... One of them, Carl Steger, seemed to have eyes on the side of his head as he greeted people with fanfare coming through the door while still tickling the keyboard.

June 14, 1996

MAKING ROUNDS of yesteryears to hear ... Gary Jon Primo and Staff at the Winery ... Tony and Carolyn at Mr. L's Silent Woman ... Billy Rose Trio at Danny's Gin Mill ... Dottie Dunn and the Gypsies at Mitch Housey's ... Charley Dubin at Kingsley Inn ... Don Hill at Gold Key Inn ... Carl Steger at Scotch and Sirloin ... Fred Boyne at Farm House ...: Saucy Sylvia Stoun at Royal Ascot ... Mel Ball Quartet at Ralph's ... Vince Ramo Trio at the Oak Barrel

August 18, 2005

QUESTION & ANSWER ...
"Hope you can stop us from arguing with an answer for our question. Where did Carl Steger play piano?" ... *Irving and Lois Susman*
[If either said Scotch 'n Sirloin or Jakk's Lounge, you both win. Carl made everyone a celebrity with "Direct from Las Vegas" and other welcoming remarks as they came through the doors at the Scotch in Detroit and later at Jakk's in Oak Park.]

August 12, 2010

CARL STEGER, 96, formerly of Detroit of Sarasota, Fla., passed away March 31, 2022.

He was a longtime entertainment fixture in the Detroit area for decades, and one of his biggest fans was the late Danny Raskin. Danny wrote of Carl many times in his "Best of Everything" columns. Once, he observed, "Carl Steger thrives on the 88 ivories and it seems to put renewed vigor in him as time goes by." Mr. Steger was best noted for his style of interweaving familiar names and places in his songs.

He is survived by his beloved wife, Carol; children, Dawn (Ron) Davey, Todd Steger, Scott (Jorge Bardowell) Steger, Kim (Wayne) Sherrill, Tim (Mimi) Steger and Ann (Tom) Goshorn; 11 grandchildren; five great-grandchildren.

April 21-27, 2022

APPENDICES

Gordon William Steger—
Carl's Father in Photographs

ca. mid 1910s – early 1920s. The photographs are from the
Phyllis (Stegar) Torrence photograph collection.

Gordon Steger (left) poses with his young half-uncle Charles
Bohanon.

Carl Gordon Herbert Steger's
1942 World War II Draft Registration Card

Public Domain.

Gordon H. Steger's (alias Carl Steger) Military Enlistment Reference Record

Gordon H Steger

United States World War II Army Enlistment Records

Name	Gordon H Steger
Name (Original)	STEGER GORDON H
Event Type	Military Service
Event Date	04 Oct 1946
Term of Enlistment	Enlistment for Hawaiian Department
Event Place	Dearborn, Michigan, United States
Race	Negro
Citizenship Status	citizen
Birth Year	1926
Birthplace	MICHIGAN
Education Level	3 years of high school
Marital Status	Single, with dependents
Military Rank	Private
Army Branch	Air Corps
Army Component	Regular Army (including Officers, Nurses, Warrant Officers, and Enlisted Men)
Source Reference	Enlisted Man, Regular Army, after 3 months of Discharge
Serial Number	16222568
Affiliate ARC Identifier	1263923
Box Film Number	02362.93

CITING THIS RECORD

"United States World War II Army Enlistment Records, 1938-1946," database, *FamilySearch* (https://familysearch.org/ark:/61903/1:1:K8GZ-K1C : accessed 31 December 2015), Gordon H Steger, enlisted 04 Oct 1946, Dearborn, Michigan, United States; citing "Electronic Army Serial Number Merged File, ca. 1938-1946," database, *The National Archives: Access to Archival Databases (AAD)* (http://aad.archives.gov : National Archives and Records Administration, 2002); NARA NAID 126323, National Archives at College Park, Maryland.

   No image available

UNITED STATES WORLD WAR II ARMY ENLISTMENT RECORDS, 1938-1946 ❶

Affiliate Publication Title Electronic Army Serial Number Merged File, ca. 1938-1946

CITING THIS RECORD

"United States World War II Army Enlistment Records, 1938-1946," database, *FamilySearch* (https://familysearch.org/ark:/61903/1:1:K8GZ-K1C : accessed 31 December 2015), Gordon H Steger, enlisted 04 Oct 1946, Dearborn, Michigan, United States; citing "Electronic Army Serial Number Merged File, ca. 1938-1946," database, *The National Archives: Access to Archival Databases (AAD)* (http://aad.archives.gov : National Archives

Carl's Mother Dorothy Steger
Detroit Free Press, September 17, 1922

POPULAR MUSIC PLEASES FANS

Harmonica Selections, Whistling Numbers Are Novelties on WCX Program.

The Saturday evening WCX radio program, broadcast by The Detroit Free Press, was especially planned for the folks who like the popular and ballad types of music. Five specialists in this sort of melody gave an attractive and enjoyable performance.

Mrs. Dorothy Steger, Negro mezzo-soprano, who possesses a voice of great sweetness, gave a group of familiar songs that included "Love Like the Dawn Comes Stealing," (Cadman); "Dear Old Southland" (Layton), and 'A Little Pink Rose" (Bard)). "Only a Bowl of Roses," (Clarke). Mrs. Steger handled these numbers with the sympathetic attitude and the touch of pathos which the people of her race lend to their music. In addition to the vocal solos, Mrs. Steger gave two whistling selections, "Florine Waltzes, "The Sheik" and "Nobody Lied." The versatile artist was applauded by telophone for both of her groups of music.

MRS. DOROTHY STEGER

Carol Elaine Channing
(1921-2019)

Carol Channing, a noted Hollywood celebrity and former Broadway musical and film sensation, revealed in 2002 at age 81 that she passed as "white" since the age of 16. Courtesy of International News Photos, June 16, 1952.

ENDNOTES

Introduction

1. Nick Bowhannon Household, June 16, 1900 U.S. Census, Madison County, Alabama, Population Schedule, Huntsville Precinct, Supervisor's District No. 8, Enumeration District No. 98, Sheet No. 22 B; Leroy Steger's WWI Draft Registration Card, June 5, 1917, Ward 7, Precinct 2, No. 358, Serial No. A 21-1-8; Stinson Funeral Home record for Leroy Steger, informant: Susie Steger; Interview with Patricia Taylor on January 8, 2002; Interview with Brenda Willis on October 13, 2015.
2. Nina Renata Aron, "When this black woman shot a white doctor in the 1950s, an ugly Southern secret came to light," Timeline, accessed on June 27, 2017, https://timeline.com/when-this-black-woman-shot-a-white-doctor-in-the-1950s-an-ugly-southern-secret-came-to-light-78d343dba7ac
3. June 16, 1900 U.S. Census, Madison County, Alabama.
4. William D. Steger Household, June 15, 1900 U.S. Census, Madison County, Alabama, Population Schedule, Huntsville Precinct, Supervisor's District No. 8, Enumeration District No. 98, Sheet No. 17A.
5. June 16, 1900 U.S. Census, Madison County, Alabama.
6. Stinson Funeral Home record for Leroy Steger.
7. Leroy Steger photograph from the Linda Scandrick photograph collection.

Chapter One: A Carousel of Yesterday's Detroit Jazz Greats

1. Interview with Dr. Jiam Desjardins on November 19, 2003.
2. Interviews with Lars Bjorn and Jim Gallert on March 30, 2005 and April 2, 2005.
3. Interview with Jim Gallert on April 2, 2005; Naima Shamborguer – Biography, accessed September 1, 2014, http://www.naimashamborguer.com/bio.html.
4. Naima Shamborguer – Biography, website.
5. Veterans' Administration Letter, August 3, 1945 and 1944 Withholding Receipt for Gordon Steger, Dearborn, Michigan, FOIA.
6. Lars Bjorn and Jim Gallert, "Alma Smith Passes," *SEMJA Update*, June/July 2012, accessed October 13, 2014, https://www.semja.org/jun2012/smith.html.
7. Interview with Charles Boles on September 29, 2015.
8. About Us, *Michigan Chronicle*, accessed April 11, 2017, https://michronicleonline.com/about-us.
9. Interviews with Charles Boles on April 7, 2005, September 29, 2015 and October 2, 2015.
10. "Fats Waller Biography," Biography.com, July 30, 2019, accessed on October 25, 2019, https://www.biography.com/musician/fats-waller; Scott Yahow, "Fats Waller: Profiles in Jazz," *The Syncopated Times*, June 1, 2017, accessed October 25, 2019, https://syncopatedtimes.com/fats-waller-profiles-in-jazz; Taylor, Steven, *Fats Waller on the Air: The Radio Broadcasts & Discography*, (Lanham, Maryland, Toronto and Oxford, The Scarecrow Press, 2006), 1-2.
11. Interview with Jim Gallert on April 2, 2005; *The Oakland Press*, Charles Boles, Detroit jazz icon, releases first album – at age 81, Gary Graff, January 27, 2014.
12. "Charles Boles Receives 2019 SEMJA Award," SEMJA, Southeastern Michigan Jazz Association, May 8, 2019, Facebook, accessed on July 1, 2019, https://www.facebook.com/127677617265941/posts/charles-boles-receives-2019-semja-awardpianist-charles-boles-is-the-2019-recipie/2512075632159449.
13. Interviews with Charles Boles on October 2, 2015 and January 29, 2016.
14. What is Bell's Palsy?, WebMD, Brain & Nervous System, accessed on June 2, 2018, https://www.webmd.com/brain/understanding-bells-palsy-basics.
15. Interview with Josephine Thompson on April 15, 2005.
16. Danny Raskin, "The Best of Everything," *The Detroit Jewish News*, May 14, 1976, 29.
17. Tom Dworetzky, "Jo Thompson, now in her 80s, reflects on cabaret past and present," *New York Daily News*, March 22, 2013, accessed on December 6, 2014.

http://www.nydailynews.com/entertainment/music-arts/jo-thompson-reflects-cabaret-article-1.1295897; Betsyann Faiella, "At 82, Pianist/Singer Jo Thompson Swings her Way to Grammy Consideration," *PRWeb*, October 21, 2010, accessed on December 6, 2014, http://www.prweb.com/releases/jo_thompson/grammy_consideration/prweb4679594.htm.

18. Greg Dunmore, Bio – History About the Fabulous Ms. Jo Thompson, Jazz Jewels.tv, NABJ Arts & Entertainment Task Force, accessed on December 6, 2014, http://www.jazzjewels.tv/jothompsonepk.html; Tom Dworetzky, "Jo Thompson, now in her 80s, reflects on cabaret past and present," *New York Daily News*, March 22, 2013, accessed on December 6, 2014, http://www.nydailynews.com/entertainment/music-arts/jo-thompson-reflects-cabaret-article-1.1295897.

19. Interview with Jo Thompson.

20. Interview with Kenn Cox on October 19, 2005.

21. Judy Adams, "Detroit Jazz Birthdays for November 2015," *The Dirty Dog Jazz Café Blog*, November 12, 2015, accessed on October 12, 2014, http://dirtydogjazz.com/Blog/index.php/detroit-jazz-birthdays-for-november-2015; Michael Ricci, "Detroit Jazz Composer and Pianist Kenn Cox, 68, Dies", All About Jazz, Jazzstage Productions, December 20, 2008, accessed on October 12, 2014, https://news.allaboutjazz.com/detroit-jazz-composer-and-pianist-kenn-cox-68-dies.php?width=1024.

Chapter Two: The Milieu

1. Interview with Kimberly Steger-Sherrill on May 21, 2005.

2. Gordon Steger and Dorothy Williams, State of Michigan, Return of Marriages in the county of Calhoun, Record No. 485, July 21, 1921, 306-307.

3. Battle Creek, History, accessed on October 31, 2018, https://www.battlecreekmi.gov/377/History; People of Faith: Sojourner Truth, PBS.org, accessed on October 31, 2018, https://www.pbs.org/thisfarbyfaith/people/sojourner_truth.html; Sojourner Truth: A Life of Legacy and Faith, Sojourner Truth Institute of Battle Creek, accessed on October 31, 2018, https://sojournertruth.org/sojourner-truth.

4. Return of Marriages in the county of Calhoun.

5. Merze Tate (1905-1996), Michigan Women's Hall of Fame; "Merze Tate," Merze Tate Explorers, accessed on June 18, 2019, https://merzetate.com/merzetate.

6. "Diplomatic Historian Merze Tate Dies at 91," *The Washington Post*, 1996, accessed on June 25, 2019, https://www.washingtonpost.com/archive/local/1996/07/08/diplomatic-historian-merze-tate-dies-at-91/8afda8e3-6561-4c94-be9f-ba41e867ac48/?noredirect=on&utm_term=.4172e1a0065a; Jon Harrison, "February 6, 1905: Merze Tate Born, First African American Graduate at Western Michigan University," Michigan State University Libraries, Blogs, February 6, 2018, accessed on June 25, 2019, https://blogs.lib.msu.edu/red-tape/2018/feb/feburary-6-1905-merze-tate-born-first-african-american-graduate-western-michigan; Merze Tate, Merze Tate Explorers.

7. "Rediscovering Merze Tate: A remarkable African-American woman who grew up in our own backyard," *The Rapidian*, March 10, 2014, accessed on June 25, 2019, https://therapidian.org/rediscovering-merze-tate-remarkable-african-american-woman-who-grew-our-backyard.

8. Blanchard Community Centennial, Blanchard, Michigan, 1873-1973, 5, Clarke Digital Collections, Central Michigan University, accessed on June 22, 2019, https://clarkedigitalcollections.cmich.edu/?a=d&d=Clarke1973-02.1.6&; Merze Tate (1905-1996), Michigan Women's Hall of Fame; "Merze Tate," Merze Tate Explorers; Merze Tate Award, American Political Science Association, accessed on June 25, 2019, https://www.apsanet.org/awards/merze-tate; Sonya Bernard-Hollins, Merze Tate, Character Clearinghouse, Florida State University, accessed on June 26, 2019, https://characterclearinghouse.fsu.edu/article/merze-tate.

9. *Transcript of Certificate of Death*, Dorothy Steger, Registration No. 5894, informant: Gordon Steger; "Melena Neonatorum," *The Free Dictionary*, Medical Dictionary, Farlex, 2003-2016, accessed on April 21, 2016, http://medical-dictionary.thefreedictionary.com/melena+neonatorum.

10. Interviews with Kimberly Steger-Sherrill and Dawn Steger-Davey on May 21, 2005; Gordon Steger Household, 1930, U.S. Census, Wayne County, Michigan, population schedule, Precinct

21, Detroit City, Ward of City 14, Block No. 212, enumeration district [ED] 82-429, supervisor's district [SD] 20, dwelling 2, family 2, National Archives micro-publication; *Veteran's Application for Pension for Disability*, Gordon W, Steger, May 1, 1945, Dearborn, MI., Form No. 526b; *Polk's Detroit West Side City Directory 1923-1924*, R.L. Polk & Co., 1923, Detroit, Michigan, 2106; *Polk's Detroit West Side City Directory 1924-1925*, R.L. Polk & Co., 1924, Detroit, Michigan, 1684.

11. *Main Causes of the Depression*, Paul Alexander Gusmorino 3rd, May 13, 1996, accessed on June 10, 2010, http://www.gusmorino.com/pag3/greatdepression; John Hope Franklin and Alfred A. Moss, Jr , *From Slavery to Freedom: A History of African Americans*, Eighth Edition, 421.

12. Williams, Jeremy, *Detroit: The Black Bottom Community*, (Charleston, Chicago and San Francisco, Arcadia Publishing, 2009), 7.

13. *From Slavery to Freedom*, 421-422.

14. *Disability Allowance Application*, Gordon Steger, August 6, 1932, No. 15-230; *Veteran's Application for Pension for Disability*; December 20, 1947, *Michigan Chronicle*, Detroit, Michigan, Volume 12, Number 39, "Death Takes Mrs. Steger" front page.

15. 1930, U.S. Census, Wayne County, Michigan; Certificate of Marriage, Wayne County, Michigan, No. 68031, Gordon W. Steger and Dorothy Steger, November 26, 1935. "Mrs. Dorothy Steger," Death Notices, *Detroit Free Press*, December 16, 1947, 25 and "Music Teacher for City Dies," *Detroit Times*, December 1947, 35, Note: Listed as in both newspapers as "Gordon C. Steger" and as "Gordon Carl, Jr." in *The Detroit News*, December 16, 1947, 28; *Polk's Detroit 1951 Telephone Directory*, 1208, R.L. Polk & Co., Note: Listed as "Gordon H Steger" in the *Polk's Detroit 1952 Telephone Directory*, 1239 and his 1952 Marriage License Application and Certificate; *Catalog of Copyright Entries, Third Series, Unpublished Music*, January-June 1952, (Washington: The Library of Congress, 1952), 718., Note: Listed as "Gordon Herbert Steger and pseudonym as "Carl Steger;" *Polk's Detroit 1953 Telephone Directory*, 1244, R.L. Polk & Co., Note: Listed as "Carl G Steger" and in the city's directories between the years 1953 and 1957.

16. Interview with Kimberly Steger-Sherrill.

17. Thomas J. Sugrue, *The Origins of the Urban Crisis: Race and Inequality in Postwar*, (Princeton: Princeton University Press, 1996), 23-24.

18. "May 01, 1926: Ford Factory Workers Get 40-Hour Week," History, 2009, A&E Television Networks, accessed on February 16, 2019, https://www.history.com/this-day-in-history/ford-factory-workers-get-40-hour-week/print; "Henry Ford," History, November 9, 2009, A&E Television Networks, accessed on February 16, 2019, https://www.history.com/topics/inventions/henry-ford.

19. "George Washington Carver," History, October 27, 2009, A&E Television Networks, accessed on February 16, 2019, https://www.history.com/topics/black-history/george-washington-carver; "Black Men Built Cars Before Henry Ford & The History of George Washington Carver," accessed on February 16, 2019, https://www.youtube.com/watch?v=XtkXsG4KZdo.

20. "Henry Ford," History; Allan Nevins and Frank Ernest Hill, *Ford: The Times, The Man, The Company*, (New York: Scribner's Sons, 1956), 409-436.

21. Bill Shea, "Timeline: Detroit, 1917 to 1967," Crain's, accessed on January 25, 2019, https://crainsdetroit.com/article/20170617/news/631731/timeline-detroit-1917-1967; U.S. *United States Census of Population, 1910-1970*, Department of Commerce, Bureau of the Census, (Washington, D.C., U.S. Government Printing Office, various years).

22. Sugrue, *The Origins of the Urban Crisis: Race and Inequality in Postwar, 23-24.*

23. Thomas J. Sugrue, "From Motor City to Motor Metropolis: How the Automobile Industry Reshaped Urban America," accessed on January 25, 2019, http://www.autolife.umd.umich.edu/Race/R_Overview/R_Overview2.htm.

24. "Black Bottom Neighborhood," Encyclopedia of Detroit, Detroit Historical Society, accessed on September 30, 2015, https://detroithistorical.org/learn/encyclopedia-of-detroit/black-bottom-neighborhood; Sugrue, *The Origins of the Urban Crisis: Race and Inequality in Postwar, 23-24*; Jeremy Williams, *Images of America – Detroit: The Black Bottom Community*, (Charleston, Chicago, Portsmouth and San Francisco: Arcadia Publishing, 2009), 17.

25. Kevin Boyle, *Arc of Justice: A Saga of Race, Rights and Murder in the Jazz Age*, (New York: Henry Holt and Company, 2004), 150-151.

26. Boyle, *Arc of Justice: A Saga of Race, Rights and Murder in the Jazz Age*, 145, 168, 183, 213; "Timeline: Detroit, 1917 to 1967."

27. Boyle, *Arc of Justice: A Saga of Race, Rights and Murder in the Jazz Age*, 146, 212.

28. Boyle, *Arc of Justice: A Saga of Race, Rights and Murder in the Jazz Age*, 207, 209.
29. Boyle, *Arc of Justice: A Saga of Race, Rights and Murder in the Jazz Age*, 6-8.
30. "Dr. Carter G. Woodson," Dr. Carter G. Woodson African American Museum, accessed on February 15, 2019, http://www.woodsonmuseum.org/about-us#dr-carter-g-woodson; Carter G. Woodson: "Father of Black History," NAACP, accessed on February 15, 2019, https://www.naacp.org/naacp-history-carter-g-woodson.
31. "Purple Gang," Encyclopedia of Detroit, Detroit Historical Society, accessed on September 30, 2015, http://detroithistorical.org/learn/encyclopedia-of-detroit/purple-gang.
32. "From Motor City to Metropolis: How the Automobile Industry Reshaped Urban America."; "Populations of Various Ethnic Groups," Detroit Statistics, *The Detroit Almanac, Detroit Free Press*, accessed on January 25, 2019, http://historydetroit.com/statistics.
33. Robert W. Bagnall, "Bagnall Reviews Early Progress of Race in Michigan," *Detroit Tribune*, August 19, 1939, 10-11.
34. Elaine Latzman Moon, *Untold Tales, Unsung Heroes: An Oral History of Detroit's African American Community, 1918-1967*, (Detroit: Wayne State University Press, 1994), 60-66.
35. *Polk's Detroit West Side City Directory 1925-1926*, R.L. Polk & Co., 1926, Detroit, Michigan, 1793; *Polk's Detroit West Side City Directory 1926-1927*, R.L. Polk & Co., 1927, Detroit, Michigan, 1945; *Polk's Detroit West Side City Directory 1927-1928*, R.L. Polk & Co., 1928, Detroit, Michigan, 2061; *Polk's Detroit West Side City Directory 1928-1929*, R.L. Polk & Co., 1929, Detroit, Michigan, 1928; *Polk's Detroit West Side City Directory 1929-1930*, R.L. Polk & Co., 1930, Detroit, Michigan, 1946; *Polk's Detroit West Side City Directory 1930-1931*, R. L. Polk & Co., 1931, Detroit, Michigan, 1774; *Polk's Detroit West Side City Directory 1931-1932*, R.L. Polk & Co., 1932, Detroit, Michigan, 1581.
36. Gordon and Dorothy Steger, Divorce Record, May 8, 1933 (State of Michigan: Circuit Court for the County of Wayne - In Chancery), Liber No. 211, 351; Dorothy Anna Steger, Application for Pension Form, October 19, 1945.
37. "Society and Woman's Page," *Detroit Tribune*, July 22, 1933, 4.
38. Marriage License, Wayne County, Michigan, No. 68031, Gordon W. Steger and Dorothy Steger, November 21, 1935; Certificate of Marriage, Wayne County, Michigan, No. 68031, Gordon W. Steger and Dorothy Steger, November 26, 1935.
39. *Polk's Detroit Directory of Householders, Occupants of Office Buildings and Other Business Places, including a Complete Street and Avenue Guide 1931-32*, 1931, R.L. Polk & Co., 2043.
40. Lars Bjorn and Jim Gallert, *Before Motown: A History of Jazz in Detroit, 1920-1960*, (University of Michigan Regional, 2001), 38.
41. Gordon Steger Household, 1940, U.S. Census, Wayne County, Michigan, population schedule, Detroit City, Ward of City 1, Block No. 12, enumeration district [ED] 84-17, supervisor's district [SD] 13, household 251, National Archives micro-publication.
42. *Detroit, Michigan General & Business Directory* 1941, 1709, R. L. Polk & Company; *Detroit, Michigan General & Business Directory* January 1942, 677, R. L. Polk & Company; *Detroit, Michigan General & Business Directory* July 1944, 769, R.L. Polk & Company; Carl Gordon Herbert Steger's World War II Draft Registration Card, Serial Number No. W347.
43. Interview with Kimberly Steger-Sherrill and Dawn Steger-Davey.
44. Veterans' Administration Letter, August 3, 1945, Dearborn, Michigan; *Detroit, Michigan General & Business Directory*, July 1944, 769, R.L. Polk & Company.
45. *Notice of Death and Information for Disposition of Remains*, August 31, 1945, Veterans Administration Supply Form 2237a, Rev. Sept. 1940; Death Certificate, No. 66, Gordon W. Steger, August 31, 1945, Informant: Records Veterans Administration; "Death Notices," Gordon Steger, *Detroit Free Press*, September 2, 1945, 4, Part 4; Dorothy Steger, *Application for Burial Allowance*, September 4, 1945, Claim No. XC 1840 168.
46. Dorothy Anna Steger's *Application for Pension or Compensation by Widow and/or Child of a Deceased Person Who Served in the Active Military or Naval Service of the United States*, Veterans Administration Adjudication Form 534, October 19, 1945.
47. United States World War II Army Enlistment Records, 1938-1946," database, *FamilySearch*, (https://familysearch.org/ark:/61903/1:1:K8GZ-K1C : 5 December 2014), Gordon H Steger, enlisted 04 Oct 1946, Dearborn, Michigan, United States; citing "Electronic Army Serial Number Merged File, ca. 1938-1946," database, *The National Archives: Access to Archival Databases (AAD)* (http://aad.archives.gov: National Archives and Records Administration, 2002); NARA NAID 126323, National Archives at College Park, Maryland; Obituaries, *Detroit Free Press*, December 16, 1947, 25; "Death Takes Mrs. Steger," *Michigan Chronicle*, December 20,

1947, 1.

48. "Gerri Major's Society," Weddings, *Jet*, May 14, 1953, 42.

49. Interview with Kimberly Steger-Sherrill and Dawn Steger-Davey; Gordon H. Steger and Onameega Varner Marriage Record, Marriage Records, Ohio Marriages, *FamilySearch*, Salt Lake City, UT., 1774-1993, Film No. 002251964, online database, Ancestry.com, last accessed on March 26, 2017.

50. Gordon H. Steger and Onameega Varner Marriage Record, Marriage Records, Ohio Marriages, FamilySearch, Salt Lake City, UT., 1774-1993, Film No. 002251964, online database, Ancestry.com, last accessed on March 26, 2017

51. Interview with Kimberly Steger-Sherrill and Dawn Steger-Davey.

52. "Gerri Major's Society,"

53. *1947 Paean Battle Creek Central High School Yearbook*, Ancestry.com, U.S. School Yearbooks, 1880-2012, online database, accessed on March 26, 2017.

54. Gordon H. Steger and Onameega Varner Marriage Record, Marriage Records, Ohio Marriages, FamilySearch, Salt Lake City, UT., 1774-1993, Film No. 002251964, online database, Ancestry.com, last accessed on March 26, 2017.

55. Interview with Kimberly Steger-Sherrill and Dawn Steger-Davey; "United States Public Records, 1970-2009," database, *FamilySearch* (https://familysearch.org/ark:/61903/1:1:KG5J-X35 : 22 May 2014), Carol Steger, Residence, Highland, Michigan, United States; *Detroit Free Press*, May 27, 1974, 8.

56. *Catalog of Copyright Entries, Third Series, Unpublished Music*, January-June 1952, (Washington: The Library of Congress, 1952), 718, 818.

57. *Polk's Detroit West Side City Directory 1957*, R.L. Polk & Co., 1956, Detroit, Michigan, 938.

58. *Catalog of Copyright Entries: Third Series, Music: Current and Renewal Registrations*, July-December 1966, (Washington: The Library of Congress, 1968), 2025, 2130.

59. "Jewell Records - Custom 900 Series & More," 45 RPM Records, accessed on March 2, 2019, http://www.45rpmrecords.com/OH/Jewel2.php.

60. Interview with Kimberly Steger-Sherrill and Dawn Steger-Davey.

61. Interview with Kimberly Steger-Sherrill and Dawn Steger-Davey; "United States Public Records, 1970-2009," database, *FamilySearch* (https://familysearch.org/ark:/61903/1:1:KG5J-X35 : 22 May 2014), Carol Steger, Residence, Highland, Michigan, United States.

62. "Carl Steger Week at the Red Cedars," *The Detroit Jewish News*, September 30, 1983, 32; "Memories of Europe," Saint Georges Restaurant-Pianobar, *Sarasota Herald Tribune*, November 11, 1983, 4-D; "Newtown: Past and Present: 1914-2014," *Newtown Conservation Historic District—Phase 1* Report, Newtown Alive, 13; "Meet the Oral History Interviewees," Newtown Alive, accessed on November 12, 2018, http://www.newtownalive.org/people.

63. "Newtown: Past and Present: 1914-2014," *Newtown Conservation Historic District—Phase 1* Report, Newtown Alive, 4.

64. *Newtown Conservation Historic District—Phase 1* Report, 13, 49-51.

65. *Newtown Conservation Historic District—Phase 1* Report, 13, 51, 55-57, 71, 79.

66. Carl Steger, *Sarasota: Carl Steger - Live at Café L'Europe*, July 10, 1998, Opy Records CD-700-71, 1998, compact disc.

Chapter Three: Dorothy Steger: Like Mother, Like Son—Musically Speaking

1. "Musical Notes," *Detroit Tribune*, August 19, 1933, 4; Gordon Steger and Dorothy Williams, *State of Michigan, Record of County of Calhoun Marriages*, Record No. 485, July 21, 1921, 306-307; Dorothy Anna Steger, *Application for Pension or Compensation by Widow and/or Child of a Deceased Person Who Served in the Active Military or Naval Service of the United States*, Veterans Administration Adjudication Form 534, October 19, 1945; Dorothy Steger, death certificate no. 15151, Michigan Department of Health and Human Services.

2. Robert K. Williams Household, 1900, U.S. Census, Wayne County, Michigan, population schedule, Detroit, enumeration district [ED] 3, supervisor's district [SD] 1, dwelling 82, family 108, National Archives micro-publication.

3. Robert K. Williams Household, 1910, U.S. Census, Hamilton County, Indiana, population schedule, Noblesville Township, enumeration district [ED] 106, supervisor's district [SD] 9, dwelling 87, family 87, National Archives micro-publication; Robert Williams Household, 1920,

U.S. Census, Calhoun County, Michigan, population schedule, Battle Creek Township, enumeration district [ED] 37, supervisor's district [SD] 3, dwelling 253, family 284, National Archives micro-publication; The NOR'WESTER, June 1923, yearbook, Detroit Northwestern High School, 56.

4. Interview with Arthur LaBrew on January 8, 2004.

5. *The NOR'WESTER*, 56.

6. Clarence Monroe Burton, William Stocking, Gordon k. Miller, The City of Detroit, Michigan, 1701-1922, Volume 5, Detroit—Chicago, The S. J. Clarke Publishing Company, 1922, 588.

7. Interview with Arthur LaBrew.

8. Hilanius Phillips, "Statement of Significance," Bertha Hansbury School of Music Historic Designation application, 1975, "James Owen House/Bertha Hansbury Music School," Detroit—The History and Future of the Motor City, accessed on December 28, 2003, http://www.detroit1701.org/Owen-Hansbury%20Home.html.

9. Ibid.

10. "Death Takes Mrs. Steger," *Michigan Chronicle*, December 20, 1947, Detroit, Michigan, Volume 12, Number 39, 1.

11. Interview with Arthur LaBrew.

12. Interview with Patricia Taylor on November 1, 2015.

13. "A.M.E. Conference Here," *The Detroit Independent*, September 16, 1927, 3.

14. *Battle Creek Enquirer*, August 25, 1931.

15. "Social Notes," *Detroit Tribune*, July 22, 1933, 4; "Social Notes," *Detroit Tribune*, January 18, 1936, 5; "Death Takes Mrs. Steger," *Michigan Chronicle*, December 20, 1947, 1; Mission, Heckscher Foundation for Children, accessed on August 25, 2018, https://www.hecksrcherfoundation.org/mission.

16. "Musicians' Association to Sponsor Negro Music Night," *Detroit Tribune*, August 5, 1933, 1; "Belle Isle Musicale Grand Success," *Detroit Tribune*, August 19, 1933, 2.

17. "Music Notes," *Detroit Tribune*, August 19, 1933, 4.

18. Second Baptist Church Historic Site marker, Michigan History Division, Department of State, Registered Local Site No. 346.

19. "Second Baptist Church of Detroit," Detroit: A National Register of Historic Places Travel Itinerary, National Park Service, accessed on October 8, 2017, https://www.nps.gov/nr/travel/detroit/d13.htm.

20. "Social Notes," *Detroit Tribune*, January 18, 1936, 5; August 23-27, 1936 National Convention of The National Association of Negro Musicians, Inc., Detroit, Michigan

21. "Symphonic Hour" to be Sponsored by Clef Club," *Detroit Tribune*, May 16, 1936, 1.

22. "This Is For the Grownups," *Detroit Tribune*, December 10, 1938, 5; "Brewster Center to Start Schedule for Summer Next Week," *Detroit Tribune*, April 1, 1939, 4.

23. "New Light Sr. Choir to Present All Star Musicale," *Detroit Tribune*, March 5, 1938, 9.

24. "Musicians Will Present Musicale at Second Baptist," *Detroit Tribune*, May 14, 1938, 1; "D.M.A. Musicale At Second Bapt. A Fine Success," *Detroit Tribune*, May 21, 1938, 5.

25. "Ancient Songs Mix with the Modern Tunes: Musical Elaboretta Presented at the Art Institute," *Detroit Tribune*, June 4, 1938, 2.

26. Detroit, Michigan General & Business, R.L. Polk & Company, 1938, (p. 1626), 1939 (p. 1589), 1940 (p. 1633), 1941 (p. 1709); "Brewster Center to Start Schedule for Summer Next Week," 4.

27. "Brewster Homes," Michigan Historical Markers, 1995, accessed on October 6, 2005, http://www.michmarkers.com; History.com Staff, "New Deal," 2009, A+E Networks, accessed on October 7, 2017, http://www.history.com/topics/new-deal.

28. Terry Gross, "A 'Forgotten History' Of How the U.S. Government Segregated America," Fresh Air, May 3, 2017, accessed October 7, 2017, http://www.npr.org/2017/05/03/526655831/a-forgotten-history-of-how-the-u-s-government-segregated-america; Robin Schwartz, "Built to separate black and white neighborhoods, the concrete wall still stands today," *The Detroit Jewish News*, January 25, 2017, accessed on June 16, 2018, https://thejewishnews.com/2017/01/25/built-separate-black-white-neighborhoods-concrete-wall-still-stands-today.

29. Gross, "A 'Forgotten History' of How the U.S. Government Segregated America"; Schwartz, "Built to separate black and white neighborhoods, the concrete wall still stands today"

30. The pictures are from the author's collection and were photographed as the "Detroit Wall" faces the Alfonso Wells Memorial Playground on Birwood Street; *The Detroit Jewish News*, January 25, 2017; "The 8 Mile Wall," The Detroiturbex.com, accessed on June 30, 2018, http://www.detroiturbex.com/content/neighborhoods/8milewall/index.html.

31. "Brewster Homes," Michigan Historical Markers.
32. "In Center of Brewster," *Detroit Tribune*, November 7, 1942, 10.
33. "Brewster Group Prepare for Colorful Eve," *Detroit Tribune*, October 31, 1942, 3.
34. "Music Teacher for City Dies," *Detroit Times*, December 1947, C-25.
35. "Musical Benefit for Paralysis Victim to be Held on Jan 26," *Detroit Tribune*, January 23, 1943, 2.
36. "The 'Stars' Shine Bright and Musically," *Detroit Tribune*, March 21, 1943, 5.
37. Dorothy Anna Steger's *Application for Pension or Compensation by Widow and/or Child of a Deceased Person Who Served in the Active Military or Naval Service of the United States*, Veterans Administration Adjudication Form 534, October 19, 1945; "'On the Beam' With Youth Councils," *The Crisis*, December 1945, 360.
38. "Musical Program of Jubilee Filled with Famed Stars," *Detroit Free Press*, May 26, 1946, 18.
39. Interview with Dr. Jiam Desjardins on November 27, 2003; Interview with Patricia Taylor on November 1, 2015.
40. Interview with Arthur LaBrew.
41. "History," National Association of Negro Musicians, accessed on February 18, 2018, https://www.nanm.org/about.
42. "History," National Association of Negro Musicians; Adam Green, "National Association of Negro Musicians," *The Electronic Encyclopedia of Chicago*, 2005, Chicago Historical Society; The Encyclopedia of Chicago, 2004, The Newberry Library, accessed on February 18, 2018, http://www.encyclopedia.chicagohistory.org/pages/871.html.
43. "National Association of Negro Musicians," *Encyclopedia of African-American Culture and History*, Encyclopedia.com, accessed on February 18, 2018, http://www.encyclopedia.com/history/encyclopedias-almanacs-transcripts-and-maps/national-association-negro-musicians; Cary D. Wintz and Paul Finkelman, *Encyclopedia of the Harlem Renaissance: Volume 2, K-Y*, Routledge, New York, London, Taylor & Francis Books, Inc., 2004, 901.
44. "Death Takes Mrs. Steger," 1, Photographer unknown.
45. Dorothy Steger, death certificate.
46. "Music Teacher for City Dies," C-25.
47. Fred Hart Williams, Historic Elmwood Cemetery & Foundation, accessed on July 22, 2018, https://www.elmwoodhistoriccemetery.org/biographies/fred-hart-williams.

Chapter Four: The Conversion

1. Interview with Gerald Steger on April 8, 2001.
2. Interview with Patricia Taylor on November 2, 2015.
3. Interview with Kimberly Sherrill on May 21, 2005 according to the family's oral history.
4. "Our Clergy at Adat Shalom Synagogue," Adat Shalom Synagogue, accessed on October 14, 2016, http://adatshalom.org/about/clergy; Interview with Rabbi Aaron Bergman on August 29, 2016.
5. "Charles E. Coughlin," Holocaust Encyclopedia, United States Holocaust Memorial Museum, accessed on October 1, 2016, https://encyclopedia.ushmm.org/content/en/article/charles-e-coughlin.
6. Patricia Montemurri, "Shrine's glory comes with shadows from its past," *Detroit Free Press*, April 20, 2015, accessed on October 1, 2016, http://www.freep.com/story/news/local/michigan/2015/04/20/shrines-glory-comes-shadows-past/26051945.
7. Montemurri, "Shrine's glory comes with shadows from its past."
8. Interview with Rabbi Aaron Bergman; gotQuestions?org, "What is Judaism and what do Jews believe?," Got Questions Ministries, accessed on August 27, 2016, SOURCEhttp://www.gotquestions.org/Judaism.html.
9. Ibid.
10. Campbell Robertson, Christopher Mele and Sabrina Tavernise, "11 Killed in Synagogue Massacre; Suspect Charged With 29 Counts," *The New York Times*, October 27, 2018, accessed on November 7, 2018, https://www.nytimes.com/2018/10/27/us/active-shooter-pittsburgh-synagogue-shooting.html; Shelly Bradbury, "Timeline of terror: A moment-by-moment account of Squirrel Hill mass shooting," *Pittsburgh Post-Gazette*, October 28, 2018, accessed on November 7, 2018, http://www.post-gazette.com/news/crime-courts/2018/10/28/

TIMELINE-20-minutes-of-terror-gripped-Squirrel-Hill-during-Saturday-synagogue-attack/
stories/201810280197.

11. Mallory Simon and Sara Sidnor, "A gunman slaughtered 11 Jewish worshippers. Then people hunted for hate online," CNN, May 15, 2019, accessed on May 18, 2019, https://www.cnn.com/2019/05/15/us/anti-semitic-searches-pittsburgh-poway-shootings-soh/index.html.

12. Interview with Rabbi Aaron Bergman; Kate Connolly, *the guardian*, "Joseph Goebbels' 105-year-old secretary: 'No one believes me now, but I knew nothing,'" August 15, 2016, accessed on October 11, 2016., https://www.theguardian.com/world/2016/aug/ 15/brunhilde-pomsel-nazi-joseph-goebbels-propaganda-machine.

13. The United States 38th president Gerald Ford pardoned his predecessor Richard Nixon for his involvement with the infamous Watergate scandal. His decision was met with major controversy and "some critics charged that Ford issued the pardon as part of a pre-arranged deal to reach the Oval Office, but Ford insisted that the nation's future hinged on ending the ordeal of Watergate and beginning the process of healing."; "Gerald Ford," HISTORY, A&E Television Networks, February 15, 2019, accessed on March 28, 2019, https://www.history.com/topics/us-presidents/gerald-r-ford.

14. The "birther" or "birtherism" conspiracy theory was reported to have begun in 2004 and claimed that Barack Obama was a private Muslim was not born in United States. During Obama's 2008 presidential campaign, "some hardcore (Hillary) Clinton backers circulated the rumors," but her campaign said they were not involved. However, Donald Trump continued in 2011 to discredit President Obama by bringing into question his legitimacy to be the United States President because of his lack of proof of being a natural-born citizen which is a requirement for the elected position; After Obama released his long-form birth certificate on April 27, 2011, Trump conceded several months later that "President Barack Obama was born in the United States. Period." Afterward, Trump falsely blamed his 2016 presidential opponent Hillary Clinton of originating the birther issue.

15. Interview with Rabbi Aaron Bergman.

16. MJL Staff, "Judaism," My Jewish Learning, accessed on October 1, 2016. http://www.myjewishlearning.com/article/judaism.

17. MJL Staff, "Conversion 101," My Jewish Learning, accessed on October 1, 2016, http://www.myjewishlearning.com/article/conversion-101.

18. Interview with Charles Domstein on August 29,2019.

19. "Arlyn Meyerson," *Jewish Deaf Community Center*, Jewish Deaf Business, November/December 2000 Issue, accessed on April 15, 2005, http://www.jdcc.org/index.php?option=com_content&view=article&id=736:jewish-deaf-business&catid=282&Itemid=283.

20. Ibid.

21. "Arlyn Meyerson."; Kathleen Brockway, *Images of America: Detroit's Deaf Heritage*, (Charleston, South Carolina: Arcadia Publishing, 2016), 88, 100, 104.

22. Danny Raskin, "The Best of Everything," *The Detroit Jewish News*. March 2, 1973, 22.

23. "Arlyn Meyerson."

24. "Dedicated to Family, the Deaf Community and his Diners," Soul of blessed Memory, *Detroit Jewish News*, October 4-10, 2018, 66.

25. Interview with Charles Boles on September 29, 2015.

26. Interview with Mark Meyerson on October 28, 2014.

27. Interview with Kimberly Steger-Sherrill.

28. Scott Burnstein, "Mafia associate's death remains a mystery after almost 40 years (with video)," *Macomb Daily*, September 30, 2013, accessed on March 9, 2016, http://www.macombdaily.com/article/MD/20130930/NEWS/130939998; Scott Burnstein, "Detroit LCN Leach Hit Will Never Be Solved: Schultz's Death Closes Book on Ever Cracking Case," Gangster Report, 2014, accessed on March 9, 2016, http://gangsterreport.com/detroit-lcns-leach-slaying-will-never-solved.

29. Interview with Kimberly Steger-Sherrill.

30. Interview with Charles Boles.

31. "Jimmy Hoffa Biography," Biography.com, April 27, 2017, accessed on November 11, 2018, http://www.biography.com/people/jimmy-hoffa-9341063.

32. "A Worker's Hero: The Life and Legacy of James R. Hoffa," Teamsters, accessed on November 14, 2018, https://teamster.org/content/worker%E2%80%99s-hero-life-and-legacy-james-r-hoffa.

33. "Jimmy Hoffa," Federal Bureau of Investigation, 55, 79; "Jimmy Hoffa disappeared 40 years ago, *The Detroit News*, July 30, 2015, accessed on November 14, 2018, https://www.detroitnews.com/story/news/local/michigan/2015/07/30/jimmy-hoffa-disappeared-years-ago/30871061.

34. Ibid.

35. Jonathan Kwitny, "Suspects in Hoffa's Disappearance Are Really Feeling the Heat," *Wall Street Journal*.

36. "Jimmy Hoffa," Federal Bureau of Investigation, Freedom of Information/Privacy Acts Section document, 87, accessed on October 9, 2018.

37. "Jimmy Hoffa" 22-23, 79.

38. "Jimmy Hoffa" 35, accessed on October 31, 2018.

39. "Jimmy Hoffa" 95.

40. "Jimmy Hoffa" 97.

41. Ibid.

42. "A Worker's Hero: The Life and Legacy of James R. Hoffa."

43. "Jimmy Hoffa disappeared 40 years ago."

44. "Jimmy Hoffa" headlines in various newspaper pages.

Chapter Five: "Guess Who's Coming to Dinner?"

1. Interview with Charles Boles on October 2, 2015.

2. Interview with an unidentified and former Highland, Michigan neighbor of Carl Steger on May 1, 2005.

3. Interview with Fred Lemke on May 1, 2005.

4. Interview with Lois Moore on May 1, 2005.

5. Interview with Barbara Wolfe on May 1, 2005.

6. Interviews with Dawn Steger-Davey and Kimberly Steger-Sherrill on May 2, 2005.

7. Interview with Kimberly Steger-Sherrill on May 3, 2005.

8. "Guess Who's Coming to Dinner (1967)," IMDb, last accessed on May 15, 2017, http://www.imdb.com/title/tt0061735; Jeffrey Fleishman, "'Guess Who's Coming to Dinner is 50' and racial tension still a problem in America," *Los Angeles Times*, February 2, 2017, last accessed on May 15, 2017, http://www.latimes.com/entertainment/movies/la-ca-guess-dinner-anniversary-20170131-story.html; Roger Ebert, "Guess Who's Coming to Dinner," Roger Ebert.com, January 25, 1968, last accessed on May 15, 2017, http://www.rogerebert.com/reviews/guess-whos-coming-to-dinner-1968.

9. Interviews with Dawn Steger-Davey and Kimberly Steger-Sherrill on May 21, 2005.

10. Sammy Davis, Jr., "Is My Mixed Marriage Mixing Up My Kids?" *Ebony*, October 1966, Johnson Publishing Company, 124, 130-131.

11. "Sammy Davis Jr. (1925-1990)," Jewish Virtual Library, accessed on December 16, 2014, http://www.jewishvirtuallibrary.org/jsource/biography/sammydavis.html.; "Sammy Davis Jr.," Biography, accessed on December 16, 2014, http://www.biography.com/people/sammy-davis-jr-9268223#commercial-success; "Eddie Cantor (1882-1964)," Jewish Virtual Library, accessed on December 16, 2014, http://www.jewishvirtuallibrary.org/jsource/biography/Cantor.html; Interview with Rabbi Aaron Bergman on August 29, 2016 concerning Judaism as a "peoplehood" comprising of a faith, nationality and culture.

12. The Official Sammy Davis Jr website, Bio, accessed on December 16, 2014, http://www.sammydavis-jr.com/#!?page_id=6; "Spingarn Medal Winners: 1915 to Today," 1968: Sammy Davis, Jr., accessed on December 16, 2014, http://www.naacp.org/awards/spingarn-medal/winners.

13. Interviews with Dawn Steger-Davey and Kimberly Steger-Sherrill on May 21, 2005; Note: Portions of the interview could not be transcribed due to some of the audio recording being undistinguishable because of occasional background noise.

14. JC Reindl, "Ollie Fretter, colorful founder of Fretter Appliances, dead at 91," *Detroit Free Press*, July 1, 2014, accessed on December 3, 2015; Oliver Fretter Obituary, A.J. Desmond & Sons Funeral Director, accessed on December 3, 2015, www.desmondfuneralhome.com/obituary/Oliver-Ollie-Fretter/_/1395210; Note: Ollie Fretter was the "colorful" founder and president of the major Detroit area appliance and electronics

retail store chain during the early 1950s. He "was a pioneer for zany marketing and advertising" and known for the phrase "I'll give you five pounds of coffee if I can't beat your best deal."; Interview with Dawn Steger-Davey and Kimberly Steger-Sherrill.

15. Susan Whitall, "Bill Bonds, iconic Channel 7 news anchor, dies," *The Detroit News*, December 14, 2014, accessed on August 5, 2018, https://www.detroitnews.com/story/entertainment/television/2014/12/13/bill-bonds-veteran-channel-action-news-anchor-dies/20372045; Bill Bonds was best known as a television news anchor and reporter in Detroit, Michigan between mid-1960s and until 1995 after his dismissal from WXYT-Channel 7 due to his alcoholic substance abuse.; Interviews with Dawn Steger-Davey and Kimberly Steger-Sherrill.
16. Interview with Dawn Steger-Davey and Kimberly Steger-Sherrill.

Chapter 6: Racial Passing: The Dark Secret in Whiteface

1. "Blackface: The Birth of An American Stereotype," National Museum of African American History & Culture, Smithsonian, accessed on May 19, 2019; https://nmaahc.si.edu/blog-post/blackface-birth-american-stereotype.
2. *Oxford English Dictionary*, (United Kingdom: Oxford University Press, 1989).
3. Gordon W. Steger's August 31, 1945 Death Certificate, No. 66, Informant: Records Veterans Administration; Dorothy Steger's Death Certificate, No. 15151, Informant: Arley Williams; "Death Takes Mrs. Steger," *Michigan Chronicle*, December 20, 1947, 1; Interview with Patricia Taylor on November 2, 2015.
4. Jennifer Soong, "6 Common Depression Traps to Avoid," WebMD, accessed on February 24, 2016, http://www.webmd.com/depression/features/depression-traps-and-pitfalls.
5. "Death Notices," *Detroit Free Press*, September 2, 1945, 4, Part 4.
6. Alice Walker, *In Search of Our Mothers' Gardens: Womanist Prose*, (San Diego: Harcourt Brace Jovanovich, 1983), 291.
7. Ibram x. Kendi, "Colorism as Racism: Garvey, Du Bois and the Other Color Line," Black Perspectives, May 24, 2017, accessed on May 24, 2017, http://www.aaihs.org/colorism-as-racism-garvey-du-bois-and-the-other-color-line.
8. "The Back Story: How the Brown Paper Bag Carried 'The Color Complex' From Slavery Forward," April 22, 2018, accessed on October 7, 2018, https://blackthen.com/the-back-story-how-the-brown-paper-bag-carried-the-color-complex-from-slavery-forward; Skin-Deep Discrimination, ABC News, March 4, 2005, last accessed on October 7, 2018https://abcnews.go.com/2020/GiveMeABreak/story?id=548303&page=1.
9. Charles W. Chesnett, *The Wife of His Youth and Other Stories of the Color Line*, (Cambridge: The Riverside Press, 1901), 1-2.
10. Ibid.
11. Ibid.
12. Henry Louis Gates Jr. and Cornel West, *Future of the Race*, (New York City: Vintage, 1996). Dr. David Pilgrim, "Brown Paper Bag Test – February 2014," Jim Crow Museum of Racist Memorabilia, Ferris State University, accessed on October 7, 2018, https://ferris.edu/HTMLS/news/jimcrow/question/2014/february.htm.
13. "Brown Paper Bag Test – February 2014."
14. Elaine Latzman Moon, *Untold Tales, Unsung Heroes: An Oral History of Detroit's African American Community, 1918-1967*, (Detroit: Wayne State University Press, 1994), 82.
15. Interview with Charles Boles on October 2, 2015.
16. "The Significance of 'The Doll Test,'" Legal Defense and Educational Fund, accessed on October 25, 2019, https://www.naacpldf.org/ldf-celebrates-60th-anniversary-brown-v-board-education/significance-doll-test.
17. "The Significance of 'The Doll Test.'"; "Key Excerpts from the Majority Opinion, Brown I (1954)," Landmark Cases of the U.S. Supreme Court, Street Law, accessed on October 25, 2019, https://www.landmarkcases.org/brown-v-board-of-education/key-excerpts-from-the-majority-opinion-brown-i-1954; "The Doll Test for Racial Self-Hate: Did It Ever Make Sense?," The Root, May 17, 2014, accessed on October 25, 2019, https://www.theroot.com/the-doll-test-for-racial-self-hate-did-it-ever-make-se-1790875716.
18. Interview with Charles Boles.
19. Rebekah Kebede, "Why Black Women in a Predominately Black Culture Are Still Bleaching Their Skin," Marie Claire, June 21, 2017, accessed on September 3, 2018,

https://www.marieclaire.com/beauty/a27678/skin-bleaching-epidemic-in-jamaica; Britni
Danielle, "Proof We're Not Post-Racial: People Are Paying $10 Billion a Year to Be Lighter,"
TakePart, January 23, 2015, accessed on September 3, 2018, http://www.takepart.com/article/
2015/01/23/beauty-companies-are-making-bank-selling-skin-lighteners-around-globe; G.P.
"Lighter Shades of Skin," The Economist, September 28, 2012, accessed on September 3, 2018,
https://www.economist.com/baobab/2012/09/28/lighter-shades-of-skin.

20. "Black America's 'bleaching syndrome,'" The Conversation, February 2, 2018, last accessed on
September 3, 2018, https://theconversation.com/black-americas-bleaching-syndrome-82200.

21. Interview with Brenda (Steger) Willis and Carolyn (Steger) Kimball on August 22, 2018.

22. Ibram x. Kendi, "Colorism as Racism: Garvey, Du Bois and the Other Color Line," Black
Perspectives, May 24, 2017, accessed on May 24, 2017, http://www.aaihs.org/colorism-as-
racism-garvey-du-bois-and-the-other-color-line.

23. Interviews with Charles Boles on April 7, 2005 and October 2, 2015.

24. Allyson Hobbs, A Chosen Exile: A History of Passing in American Life, (Cambridge and
London: Harvard University Press, 2014), 7; IMDb, accessed February 25, 2016,
http://www.imdb.com.

25. "Movie Fame and Fortune Await Unknown Negro Lass," Jet, November 13, 1958,
60-61.

26. Willis Steger household, 1880 U.S. census, Madison County, Alabama, population schedule,
Township 3, R 2. W. Beat 3, Page 17, enumeration district [ED] 222, supervisor's district [SD]
1, dwelling 2, family 2, National Archives micro-publication; Molly Steger household, 1900 U.S.
census, Madison County, Alabama, population schedule, Maysville, enumeration district [ED]
104, supervisor's district [SD] 8, sheet 6 A, dwelling 97, family 97, National Archives micro-
publication; Death related records for Leroy and Gordon Steger name their father as "William
Steger"; Richard Bohannon household, 1910 U.S. census, Madison County, Alabama,
population schedule, Precinct 1, East of Meridian and Whitesburg excluding Huntsville town,
enumeration district [ED] 113, supervisor's district [SD] 8, sheet 3 B, dwelling 68, family 70,
National Archives micro-publication, Note: Nicholas Bohanon was listed by his middle name as
"Richard" in the record; Gordon Steger and Dorothy Williams, State of Michigan, Record of
County of Calhoun Marriages, Record No. 485, July 21, 1921, 306-307; Gordon William
Steger's Social Security Application, January 1937.

27. Interview with Ophelia Steger on November 26, 2001.

28. Lorraine Elena Roses and Ruth Elizabeth Randolph, Harlem's Glory: Black Women Writing,
1900-1950 (Cambridge, Massachusetts and London, England: Harvard University Press, 1996),
59; Quoted from Mary Church Sherrill's unpublished manuscript Why, How, When and Where
Black Becomes White, Moorland-Spingarn Research Center, Howard University, n.d.

29. Interview with Patricia Taylor January 8, 2002.

30. Interview with Ophelia Steger.

31. Interviews with Patricia Taylor on January 8, 2002 and November 1, 2015; The Detroiter,
Volume 11, April 24, 1916, 6.

32. Allyson Hobbs, A Chosen Exile: A History of Passing in American Life [Cambridge and
London: Harvard University Press, 2014]; Dana Christine Volk, "Passing: Intersections of Race,
Gender, Class and Sexuality," 2017, accessed on February 9, 2019,
https://vtechworks.lib.vt.edu/bitstream/handle/10919/78449/Volk_DC_D_2017.pdf?sequence=1.

33. Lisa Page, "Before Passing Away, Carol Channing Passed for White," Beacon Broadside-
Beacon Press, January 24, 2019, accessed on February 9, 2019;
https://www.beaconbroadside.com/broadside/2019/01/before-passing-away-carol-channing-
passed-for-white.html; Carol Channing, Just Lucky I Guess: A Memoir of Sorts, [New York:
Simon & Schuster, 2002]; Jane Wollman Rusoff, "At 82, Channing still in step," Chicago
Tribune, May 22, 2003, accessed on February 9, 2019, https://www.chicagotribune.com/news/ct-
xpm-2003-05-22-0305220078-story.html.

34. "Before Passing Away, Carol Channing Passed for White"; Gentlemen Prefer Blondes, lyrics by
Leo Robin, music by Jule Styne, dir. John C. Wilson, Ziegfeld Theatre, New York, NY,
December 8, 1949; Note: The "Great White Way" is a nickname for the theatre district of
Broadway in the Midtown section of New York City between 42nd and 53rd Streets.

35. "Before Passing Away, Carol Channing Passed for White"

36. "At 82, Channing still in step."; "Before Passing Away, Carol Channing Passed for White."

37. Hobbs, A Chosen Exile: A History of Passing in American Life, 18.

38. Ibid.

39. Hobbs, *A Chosen Exile: A History of Passing in American Life*, 27.
40. Robert P. Stuckert, "African Ancestry of the White Population," [The Ohio Journal of Science. V58 n3, May 1958], 155, 159, accessed on July 30, 2016, https://kb.osu.edu/dspace/bitstream/handle/1811/4532/V58N03_155.pdf.
41. African Ancestry of the White Population, 158.
42. Nathan Irvin Huggins and Brenda Smith Huggins, *Revelations: American History, American Myths*, (New York & Oxford: Oxford University Press, 1995), 245-246.
43. Robert Fikes, Jr., "The Passing of Passing: A Peculiarly American Racial Tradition Approaches Irrelevance," BlackPast.org, December 30, 2014, accessed on June 3, 2017, http://www.blackpast.org/perspectives/passing-passing-peculiarly-american-racial-tradition-approaches-irrelevance.
44. 23andMe, "An analysis of the ancestry make-up of people across the United States," 23andMeBlog, December 18, 2014, accessed on May 22, 2018, https://blog.23andme.com/23andme-research/history-written-in-our-dna.
45. Henry Louis Gates Jr., "How Many 'White' People Are Passing?," The Root, March 17, 2014, accessed on June 3, 2017, http://www.theroot.com/how-many-white-people-are-passing-1790874972; Scott H, "DNA USA," 23andMeBlog, accessed on June 3, 2017, https://blog.23andme.com/23andme-research/dna-usa-2.
46. "How Many 'White' People Are Passing?"
47. Michelle Gordon Jackson, *Light, Bright and Damn Near White*, [JacksonScribe Publishing Company, 2014], 1.
48. Gordon Jackson, *Light, Bright and Damn Near White*, 329.
49. Ibid.
50. "Loving v. Virginia, 388 U.S. 1 (1967)," Justia, accessed on January 13, 2019, https://supreme.justia.com/cases/federal/us/388/1; "Loving V. Virginia," HISTORY, A&E Television Networks, November 17, 2017, accessed on January 13, 2019, https://www.history.com/topics/civil-rights-movement/loving-v-virginia.
51. Langston Hughes, *The Big Sea: An Autobiography by Langston Hughes*, (New York & London: Alfred A. Knopf, 1940), 36.
52. Langston Hughes, *The Collected Works of Langston Hughes: Essays on Art, Race, Politics, and World Affairs, Volume 9*, (Columbia & London: University of Missouri Press, 2002), 314.
53. Note: The 44th president of the United States Barack Hussein Obama is widely recognized as the first black person to hold the position. However, debates exist among historians as to which persons were the country's first black president from John Hanson to Dwight D. Eisenhower. If the DNA testing technology existed back then as it does today, perhaps Obama may not be the first president with African ancestry; Interview with Charles Boles on October 2, 2015.
54. Ibid.
55. Hobbs, *A Chosen Exile: A History of Passing in American Life*, 159.
56. Obituaries of Blessed Memory, *Detroit Jewish News, The*, April 21-27, 2022, 69.
57. "In Depth with Imani Perry," C-SPAN 2, Book TV, November 3, 2019, accessed on November 14, 2019, https://www.c-span.org/video/?465328-1/depth-imani-perry.
58. "Dr. Martin Luther King's visit to Cornell College," quote from speech at Cornell College, Mount Vernon, Iowa, October 15, 1962, accessed on November 12, 2019, https://news.cornellcollege.edu/dr-martin-luther-kings-visit-to-cornell-college; Martin Luther King, Jr., *Strength to Love*, [New York, Evanston & London: Harper & Row, 1963]; Martin Luther King, Jr, "A Proper Since of Priorities," Washington, D.C, February 6, 1968, African-American Involvement in the Vietnam War, accessed on November 12, 2019, http://www.aavw.org/special_features/speeches_speech_king04.html; Martin Luther King, Jr., quote from "I Have a Dream" speech in Washington, D.C., 1963, accessed on November 12, 2019; https://www.archives.gov/files/press/exhibits/dream-speech.pdf; Clayborne Carson et al., *The Papers of Martin Luther King, Jr., Volume VI: Advocate of the Social* Gospel, September 1948-March 1963, [Berkeley & Los Angeles: University of California Press, 2007]; Dr. Martin Luther King, Jr., quote from speech in St. Louis, March 22, 1964 in *St. Louis Post-Dispatch*, March 23, 1964; Martin Luther King, Jr., "Live together as brothers or perish together as fools," video excerpt of King's March 22, 1964 speech in St. Louis, YouTube, accessed on November 12, 2019. https://www.youtube.com/watch?v=bNPpEQkep2k, audio transcribed by the author.
59. Clayborne Carson et al., *The Papers* . . .

Chapter Seven: A Tribute and Historical Collage through
Newspaper Advertisements and Articles

1. Elaine Latzman Moon, *Untold Tales, Unsung Heroes: An Oral History of Detroit's African American Community, 1918-1967*, (Detroit: Wayne State University Press, 1994), 322.
2. Ila Mae Boyd, "Brewster Notes," *Michigan Chronicle*, February 19, 1939, 9.
3. *The Detroit Free Press*, March 29, 1960, 20.
4. "Places to Go...to Dine and Dance...," *The State Journal*, July 16, 1960, 16.
5. *The Detroit Free Press*, October 7, 1960, 19.
6. *The Detroit Free Press*, March 25, 1973, 136.

BIBLIOGRAPHY

Austin Powers in Goldmember. Directed by Jay Roach. 2002. Los Angeles, CA: Warner Bros. Film.

Bjorn, Lars, and Jim Gallert. *Before Motown: A History of Jazz in Detroit, 1920 to 1960*. Michigan: University of Michigan Regional, 2001.

Carson, Clayborne, Susan Carson, Susan Englander, Troy Jackson and Gerald L. Smith. *The Papers of Martin Luther King, Jr., Volume VI: Advocate of the Social Gospel, September 1948-March 1963*. Berkeley & Los Angeles: University of California Press, 2007.

Gentlemen Prefer Blondes. Directed by John C. Wilson. 1949. New York, NY: Ziegfeld Theatre. Musical.

Guess Who's Coming to Dinner? Directed by Stanley Kramer. 1967. Los Angeles, CA: Columbia Pictures. Film.

Hello, Dolly! Directed by Gower Champion. 1963. Detroit, MI: Fisher Theater. Musical.

Hobbs, Allyson, *A Chosen Exile: A History of Racial Passing in American Life*. Massachusetts: Harvard University Press, 2014.

Huggins, Nathan Irvin, *Revelations*. New York & Oxford: Oxford University Press, 1995.

Hughes, Langston, The Big Sea: An Autobiography, New York: Hill and Wang, 1940.

Imitation of Life. Directed by John M. Stahl. 1934. Universal City, CA: Universal Studios. Film.

Imitation of Life. Directed by Douglas Sirk. 1959. Universal City, CA: Universal Studios. Film.

I Passed for White. Directed by Fred M. Wilcox. 1960. Los Angeles, CA: Allied Artists Pictures. Film.

King, Martin Luther, Jr., *Strength to Love*. New York, Evanston & London: Harper & Row, 1963.

Lost Boundaries. Directed by Alfred L. Werker. 1949. Newington, NH: Louis De Rochemont Associates. Film.

Marchese, David, "In Conversation: Quincy Jones," *Vulture*, February 7, 2018, http://www.vulture.com/2018/02/quincy-jones-in-conversation.html.

Moon, Elaine Latzman, *Untold Tales, Unsung Heroes: An Oral History of Detroit's African American Community, 1918-1967*. Michigan: Wayne State University Press, 1994.

Pinky. Directed by Elia Kazan. 1949. Los Angeles, CA: 20th Century Fox. Film.

Sachar, Abram Leon, *A History of the Jews*. New York: Alfred A. Knopf, 1940.

Willis, Eric B., *The Willis Handbook: An Intersection of Genealogy, Memoirs and History of a Black American Family – 1835-2003*. Michigan: Panoply House of Publishing, 2014.

ACKNOWLEDGMENTS

- Linda (Robinson) Scandrick—for your kindness with allowing me to see the likeness of my great-grandfather Leroy Steger, Sr. for the very first time

- Gerald Steger—who being the first to express your insightful memory of our cousin Carl Steger

- Patricia Taylor—for your openness with sharing the wonderful history of our Steger ancestors

- Dr. Jiam Desjardins—for your shared memories of Carl and a part of Detroit's history involving Paradise Valley during the 20th century

- Lars Bjorn and Jim Gallert—for your vast knowledge of Detroit's jazz history and for sharing your early and helpful suggestions which put me on a path of immense discovery

- Naima Shamborguer—for providing me with key bits of knowledge which assisted me with connecting one puzzle piece to another—crossing one bridge over to another

- Charles Boles—for being very hospitable and inviting me into your workspace and into your lovely home; for being an invaluable source of information; for allowing me to enjoy and listen as you and your wife iterate a hodgepodge of gratifying and sometimes troubling memories of your lives long past; and for entertaining me and the masses with your tremendous gift of musical creativity

- Kimberly Steger-Sherrill and Dawn Steger-Davey—for having an enthusiastic quest for knowledge and for the suggestion to make face-to-face familial connections under uncomfortable and unforeseen circumstances

- Rabbi Aaron Bergman—for your willingness to share with me the breadth and depth of your culture, nationality, faith, and other personal ideologies

- The Motown Writers Network group in Detroit which I am a member of, including my crew Sylvia Hubbard (founder and host), Walter O'Bryant and Wayne Bibbs, and a myriad of writers from the novice to the professional—supporting and networking with one another

- Andrea Gallucci—for providing me with your knowledge of wonderful and additional untapped areas of research sources

- Dr. Charles Domstein—for the review of your archived material and for your additional and personal insight into Rabbi Aaron Bergman

- Phyllis (Steger) Torrence—for our wonderful conversations and incites about the Steger family history and the invaluable family photographs

- Tia Ross and Gary Torgerson—for your magnificent editorial enhancements for this project

- My beta readers, i.e., Wayne A. Bibbs, Kathryn Curreathers, and Walter O'Bryant—for your wonderful reviews and helpful incites

- Samuel and Brenda Willis—my parents—for your love and continuous encouragement and support

- Patricia Willis—my beautiful wife and treasure—for your love and unwavering support during this journey; my beautiful daughter Tanessa—for your patience while listening intently as I proof read my draft copies; my beautiful daughter Marissa—for me believing that you will be gratified by this project's results; and my 80 lb. plus pyredoodle Gabriel who eagerly seeks my attention for a daily fur-rub-down after my arrival home from work

INDEX

Allen, Johnny, 227
Allinger, Charles E., 208-209

Battle Creek Central High School, 31-32, 58, 65
Battle Creek, Michigan, 31, 56, 65, 72, 164
    Reese Cemetery, 57, 89-90, 189
    Sojourner Truth's home in (1866), 31
Battle Creek Enquirer, 54, 72, 90
Beethoven, Ludwig van, 237
bell's palsy, 26
Bergman, Aaron. *See* Judaism
Bjorn, Lars, 4-7
Black Bottom. *See* Detroit, Michigan
Black Hebrews. *See* Judaism
Boles, Charles, 6, 9-26, 128, 135, 141, 149-150, 166, 168, 196-198, 200, 206, 212, 224-234, 237-240
    career of, 10, 12-20, 24-25, 128, 195-198, 200, 212, 224-234, 237-239
    family history of, 13, 195, 228, 231-232, 234, 237, 240
Bohanon, George R., 31, 189
Bohanon, Nicey, 2, 207, 212
Bohanon, Nicholas, 2, 207, 212
Brewster Homes. *See* Detroit, Michigan
Brown v. Board of Education of Topeka (1954), 199
Bryc, Katarzyna "Kasia." *See* Racial Passing
    DNA studies and revelations
Byrd, Sarah Anna, 54

Carver, George Washington, 36
Channing, Carol. *See* racial passing
Chesnutt, Charles Waddell, 190-191
Clark, Kenneth and Mamie, 198-200
Cortez, Carlos, 227
Cox, Kenneth, II, 28-29

Davis, Sammy, Jr., 146-149, 255-256
    see also Judaism
Desjardins, Jiam, 3-4, 87, 212
Detroit Conservatory of Music (formally Detroit College of Music), 28, 65-68
    Hahn, J. H., 65, 68
    history of, 65, 68-69
Detroit Federation of Musicians – AFM Local 5 (union), 6-7, 9, 11, 172
Detroit Free Press, 6, 63, 134, 150, 189, 247-248, 266
Detroit Jewish News, The, 27, 80, 131, 148, 156, 173-174, 245, 255

Detroit, Michigan, 36, 41, 49-50
    demographics, 37, 41, 43
        blacks, 36-38, 41
        southern migration into, 37, 44, 46
    history of (since 1926), 42-46
    jobs in the automobile industry, 36-37, 43
        Ford Motor Company, 36, 43
        mass production, 36, 43
    Paradise Valley, 3-4, 52
        Hastings Street, 4, 24, 52
        map, 53
    open-shop town (no unions), 49-50
    racism,
        discrimination in:
            jobs, 40
            judicial system, 48-50
            police and violence, 45, 50
        Ku Klux Klan (KKK), 41, 45
        segregation in housing, 36-38, 45
            A.L. Turner riot, 45
            Black Bottom, 23, 38, 37-38, 52-53, 195
            FHA (Federal Housing Administration), 79-80
            Brewster Homes, The, 78
                history of, 79, 82
            Detroit Wall. *Also known as* "Wailing Wall" and "Eight Mile Wall," 79-81
            New Deal, The (President Roosevelt), 50, 79
            redlining policy, 79
        Jewish and black ghettos, 47
        Ossian Sweet case, 38-40, 45-46
Detroit News, The, 6, 91, 150
Detroit Tribune, 41-42, 77-78, 85, 87, 94, 205, 246
Dockstader, Lew, 188
Duke, John. *Also known as* John Samuel, 10, 26

Farrakhan, Louis, 17
Fikes, Robert, Jr., 218-219
Ford, Henry, 36, 40, 43
Franklin, Aretha, 18-19, 24

Gallert, Jim, 4-7, 10
Gates, Henry Louis, Jr., 193, 220-221
Giacalone, Anthony, 18, 131-133
    see also James Hoffa's mobster associations
Goodman, Ernest, 47-51
    National Lawyers Guild, 47, 49
Great Depression, The, 33, 48, 79

Great Depression, The, (continued)
effects on the black population, 35, 48,
69-70
New Deal, The, 79
Green, Pauline, 206-207
"Guess Who's Coming to Dinner?" (film), 146

Hansbury, Bertha, 69
Bertha Hansbury School of Music, 69, 71
Household Art Guild, The, 69-70
Hitler, Adolph, 237
Hobbs, Allyson, 187, 215-216, 240
Hoffa, James Riddle. Also known as Jimmy
Hoffa, 133, 135-139
his disappearance, 135-136, 138, 210,
229
International Brotherhood of Teamsters
(union), 135-138
Labor's International Hall of Fame, 138
mobster associations of, 136-138
Huggins, Nathan Irvin, 216-218
Hughes, Langston, 222-224

I Passed for White (film), 206-207

Judaism, 104
anti-Semitism, 105, 108, 116, 118
Coughlin, Charles E., 105-106
Ford, Henry, 43, 106
see also Henry Ford
Goebbels, Herman Joseph, 118-119
Brunhilde Pomsel (secretary of), 119
threats and violence, 116-117
increase in, 117
worst Jewish massacre in U.S.
history, 117
Bergman, Aaron (rabbi), 104-124, 126-127
Black Hebrews (Black Israel Movement),
120; Capers, Funnye (rabbi), 120-121
Cantor, Eddie, 148
conversion into, 108, 125-126
black Americans, 120-121, 146; see also
Carl Steger
Davis, Sammy Davis, Jr., 146-147, 163
ideology of, 106-116, 125-126
denominations, 109-111, 121, 125
holidays, 113-116, 125; see also
Carl Steger
"Jew" vs "Jewish," 116
life cycle events, 113-116, 125-127
worldwide demographic of Jewish
people, 113

Kimball, Carolyn, 202, 205
King, Martin Luther, Jr., (Dr.) 135, 242-244
KKK (Ku Klux Klan), 40-41, 220
expansion beyond the South, 41
see also Detroit, Michigan

Leach, Harvey, 132-134, 230

Lewis, Shirley Marie. See Steger, Shirley
Lewis and Carl Steger marriages
Loving v. Virginia (1967), 221-222

malena neonatorum, 33
McCoy, Elijah, 44
McDaniel, Hattie, 22-23
Meyerson, Arlyn, 127-128, 131-132, 144, 148,
151-152, 157
Scotch 'n Sirloin, 127, 129, 131, 143-144, 148,
151, 157-158, 173, 178; see also Carl
Steger's performance at Scotch 'n Sirloin
Meyerson, Mark, 131-132
Michigan Chronicle, 9, 15, 54, 65, 92-93, 183,
246
Muer, Charles, 174

National Association for the Advancement of
Color People (NAACP), 149, 199
see also Walter White
National Association of Negro Musicians
(NANM), 88-89
history of, 88
National Lawyers Guild. See Ernest Goodman
Nina Simone, 21-22

Oakland Press, The, 150, 173-174
Obama, Barack Hussein (44th U.S. president),
121-122, 224

Paderewski, Ignacy Jan, 19
Paradise Valley. See Detroit, Michigan
Perry, Imani, 241-242, 244
Pilgrim, David, 193
Plessy v. Ferguson (1896), 199-200, 221
politics, 241-244
Clinton, Hillary (2016 U.S. Democratic
Presidential Nominee), 119
Ford, Gerald (38th U.S. President), 119
Milliken, William "Bill" (Michigan governor),
15-16
Trump, Donald John (45th U.S. President),
116, 118-120, 122-123
Purple Gang, 41, 47

racial passing, 38-39, 121, 187-188, 196, 206,
208, 215-220, 223-224, 228,
233-234, 237, 239
Carl Steger's involvement in, 5, 101, 103-105,
146, 166, 188-189, 206, 213-214, 225-226,
228-230, 233-234, 237-238
Carol Channing involvement in, 214-215, 224
Channing's father involvement in, 214
dark secret in whiteface, the, 187-188
decline of, 216-219
disruptions to family relationships,
communities, and histories, 189, 196, 213,
215, 234, 240
DNA studies and revelations of, 219-221, 224
whites unaware of African ancestry—

passing as white, 219-221
emotional effects of, 166, 196, 213, 229, 234
in media and films, 206-207
Jews involved in, 104
population study of:
    blacks passing as white, 216
    see also Carl Steger
    see also Walter White
racism, 13, 40, 118, 167, 196, 200, 205, 208,
    221, 230-231
anti-Semitism. *See* Judaism
blackface, 187
black race skin color discrimination, 189-190,
    195-197, 203-206
    Blue Vein Societies, 190-193
    Brown Paper Bag Test, 190, 193-194,
        196-197
    colorism, 189-190, 206
    "elites" or "siddity girls,' 196
elimination of (solutions), 241-244
Jim Crow (laws), 1, 37, 64, 135, 187, 190,
    193, 221, 224
"One Drop Rule" or hypodescent, 220-221
paramour rights, 1
physiological effects of, 200-205
psychological, physiological and social
    influences of, 199-200, 230
    "Doll Tests, The," 198-200
political influences of, 122, 241-244
skin bleaching or "browning," 200-205, 220,
    230, 236
    psychological effects of, 200-201
    white vs black skin, 205-206
whiteface, 187-188
white supremacist groups, 107, 121-123, 188,
    221
        see also Detroit, Michigan
        see also KKK (Ku Klux Klan)
Robinson, Bill "Bojangles," 22

Sarasota, Florida, 63, 144, 153, 173-174, 176,
    182, 228-229, 257-258
    black history of, 63-64
Sarasota Herald Tribune, 257-258
Schwikert, Carol Ann. *See* Steger, Carol
    Schwikert and Carl Steger marriages
Scotch 'n Sirloin (restaurant, club). *See* Arlyn
    Meyerson
    see also Carl Steger
Second Baptist Church (Detroit, Michigan), 74
    history of, 74-76
    Underground Railroad, 75-76
Shamborguer, Naima, 7-8
Simone, Nina, 21-22
slavery, 31, 64, 74, 190, 193, 200, 213, 221
    results of, 1, 50, 190, 193, 200
Smith, Mary "Alma" Foster, 8-9, 212, 227
Steger, Brenda. *See* Brenda Willis
Steger, Carl. *Also known as* Gordon Carl Steger,
    Gordon Herbert Steger, Carl Gordon Steger

and Carl Gordon Herbert Steger, 2-8, 54, 56,
    72, 77, 141-144, 146, 149-150, 153-157,
    159-160, 162-173, 176-183, 210-213, 224-230,
    233, 237, 238-239, 241, 246, 251
    birth of, 35-36,
    defect in fingers, 31, 179
    career of, 10-11, 19-20, 27, 85, 131-132,
        143, 177-178, 227, 246-250, 252-259;
        Carl Steger Duo, 61; Carl Steger Trio,
        247
    childhood of, 178-179, 246, 264
    census record (1940 U.S. Federal), 55-56
    clubs and restaurants performed at:
        Au Sable Lounge (Detroit, MI), 62
        Bouche' Lounge (Detroit, MI), 247
        Café L'Europe (Sarasota, FL), 177, 181
        Café St. Louie (Sarasota, FL), 258
        Chez Sylvie (Sarasota, FL), 258
        Club 49 (Detroit, MI), 10, 12, 17, 227,
            224, 227, 247
        Excalibur (Southfield, MI), 150, 176
        Frisco's (MI), 254
        Jakks Place (Oak Park, MI), 7, 157,
            175-176, 250, 252-254
        Lounge, The (Lansing, MI), 247
        Machus Red Fox (West Bloomfield,
            MI), 135-136, 150, 175-176
        Nifty Norman's (Walled Lake, MI), 254
        Red Cedars (Union Lake, MI), 7,
            174-176, 254-256
        Saint Georges (Sarasota, FL), 257-258
        Scotch 'n Sirloin (Detroit, MI), 9, 11, 27,
            63, 128-129, 131-132, 143-144,
            150-151, 156-157, 176, 178, 247-250;
            see also Arlyn Meyerson
    death of, 240
    Judaism, conversion into, 104, 127, 149,
        152-153, 163-165, 172
        Hanukkah (holiday), celebration of,
            163
    marriages to:
        Lewis, Shirley Marie (1st wife), 57-58
        Varden, Florence Onameega (2nd wife),
            57-58; license application and
            certification, 59
        Schwikert, Carol Ann (3rd wife), 63,
            155, 162-163, 178-180
    military service, 57, 248, 250, 265
    records and compact disc (CD) releases, 62,
        64, 176-177
    songs written by, 60. 62
    voting history report, 102-103
    see also racial passing
Steger, Carol Ann, 7, 64, 142-144, 151, 153, 155,
    157, 166, 170-171, 174, 176-178, 252
    see also Carl Steger marriages
Steger, Carolyn. *See* Carolyn Kimball
Steger, Dawn Marie. *Also known as* Dawn Steger-
    Davey, 144-147, 149-185, 210, 213, 229, 233
Steger, Dorothy. *Also known as* Dorothy Anna

Steger, Dorothy, (*continued*)
  Williams, 5, 7, 36, 51, 55-56, 72, 146, 179,
    207, 210, 212
  birth and childhood of, 65-66
  daughter of Gordon and Dorothy Steger,
    Also known as Dorothy Steger, 33
  death of, 89, 188, 200; (obituaries) 90-94,
    158-159, 183, 210, 230
  educated at, 83
    Northwestern High School (Detroit),
      66
    see also Battle Creek Central High
      School
    see also Detroit Conservatory of Music
  employed at, 35, 89
    Bertha Hansbury School of Music.
      See Bertha Hansbury,
    Department of Parks and Recreation
      (Detroit), 72, 82, 84, 86-87, 89
      Brewster Community Center,
        77, 82
      Brewster Homes (Brewster
        Housing Project). *See*
        Detroit (Michigan), FHA
      Cass Technical High School,
        83
      Duffield Elementary School,
        82
      Grand Army of the Republic
        (G.A.R.) Recreation Center,
        83
      Jewish Community Center, 86
      Metropolitan Baptist Church,
        82
      Mount Vernon Recreation
        Center, 82
      St. Cyprians Parish House, 82
    Heckscher Foundation (New York),
      77
    Utopia Children's House
      (New York), 77
  musical performances of, 72-74, 77-78,
    82-87, 247, 266
  marriages to Gordon Steger, 31, 34
    (1921), 52 (1935)
  Singing Simplified (instructional singing
    book), 95-100
Steger, Florence Varden, 57-59
  see also Carl Steger marriages
Steger, Gerald, 101, 170, 212, 239
Steger, Gordon, 33, 35-36, 51, 55-56, 77, 170,
    179, 207, 210, 211- 213, 246
  death of, 57, 188-189
  marriages to Dorothy Williams, 31, 34
    (1921), 52 (1935)
  photographs of, 261-263
  son of Gordon and Dorothy Steger
    See Carl Steger
Steger, Kimberly Ann. *Also known as*
  Kimberly Steger-Sherrill, 31, 127, 144-146,

    149-185, 210, 228-230, 233
Steger, Leroy Gordon, Jr., 210-212
Steger, Leroy, Sr., 1-3, 207-212, 240-241
Steger, Lilly, 200, 202, 205, 210
Steger, Oreatha, 101, 208, 212
Steger, Sarah. *Also known as* Sarah Bradley, 1-2,
  189
Steger, Shirley Lewis, 57-59
Steger, Susie, 208, 212
Steger, William. *Also known as* William David
  Steger, 1-2, 169, 207, 212
Steger, Willis, 212
Stuckert, Robert P., 216
Swan, Ernie, 227, 248

Tate, Vernie "Merze," 31-33
  Merze Tate Award, 33
  Merze Tate Explorers, 33
Taylor, Patricia, 101
Thompson, Josephine ("Jo"), 9, 27-28, 148, 212
Trump, Donald John (45th U.S. President). *See*
  politics

Underground Railroad, 31, 43-44
  see also Second Baptist Church (Detroit)

Varner, Florence Onameega. *See* Steger, Florence
  Varner and Carl Steger marriages

Walker, Alice, 189
Waller, Thomas Wright "Fats," 24,
"white clubs," 4-5, 11, 13, 227
White, Walter, 39, 220
  NAACP (National Association for
    Advancement of Color People), 39
  racial passing (undercover), 39
Williams, Dorothy Anna. *See* Dorothy Steger
Williams, Fred Hart, 93-94
  E. Azalia Hackley Collection, 93
  Fred Hart Williams Genealogical Society,
    93-94
Willis, Brenda, 1, 202, 205, 212
Wilson, Greg, 177
Woodson, Carter Godwin, 41
  Negro History Week, 41

ABOUT THE AUTHOR

Eric B. Willis is a genealogist, writer, historian, publisher, and visual artist. He is the author of the award-winning publication *The Willis Handbook: An Intersection of Genealogy, Memoirs and History of a Black American Family – 1835-2003*. He is the founder and owner of Panoply House of Publishing, LLC, and a member of the International Society of Genetic Genealogy. His works exist in private and public collections of noted institutions throughout the United States.

Having traced his family's paternal lineage back to eight generations and encouraging others to become family historians, Willis sees genealogy like being a visual artist—as a way of drawing people together for conversation.

Willis lives in Michigan with his wife, two daughters, and an always hungry pyredoodle.

Please direct any inquiries to Panoply House of Publishing, LLC:

Web: www.panoplyhouseofpublishing.com
facebook.com/panoplyhouseofpublishing

Email: info@panoplyhouseofpublishing.com

CPSIA information can be obtained
at www.ICGtesting.com
Printed in the USA
LVHW052316300623
751244LV00001B/2